D1566675

PRAISE FOR *The Soul of the Full-Length Manuscript*

"A guide to confronting one's own life issues, it is definitely a powerful system for helping the writer complete a full-length manuscript but it also requires a serious examination of how our life stories are reflected and shaped in our work. This book should come with a warning label: 'Be ready, you are going to have to go deeper than you ever imagined.' "
— DOROTHY ALLISON, author of *Bastard Out of Carolina*

"Zelda Lockhart's soulful guide for fledgling writers is an extraordinary gift of generosity and eloquence, a treasure map of our uncharted imaginative topographies." — DANA HELLER, Eminent Scholar of English, Old Dominion University

"Rather than hiding from our past and the difficulties we have each endured, Lockhart teaches us how to shine a light on those painful memories and make sense of them through writing resolutions to those stories. Part creative writing and part therapeutic writing, Lockhart's work is open, accessible, and allows writers to gain new perspectives on life events that have shaped us." — DR. MICHELE FORINASH, director of Expressive Therapies Division, Lesley University

"The main message in this book is to transform your psychological wounds and utilize your spiritual strength in order to find your authentic voice. And like a good therapist or counselor, Lockhart is there with you all the way, providing encouraging insights and important ideas to keep you moving along the path. This is a must-read for anyone who has ever wanted to write an emotionally forceful and soulful piece of fiction, memoir, or poetry." – DR. MITCHELL KOSSAK, associate professor of counseling and expressive therapies at Lesley University and author of *Attunement in Expressive Arts Therapy: Toward an Understanding of Embodied Empathy*

THE SOUL

OF THE FULL-LENGTH

MANUSCRIPT

Turning Life's Wounds
into the Gift of Literary Fiction, Memoir, or Poetry

Zelda Lockhart, PhD

LAVENSON PRESS

HILLSBOROUGH, NC

THE SOUL

OF THE FULL-LENGTH

MANUSCRIPT

Copyright © 2017 Zelda Lockhart

All rights reserved. No part of this book may be reproduced in any form or by any electronic or mechanical means, including information storage and retrieval systems, without permission in writing from the publisher, except by reviewers, who may quote brief passages in a review.

Print ISBN 978-0-9789102-6-6
Ebook ISBN 978-0-9789102-7-3

Library of Congress Control Number 2017901616

Some characters in this book are fictitious except where otherwise stated. Any similarity to real persons, living or dead, is coincidental and not intended by the author.

The examples, interpretation, and analysis of literary works are the interpretations of one reader and not meant to suggest a truth for all readers.

Excerpt from "Play Ball" by Grey Brown. Reprinted with permission.

Front cover graphic and design by Obelia Exum
All interior graphics by Zelda Lockhart unless otherwise credited
Typesetting and editing by Lisa Hosokawa Garber

Published by LaVenson Press
P.O. Box 1432
Hillsborough, NC 27278

Visit www.LaVensonPress.com

Printed in the United States of America
First Printing March 2017
Second Printing June 2019

For Our Souls
that in our embodied-lives
endure so much shunning.

CONTENTS

PART 4: Craft Elements to Bring About Literary Plot

ACKNOWLEDGMENTS

My daughter, Alex, has seen the most, heard the most, and held vigil the longest while this book emerged from the experiences of my teaching. I thank her for her patience and innate wisdom.

A host of teachers encouraged me to say what I mean, but of greatest influence are Ms. Chambers, my seventh grade teacher who told me to walk with my head up and always look like I know where I am going even if I don't; Toi Derricotte, who over twenty years ago told me my poetry was clever but missing the difficult truth; and Dorothy Allison, who twenty-something years ago told me I had a lot of nerve and I was going to need it. They made me reach inward until I found my heart.

My students, all of them who have ever been my students in universities, community centers, libraries, coffee shops, and my living room, deserve all my gratitude for "calling me to task" and answering no when I ask, "Am I making any sense?" They helped me to seek deeper ways to communicate deeper thoughts.

For helping me make sense of this book, hold the continuity of it, and get the spelling right, I am grateful to Jade Brooks, Dawn Shamp, and Maya Corneille, who read and advised. Thank you Kim McCrea, Chaley Munn, Rose Brown, and Sophie Shaw for the marketing and publicity push.

The biggest thanks goes to the last standing, the book's production crew, Lisa Hosokawa Garber, Obelia Exum, and Alex Lockhart; I appreciate the way you saw the book process through to its send-off for printing.

I am ever so grateful for all of the writers whose works I reference in this book. Over the years, I have consumed your tales again and again until they are part of the cells of my being.

So many souls have created this book. I hope you feel them all as you consume and create and consume.

INTRODUCTION

We all "have personal stories as vast in scope and as powerful as the numen in fairy tales," but the stories associated with our shame and our secrets "contain some of the most important stories we can give our time to unravelling. . . . These secret stories . . . are personal ones, embedded, not like jewels in a crown, but like black gravel under the skin of the soul" (Estés, 374).

When I was a child and it rained in the summertime, I watched from the open window. I could smell the way the dry concrete absorbed the first drops and how much that smell was like the smell of chalk. Then I would watch and wait until the rain stopped and would go out into the yard. Even on the West Side of St. Louis, the rain refreshed the parched streets and vacant lots and brought back the brightness in the color green. I would go to the bulging green milkweed pods and watch what one could only watch in early summer after a rain. The drops rolled down, resisting the tight green skin of the pods, and in each drop, there was a universe.

When I was done observing what the rain had created, I found a good puddle, went to my stash of jelly jar tops near the basement door, and made a full spread of mud pies. I was five years old and this is how I survived the secret molestations inside the ironic safety of my childhood home. Nature was a safe place that held the lessons of life, and was my inspiration where I created mud pies and other metaphorical foods.

What does all of this have to do with writing? As I grew older, I explored other cycles of inspiration and expression that shared one container. Inspired by nature, I created in nature; and eventually inspired by reading poetry and fiction, I wrote poetry and fiction. But this transformation didn't fully happen until my college years.

As an undergraduate, I was a math and computer science major. I wrote programs while dreaming and felt like a puzzle-solving queen. One semester, I took a literature class, and it was as if someone dropped those milkweeds of childhood on the ground and inside was more than a universe, but several universes. No one told me that inside of the minds of Black folks were all of the same kinds of good days, bad days, joys, and pains that I had experienced; that inside the expressions of women's words were the programming codes of the emotional stress of being female in a world hammered on by men. How brilliantly Zora Neale Hurston, Richard Wright, and Alice Walker told their truths.

My computer science professors cringed when I said I was changing my major. My English professors cringed when they saw the first poems that I was inspired to write. Well, I cringed too; something was missing.

During the first semester of obtaining my master's degree, I was reading my poetry in a class taught by visiting writer Toi Derricotte. When I was done, my classmates clapped vigorously, but Toi just stared at me. She said, "Well, that was clever, but what is the story behind the cleverness?" I was pissed off, but it brought out the poem "Untitled," which was later titled "Granmama's Funeral" (25–27).

> I still hear her voice whispering
> in my three-year-old ear,
> "You're my baby, 'cause you were
> born here and love my greens and
> rutabagas."
> She died that summer.
> I kept eating greens and
> rutabagas and eventually
> turned four.
> I'd see her on her knees doubled

over a tub full of water
that turns into a tub
full of blood, my stomach turns.
Every night when I was
nine I thought she'd come
take me from
beneath the black chest wedging
me into the bed.
She would rise
up and smite him, smack
him hard, and he'd
disappear forever. Then
her daughter would be
able to love her baby
girl.
Still waiting.
Each night became
more silent,
the weight of his body
crushed me,
cut off my air
and my mother,
a quivering shadow
leaned across the floor,
just beyond the
door not letting me out.
Now
no chest
crushes me,
but dark clouds hover
over me.
I whimper,
I hurt,

and grandmother still
does not come.
Last night I dreamed my
grandmother died.
She was lingering in the air
not strong, but weak,
creating silence.
No one would ride to the
funeral with my father, so
to keep my grandmother's peace,
I did, he was a
pallbearer and helped to
carry grandmother's stretcher,
her covered corpse down the
cold hard steps of the church.
Her white sheet, the contour
of her "head-to-foot"
contrasted the grey clouds.
I woke the same age
as in the dream,
Twenty-one-years
after grandmother's death,
the morning
after grandmother's death.
She would never
rise up over the dark cloud
that hovered over me, that
pushed down on me. She
would never smack him hard.

I was twenty-four years of age at the time, and this expression was like pulling a string in a blanket. The whole façade of cleverness unraveled in poetry, performances, short stories, and eventually a first novel. The missing ingredient in my other poems was the emotional truth of what it is like for Zelda to live this human life, but once I used the work to tell truth, I was making art, connecting with others.

The works of writers like Sharon Olds, Lucile Clifton, and Galway Kinnell continuously inspired me, but to stay in the ecology of that creative gift giving, I had to continue to tell the truth in my creations so that others could be inspired to tell their truths. I did not know at the time that I was twirling around in a **bibliofusion** ecosystem: inhaling stories of someone's metabolized joys and pains as food, medicine, and kinship, and then exhaling story through writing, which becomes my own and others' healing.

Those years ago, Toi Derricotte's writing workshop inadvertently and slowly became a holding environment for me to express the unexpressed, to bring up from the deep consciousness and put on the outside my feelings so I could examine them in a way that gave me power over my own life.

For over twenty years, I have helped so many others to do the same, through teaching writing workshops in my studio, at colleges and universities, and as a public lecturer. I have been touched and transformed by the creations made of their blood and dirt, whole masterpieces sculpted from their experiences, and by getting personal about their lives and offering their unique thumbprints to the process of making story.

We have twirled ourselves into the ecosystem of wounded, healed, gift-givers. In order to twirl myself around with the folks who are and aren't able to show up in my living room, a classroom, or an auditorium, I offer this book, *The Soul of the Full-Length Manuscript*, so that the reader may return as many times as necessary, and proceed at a pace consistent with their own twirling.

The book acts as creative companion for individuals (those with or without writing experience) as they journey through the sharing of an impactful event in life, do exercises that help them to transform internal obstacles into external gifts, and then write resolution and outcome. I call this process **personal plot**. My own rough drafts, and excerpts from published fiction, memoir, and poetry of writers like Toi Derricotte, Helena María Viramontes, and Ta-Nehisi Coates, along with films by writers and directors like Sherman Alexie, offer kinship on the journey of unearthing and sharing a personal plot.

Want, Want, Want

"Want" is probably the most utilized word in this book other than "the" and "a," because much like with literary plot, which mirrors personal plot, want drives our emotional, psychological, and spiritual journey.

Some of us were taught that the road to getting what we want is through work and suffering, and some of us were taught that the way to get what we want is by knocking someone else down if we have to. Few of us spend time figuring out what we want and devising ways to self fulfill that want without holding others hostage. And then there are those of us who hide what we want with the behavior of a self-proclaimed martyr who can't separate what we want from what others want. I know that I've had times in my life when I thought that fulfilling what others wanted was honorable, but what I was really doing was hiding my true wants, because what I wanted reminded me too much of what I'd lost.

Hiding our wants behind other people's wants isn't sustainable and turns our blame righteous. In a very cyclical way, I have had those times when I break down under the stress of my martyrdom and become either the suffering victim or the vicious, lashing-out person who is judgmental and aware of everyone else's flaws. The self-righteous, wounded martyr trick works until I am hungry for intimacy and I forge out again, blindly seeking what I want without even knowing what I want and blaming the found relationships of love, friendship, social networks, and work for not fulfilling me. I call these cycles unresolved personal plots. I'm not so blind to these cycles anymore, because I've made a writing career out of crafting stories from the exercise of attempting to resolve (even if temporarily) personal plot through writing.

This book is designed to take the emotional and psychological *stuff* that has been making a mess of your life and use it to make art, to seek closure (temporary or perhaps permanent) for one or more of your many personal plots with revelation and outcome so that, through your own hell-bent desire to evolve, you offer a beaten path for others to evolve. This book also works with harmonizing art and craft so that art takes the lead melody and craft takes its rightful auxiliary place as a background singer rather than masquerading as the art itself.

This book is designed then to help folks utilize their emotional, psychological, and spiritual selves to produce the first draft of a full-length manuscript. At times, you will feel that the book is designed to produce a new emotional, psychological, and spiritual you and that your resulting manuscript is merely the byproduct. Both are true of the design, because the purpose of art is to make yourself vulnerable about your experiences here in life—to have *the courage to be vulnerable* about those experiences so that you can connect with others who came here solo like you and will leave solo just like you; and that process of sharing is transformative.

One particular poet who embodied the courage to be vulnerable in her art was Forogh Farrokhzad. Born Iranian and female in 1935, Farrokhzad celebrated her sexual passion, her desire to love and be loved, though her society shunned her for reveling in her womanhood rather than hiding it. She went on then to write about the pain of depression and the joys and pains of love, but had she succumbed to the shunning and not allowed herself to express, we would not have her body of work as sustenance and inspiration for others.

Some would say that this is the purpose of life, to make art, to leave something meaningful and true behind. This book supports that sentiment. Think of your emotional and psychological truth as the authentication of your birdcall. If other birds are to respond, they have to hear the undiluted truth of your call, or else what they hear won't register as being in any way relevant for them. Without authentic emotional and psychological content to your writing, there is no extension of you for people to connect with.

Spiritually, with writing and any other art making, you must work and walk in a space of what is unseen and not yet experienced, and trust both your instincts and your belief that it won't kill you to walk through the landscape of your greatest joys and greatest pains even when your greatest fears emerge. You must have faith that what you feel compelled to express will enhance your life, not expedite your death.

This is the way that I teach, by reminding you of the tools that you possess and offering you new sets of tools to get at the core, so you can utilize the best stuff for creating lots of artful raw material. Once you recognize the good, bad, and mundane of who you are, you can utilize that raw material to your best artistic, self-evolving potential. Not everything you write will be an excerpt from your life story, but there most certainly needs to be your emotional, psychological, and spiritual truth there to authenticate the work as your art.

So, that's **art**. What of **craft**? Craft in this book is defined as elements added to manuscripts that enhance the reader's experience of an already whole work. Craft is important but is secondary in my teaching, since it is embellishment to the raw, artful truth of personal plot, which could stand alone. If you think of the art as the lead singer and the craft as the doo-wop quartet in the background, then the art could go out on tour alone and do fine, but those backup singers (let's call them the Embellishments) won't draw a crowd. You can also think of craft as the nifty, clever tricks that further engage the reader; it is the intoxicating language and plot devices that entice the reader's analytical mind while the artistic mind is carried off to a deeper place. But even when utilizing the intricate tools of craft, the writer has to keep their emotional, psychological, and spiritual self engaged so that the tools of craft help tell the truth well, as opposed to the tools attempting to go off and masquerade as the art. There's nothing worse than a backup singer trying to drown out the lead.

This book works first with the art. We will get personal, work with resolving some unresolved life stuff, and use that journey toward resolution and outcome as the organic plot of a manuscript of fiction, memoir, or poetry. I will offer you prompts to pull your stories up from your base.

Once you have massive amounts of raw written material to work with, we'll apply craft, which as I said is not merely a collection of technical elements, but technical elements that are very specific to your personal plot that work with greater specificity to enhance the plot.

As we work through the exercises, I will occasionally offer short excerpts of my own raw material from these exercises. This process of creating while my students create—and sharing vulnerability—is how I come to teaching. The only way that I know to connect with you, or truly inspire you, is by sharing my personal life plot for the sake of literary plot in the same way that I will ask you to share. What is required of me in the writing of this book is the same that is required of any manuscript: I must write from my own base.

So, much like the pieces of art we create with our works of fiction and memoir, this book of nonfiction has the capacity to be food, medicine, and kinship. We will also experience the personal plots of other writers and filmmakers and how these personal plots are manifested in their works.

Now, here is what is required of you: in order for this book to have an impact on your writing that is similar to what you would gain if you were sitting in a workshop with me, you must *do* this book, not just read this book. This is a teaching and learning journey where one exercise builds on the next. You will have to do the writing exercises in the order that they are presented here. Think of this as being similar to what you might encounter with a piano instruction book. You wouldn't just skip to the last exercise and expect to brilliantly perform a concerto.

The writing prompts and exercises of this book speak to the conscious *you* while stimulating the more raw expressions of the subconscious *you*. The guidance that goes with the prompts is designed to give you the tools to intentionally utilize your conscious and subconscious expressions as needed in creating the narrative of a human experience. In short, this book helps you develop the tools to write your own movements through life by writing and living your personal plot.

With that said, before you begin the journey, it is a smart idea to put your psychological and spiritual support network in place. What do I mean by that? If you work well with other writing friends, take the journey together. If you process change and transformation well with a therapist, put that person back on payroll. If you have a spiritual leader you visit or listen to as your grounding force, make sure that person is available for their weekly sermon and not on sabbatical. We will talk more on staying grounded in Chapter 3, Spelunking and Internal Saboteurs.

Lastly, we will cover what it takes to self edit and engage peer editors so that you polish up your work for publication. The unknown audience is a profoundly essential part of the work itself. There is an entire unfulfilled dimension of the art that does not exist until an audience receives it.

I believe that practicing the art of writing can help a person self define and therefore self propel their evolution; that is, if they want for their evolution in a hell-bent sort of way. I have seen it in my own life and in the lives of others I have worked with for over two decades.

Texts in Common

Throughout this book, we will delve into connections between personal plot and literary plot as we blend and merge the two. It will be helpful to have some texts in common, as I will refer to other pieces of literature that do this blending quite well. These are but a few of the works that line my office walls and the gray matter memories in my brain, but all of our libraries can offer kinship during the parts of creating that can feel scary and difficult. I have left space for you to fill in titles of poetry, prose, and movies that are told from a personal plot base. As you journey through this book, writers you have encountered over the years will likely begin chatting with you, reminding you of their personal journeys. Feel free to email me the literature you remember. Through the stories of other writers, you will be reminded of the beauty that results from the task of expressing your truth.

MEMOIRS

- "Beauty: When the Other Dancer Is the Self" by Alice Walker
- *Rescuing Patty Hearst* by Virginia Holman
- *Between the World and Me* by Ta-Nehisi Coates
- "Indian Education" by Sherman Alexie

NOVELS

- *Fifth Born* by Zelda Lockhart
- *The Whale Rider* by Witi Ihimaera
- *Bastard Out of Carolina* by Dorothy Allison
- *Fifth Born II: The Hundredth Turtle* by Zelda Lockhart
- *Cold Running Creek* by Zelda Lockhart

SHORT STORIES

- "Rules of the Game" by Amy Tan
- "Sonny's Blues" by James Baldwin
- "The Moths" by Helena María Viramontes
- "The Empty Nest" by Zelda Lockhart

POETRY

- "my dad & sardines" by Toi Derricotte
- *The Father* by Sharon Olds
- *The Rose That Grew from Concrete* by Tupac Shakur
- *What It Takes* by Grey Brown
- *Sin* by Forough Farrokhzad

MOVIES

- *Frozen River* written and directed by Courtney Hunt
- *Smoke Signals* written by Sherman Alexie and directed by Chris Eyre
- *The Pursuit of Happyness* written by Steven Conrad, directed by Gabriele Muccino, and adapted from a memoir by Chris Gardner

OTHER WORKS YOU REMEMBER WITH PERSONAL PLOT:

_____

_____

_____

_____

_____

_____

_____

_____

Shared Vocabulary

As the lessons of the book build, you will encounter words and phrases that are used differently here than they are in other instructional books. They will pop up in the text where necessary, and either they will be in bold or you will see the tag "Vocabulary," just like you see below.

Vocabulary: For the sake of shared vocabulary, I will refer to your writings as events or scenes. This is because each memory or musing that you write should be rendered with full internal and external detail. The deeper we get into the chapters of this book, the more the terms scene and event will come to represent a fully rendered internal and external moment in fiction, poetry, or memoir.

PART 1

Jump-Starting
and Warm-Up Prompts

The prompts in this section are to warm up your heart for the type of writing to come. It's like the midwife rubbing on the newborn's chest to get the circulation going. Try not to think of it as schoolwork where the concern in those cases was if you did it right. When your heart is beating and keeping you alive, there is no listening to see which among the heartbeats sounds right; there is no listening to see which sort of breathing sounds right. The exercises are to get *your* heart beating and *your* breath in its true rhythm before we dive into the depths of a prompt that will take us through several months of writing. Before we go, I want your heart and breath acclimated to working at such depths, because down deep is where the manuscript exists.

CHAPTER 1

Creating
Raw Material

The First Layer:
Leaving Behind Strange Notions about the Time to Go Deep

My early days of writing were wrought with the busyness of everyday life. I would like to impart my survival skills to the many writers who are in the same boat that I was in, who believe that they don't have time to write because they have too many jobs, too many classes, or too many kids, or they are taking care of an elderly family member and working full-time, or any number of real-life scenarios.

There are always more internal obstacles that parallel these external obstacles to getting the work done, and we'll work on how to manage those deeper, more internal obstacles that can thwart a creative endeavor in Chapter 3.

For now, let's talk about managing and maneuvering around time.

Writing with the Time You Have

When I started writing *Fifth Born*, I was directing a not-for-profit community agency, raising my thirteen-year-old son, and working with my partner to grow her art business by attending art and craft fairs on the weekends and painting for her at night; and on top of everything else, I had taken a contract with my county's human resource department to conduct evening art-based human resource training. I thought to myself that things were shot to hell and I'd never get the first novel written, but I remembered what my brother LaVenson told me so many years ago, "If you aren't doing what you feel you were put here to do, then you aren't living. You are merely surviving. You may as well be a mouse or an ant or something."

After remembering that blunt pep talk, I started getting up a bit earlier each morning, before my partner and son woke, and started staying in the bathroom a little later each evening after they had gone to bed. I started getting to work fifteen minutes early and leaving the lights off and the office locked for those fifteen minutes. Initially, I would burn my fifteen minutes musing about what to write, or giving in to exhaustion thoughts and staring out the window, or even taking luxurious ten-minute naps. Eventually, I started carrying a few artistic, inspirational items to keep me charged. I kept these **Jump Starters** and pen and paper in my car, in my bag, and hidden in my office desk.

With these short moments in the day, sometimes ten- to fifteen-minute writing sessions, I ended up getting several scenes written, and when I wasn't writing the novel I was writing ten-minute poems. I called these writings **raw material**. I began to get the writing work done in tandem with the busy life inside and outside of my head. The connections between my fears, joys, and daily worries made their way into the authenticity of what I was writing, and I realized that was exactly what should happen: a win-win for creativity and mental health. As a byproduct, I felt more grounded; it was like doing yoga at the beginning and end of a busy day.

The key to producing soulful art in a short period of time was getting into the writing moments quickly and deeply so that the fifteen-minute session I afforded myself wasn't wasted. Before each writing moment, I would jump-start myself. Yes, think of jump-starting a car; the car is sitting there cold and needing energy, which is the way most of us feel when we sit down to write. Something has to happen to spark and inspire that engine to run.

The Second Layer:
Getting and Staying at Depth

These three Jump Starters will be used throughout the entire course of this book. To give yourself a creative jolt, first collect the following and carry them in a bag, briefcase, backpack, car, or bicycle basket, or on an electronic device:

1. *Poetry*. A book of poetry with very concentrated figurative language. My favorite for years has been Sharon Olds's *Blood, Tin, Straw*. Of course, you can always access the poetry on your electronic device as well by bookmarking a poetry website; purchasing it for your device; or going to the poet's reading, website, blog post, or social media page where you might find a poem or two. Be sure to choose from poetry that you feel gives you an emotional jolt or stirs your spirit, as opposed to poems that you like because they are cleverly constructed or because they are such neat word puzzles. The point is to stir way down at the bottom of the pot of your emotions, psyche, and spirit.

2. *Photography*. Candid photo images that speak to your heart. Think about the *Time Life* photo books, the Margaret Mead series of books, or one of my current favorites, *Sweet Breath of Life* with narrative and poetry by Ntozake Shange and photography by Kamoinge. Your local library has these to loan. You can also go to an "image of the day" section of a website like the Smithsonian, or do a web search for a particular theme like "poverty in America," which pulled up a slide show by Bill Moyer

and inspired me to write a short story last week. Pick photos related to the emotional subject matter or setting of your writing. You can bookmark these sites so that they are readily accessible to you. These photos should *not* be posed photos of humans, but humans caught off guard in real-life candid moments. This will help engage your emotional, psychological, and spiritual self.

3. *Music.* Music that inspires mood and reaction in you. Have some music downloaded to your phone, computer, or other electronic device. You can also use CDs for your laptop if you're still into that. You'll want this to be music that stirs and moves you whenever you listen to it. Again, this will help engage your emotional, psychological, and spiritual self. Many artists use music as a way of reaching into their emotions and memories for the soul-work of their creations. Maurice Sendak shares, "Useful for my work, are the childhood fantasies that were reactivated by the music and explored uninhibitedly by the pen" (130). Lately, I've been hooked on listening to Bobby McFerrin while creating, as the vocal sounds mimic the sounds of nature.

Now, what do you do with these items?

Before we write anything, I will tell you that within the pages of this book, I recommend that you write in **first person, past tense, minimal dialogue**. If you're an academic, you will really have to train yourself toward first person for these exercises and leave objective third person behind for a while. The reason is because a story well told should rely on the most primary devices that we utilized when we were two years old. Remember how your friend pushed you off the swing and you ran to your mother or another big person and began crying as loudly as possible so they would have a sense of the wound you had suffered? Then you pointed at the accused and gave the details of how you were just swinging and playing and then they came up behind you and yelled, then pushed you, and to make it all true, you showed the blood? The toddler already knows the power of telling the raw truth from their perspective of an event that occurred.

But as we grow older, we think it discredits us if we speak from our emotions (an internal obstacle we'll explore in the next chapter), so we try too hard to make our stories sound intellectually credible. The toddler would sound like a malfunctioning robot if they said, "One might imagine how swinging and falling to the ground would impact an individual and produce tears."

So, for the sake of emotional connection, I'm calling for your most honest rendering of first person, past tense.

I'm not suggesting that first person is the only perspective for rendering good art, but much like film students who are taught to produce their first films without sound so that they rely on the images to tell the story, we will rely on the emotional, psychological, and spiritual journey of the voice to tell the story by speaking only in that voice.

For those of you who want to resist this advice, think of this as a writing experiment. You've tried so many by now and have kept what works and discarded what didn't. Do the entire experiment, and in the end, assess what worked best for you. Resisting and not trying the experiment at all will mean that you have committed to trying a new method by insisting that your old methods are the way to be. This is characteristic of the hardheaded learner. I know, because I spent my twenties, thirties, and part of my forties entertaining this of my many internal saboteurs. In Chapter 3, we'll talk about our internal saboteurs that often engage just before we are about to try something new, healthy, and potentially progressive toward fulfilling our wants. For now, may I entice you to come along for the first person, past tense experiment?

Regarding dialogue, we'll work with the proper use of dialogue in later chapters, but for now, know that most writers attempt to use dialogue and internal thinking to have the voice or the characters offer the plot. I've certainly been guilty of it in my earlier writing days, but this doesn't sharpen our skills at utilizing character development and setting development in order to organically progress the plot of our memoir, fiction, and poetry in such a way that the reader is fully engaged. More on all of that later, but for now, allow yourself to trust the experiment and also create all of your raw material with no dialogue; don't fidget with "How? How?" We'll come to that momentarily and organically.

Now, let's use those Jump Starters.

CHOOSE A LINE

Fan through the pages of a poetry book that is written in very concentrated, lyrical language, or randomly pull a poem up on your electronic device. Close your eyes and open to a page, and still without looking, plop your finger down on the page. Take the three or four words that you land on (not the whole sentence or phrase) and write them at the top of your paper, or type them at the top of your document. Whatever the words remind you of, whatever emotion or image or event or memory they spark in you, write them. Don't use the words verbatim in your writing, only what they inspire. Whenever you feel you are about to stop writing, grab for three or four more words and go.

Here are examples of words I chose when choosing lines from poet Jaki Shelton Green: "larger than their dreams," "eyeless horses," and "darkness contained the stars."

Write for Ten Minutes: Now, without thinking of what you will write, instead inspired by what was sparked from the Jump Starter, write the event inspired by the Jump Starter—yes, the memory or the story behind the emotions that were stirred. Be sure to ground us in time and place (setting) and sensory details. Let us know where you were; when the memory took place; what things looked like, smelled like, tasted like, and sounded like; and the tactile sensations of the memory.

Caution: Do not use the actual lines in your work; just use the lines to inspire you. Ask yourself, what did you see, hear, taste, feel, smell, remember, or fantasize about when you landed on the words? Also, don't start reading the poem rather than choosing a line. This would defeat the purpose and become another way to distract you from getting into the zone quickly.

For Example: I chose the words "unalterable against the white," and I remembered how I felt hanging the laundry this morning. I had to go back and add smell and touch after allowing myself to first be in the zone and write it raw, but here is some of what I wrote:

> Clorox in cold water made the traction of my swirl of fingerprints disappear from my hands. I scrubbed the garden shirt in the bathroom sink, porcelain cool bowl surrounded by white tiles. I remembered to be grateful to be cooled by the tile floors and walls. I created a list of mantras: Use the ninety-degree sun to dry your clothes, harness the sun to grow the vegetables, people in Ghana wash their clothes by hand daily. But my head still felt heavy when I walked past the half-bathroom where the stack washer and dryer sat un-stacked, blocking passage to the second toilet awaiting repair. On the porch, I remembered to sing to keep the mosquitos away, to keep the sun from searing, and to keep from feeling sorry for myself.

Note: When writing raw material, my general edit rule is to add in but never take out, because you may end up deleting what will later be the valuable connection between all of your raw material. The only time deleting is a great idea is when you are not landing in an actual moment with sensory detail. I call this "not landing the plane." You are hovering around and philosophizing instead of writing the event with sensory details. An example of this would be jump-starting and landing on "unalterable against the white" and proceeding with "White isn't actually a color, but people always include it as such . . ." That's an old Zelda habit, to hover before landing the plane. You can always go back to the raw material, delete the hovering, and leave the actual tangible and emotional moment.

PHOTO INSPIRATION

Open your photo book randomly in the same way that you opened the poetry book. Or pull up the photo archive you have bookmarked on your electronic device. Just plop your hand down. Glance at the photo, then look away. Write whatever it reminded you of, whatever emotion or image, memory, or event was sparked in you. Be careful not to read the caption or text that accompanies the photo; doing that will distract you from the journey you were about to embark on with your own words. Be careful not to spend your time looking for just the right photo. Trust the magic. Also, this is not one of those exercises where you write about the photo. This is an opportunity to allow the stories, memories, and emotions that are inside of you to be inspired out of you.

Write for Ten Minutes: Now, without spending time planning out what you will write, instead inspired by what was sparked from the Jump Starter, write the event inspired by the Jump Starter; yes, the memory or the story behind the emotions that were stirred. Be sure to ground us in time and place (setting) and sensory details. Let us know where you were; when this took place; what things looked like, smelled like, tasted like, and sounded like; and the tactile sensations of the memory.

Caution: Don't write about what is happening in the photo. This isn't an exercise to write a made-up story about what you see in a photograph, but a Jump Starter where a quick look at a photograph inspires and connects with an event already living in you. That event is what you are writing. Also refrain from reading the caption, flipping through for a photo you really like, or any of those little things to distract you from the task at hand.

MUSIC IN THE SAME VEIN

Get your inspiring music. Plug it into your ears using headphones or earphones (not just music broadcasted from the speakers in the room unless, of course, you have to for health reasons) and write based on all of the memories, emotions, images, or events that are sparked by the music. This can be very transporting.

Write for Ten Minutes: Now, without thinking of what you will write, instead inspired by what was sparked from the Jump Starter, write the event inspired by the Jump Starter—yes, the memory or the story behind the emotions that were stirred. Be sure to ground us in time and place (setting) and sensory details. Let us know where you were; when this took place; what things looked like, smelled like, tasted like, and sounded like; and the tactile sensations of the memory.

Once you have done the ten-minute write and have read what you have written, go back and choose music that is of the time period or what you were listening to at that time in your life. Ask yourself what music, if any, was playing during the event, and continue to write on that event with setting-specific music playing. This is how the suggestion of so much Motown is in my novel *Fifth Born*.

Caution: If the event you wrote about was a difficult or traumatizing one, you may find it disturbing to find the music of the time. In that case, only perform the first part of the Jump Starter.

Jump Starters can help you get ten minutes of concentrated writing done in the zone. The zone is that place where you have let go of all self-consciousness and you are just creating from your depths without editing, thinking, or being on the surface of the moment.

You are essentially grabbing a zip line. You are standing on one ridge, not in the zone, and the poet, photographer, or musician who created the inspiring art is in the zone on the other side. You choose a line, look at a photo or turn on the music, and instantly you are in the zone too and can write. The goal is to end up so deep inside of the moment that you have no idea what you are writing, but you feel moved by it.

That's the zone, which most people will only experience for an hour after writing for eight hours. But you're busy and don't have time for all of that, so instead you write for ten minutes in the zone, produce some of the most authentic and inspiring raw material of your week, and are done until you take another crack at it during your next break at work, or while you are waiting to pick up Mama or Pop from the eye doctor, or waiting to pick up one of the kids from sports practice, or waiting in line at the motor vehicles office. Just reach into your bag, backpack, or glove compartment, and get writing.

When we are sleeping or meditating, we have this wonderful ability to slip in and out of images and spaces without our brain/mind trying to control it. But then as we wake up and begin to calculate our day and work on and work out our schedule, we begin to see everything in the way that a puzzle solver does: "What tense should I put this in?" "Should this piece be about my father?" rather than just writing and letting what comes out of your fingertips be whatever was called for.

With the Jump Starters, what can come out of your fingertips is what the words, images, or sounds of the Jump Starters triggered in your subconscious mind. This is being in the zone; this is letting your subconscious be awake and be the dominant force of your actions—in this case, your writing. Jump Starters alone help you to produce some quick, in-depth raw material. You can also combine the Jump Starters. For instance, I often listen to music that is inspiring, which is what I am doing right now, and I will also choose a line of poetry to get me going. Use any combination, or each one alone. Or create your own ways to let art inspire art. You may find that going to a movie, dance, music concert, or lecture gets you inspired. So, take a notepad and scribble in the dark from your audience chair.

Combining Prompts and Jump Starters

Before we do another writing exercise, let me take a minute to distinguish my meaning of the term **prompt** from my meaning of the term Jump Starter so that I am building a common language between us. Prompts are equivalent to the tiny bits of intent for your writing, a direction to go in, so to speak.

For instance, a prompt may be "Write your birth story." The Jump Starters are the artistic inspirations to get you into the writing of your prompt. I might prompt you to write your birth story, and you just sit there thinking about the fact that you don't remember being born, or thinking about the story that you've been told over and over. All that pondering, but your little car is sitting on the track and you haven't gone anywhere yet.

Jump Starters are bits of artistic inspiration from other sources like photos, music, lines of poetry that are already published or presented as being "in the creative zone." You use these if the prompt doesn't immediately spark the desire to zoom off down the track and write. Jump Starters, just like jump-starting a car, can take you from a mundane brain into the artistic zone in seconds and can prevent you from fiddling around, wondering how to start or what to say about an event.

Don't worry if you jump-start and end up writing authentic emotional, psychological, spiritual stuff from the zone, but it wasn't related to the prompt. Sometimes, the prompt doesn't move us, but there are very present emotions and memories stirring and the Jump Starter brings those memories and thoughts to the surface. The most important thing is not to think, but to follow the first impulse, memory, or words that come to you from the prompt or the Jump Starter or both. Whatever authentically comes out is what is being called for; following that impulse will produce the raw material that is most significant.

That said, when you know that choosing a line (for instance) works for you, don't allow yourself to have one of those sabotaged writing sessions where you are all moody about what doesn't work, and then spend your ten minutes choosing lines of poetry and insisting that none of them stimulate your memories or thoughts. It's likely that you are blocking the thoughts and memories that the Jump Starters are sparking, because the memories that made you—the most joyful and the most painful memories—are inside of the same cave, and it's just scary to go in there.

The most important thing for you during the course of working with this book will be for you to make time, make a creative home between the top of your head and the bottom of your feet, and get your work done. I'll close this chapter with some inspiration from Clarissa Pinkola Estés regarding your creative home:

The exact answer to "Where is home?" is more complex . . . Home is where a thought or feeling can be sustained instead of being interrupted or torn away from us because something else is demanding our time and attention. (283)

CHAPTER 2

Warm-Up Prompts

to Reveal the Irony and Tension of Your Dichotomies

It's a weird feeling for more than one opposing feeling to be present, but it's often the case. Joy and pain, for instance, are two divergent emotions that can be present in one moment and offer not just irony in art but also harmony, the beautiful sound we hear when two discordant notes are present in one space and time. On the other hand, our dichotomies occupying one space can cause a great deal of confusion and send us to our journals to work out the tension we are experiencing as a result of our divergent hopes and fears.

The dichotomies of our personal plots are held in an inextricable bond because they are the result of events in life of significant loss (negative charges) combined with our attempts to *survive* those losses (positive charges). When explored through writing, our dichotomies generate enough energy to make beautiful, raw art in much the way that nature makes art of the original dichotomies of life and death at the shoreline where the ocean meets the land, and there we find just the right combination of positive and negative charges to animate and stimulate our existence.

Joys and Pains Exercise

At some point after we are born into this world, we experience the first profound joy and profound pain, and these reactions to the world are both inevitable and indelible. My first joyous memory was sitting on my grandmother's lap with the table in front of me at eye level and her breasts and heart at the back of my head, and I could not speak coherently but remember her saying that I was her baby because I loved her greens and rutabagas. That feeling of love became the Geiger counter for detecting love in my life.

Similar to the emotional reaction from memories of joy are the first memories of pain, which can cause in us mortal fear. That same mortal fear can show up like an apparition in relationships and cause us to lose our discernment for the difference between real dangerous relationships and challenging relationships. For instance, one of my first profound incidents of pains was when I was around five years old and ran to my mother to tell her that my father hurt me sexually. The great pain was the slaps from the woman who, instinctually, I had known as my protector. Yes, there was the pain of my father hurting me, but there was something of the sin against birthed by the birther when my mother heard this truth and beat me for it. One of my great difficulties then became discerning the difference between a woman whose outward projection of pain was of no harm to me, and when a woman's outward projection of pain meant "duck!"

Ironically, there is so much in the moment of my initial joy that helped me to survive my initial pain. I possess the nurturing and sweetness of my grandmother, despite the injuries in my life that have had a negative impact. It is why I am nonviolent and it is why I am such a staunch protector of children and their right to be safe and healthy and nurtured and heard. It is why I want to be such a positive, loving figure for my children and grandchildren.

This exercise is designed to help you to identify these past joys and pains as well as current joys and pains through a series of prompts that will connect these to the life that you want and the losses you want to prevent.

JOYS AND PAINS CHART

1. Take a sheet of paper and hold it lengthwise (landscape) and fold it into thirds like a letter, or create a three-column document on your computer. At the top of one of the outside columns, write the word "Joys."

2. Think of and bullet at least three things in the past year that have brought you profound joy. Don't be general and say something like "Seeing more people recycle." Make sure that you keep the joys specific to your personal and emotional experiences.

3. At the top of the other outside column, write the word "Pains." (Leave the middle column blank for now.)

4. Think of and bullet at least three things in the past year that have brought you profound pain. Again, don't be general and say something like "warring in the Middle East," unless, of course, that warring has caused you the temporary or long-term loss of a loved one, or loss of something internal through personal impact. Make sure that you keep the pains less universal and express more of your personal and emotional experiences.

5. Look at the two lists and literally draw lines between connections that you notice on the two lists. Perhaps there is something on your Joys list that is a result of something on your Pains list: a cause-and-effect relationship. Perhaps there is an ironic relationship where there is the same thing on your Joys list as your Pains list, or perhaps there is a connection that you are aware of that I can't fathom or imagine, but you know the relationship.

6. At the top of the middle column, write the word "Connections," and write the relationship between the joy and pain on the actual connecting

PAINS

- Emotional separation from my family of origin.
- The long, long period of time without being partnered.
- Getting older & experiencing physical limitations.

CONNECTIONS

- I missed the 1st years of her life b/c of family estrangement and now want to know her.
- I have so little connection w/ the past & I don't want to repeat it.
- I so admire & experience from my daughter's physical confidence.

JOYS

- Seeing my niece grow into a woman
- Watching my daughter run track with such freedom & determination
- Getting to video call with my granddaughter and laughing with her and talking about dogs & flowers.

line in the form of something you want or want to prevent. For instance, on my Joys list I wrote, "Seeing my niece grow into a woman," and on my Pains list I wrote, "Emotional separation from my family of origin." On the line connecting the two, I wrote, "I missed the 1st yrs. of her life b/c of family estrangement and now so want to know her."

Now, what do you do with this?

PROMPT 1: JOYS AND PAINS

Your writing prompt is to consider the Joy/Pain Connections (what you wrote on the connecting line as a want or something you want to prevent). Which of these connecting wants do you have the strongest reaction to, currently care the most about, or feel the most emotional about? Write one of the events in your life associated with that Joy/Pain Connection. For instance, my prompt then is to think about "I missed the 1st yrs. of [my niece's] life b/c of family estrangement and now want to know her." After you've done this for one Joy/Pain Connection, prompt again from another Joy/Pain Connection.

Jump Starter: Choose a line, flash on a candid photo, or plug some music into your ears to jump-start you, and go. Don't worry if you jump-start and end up writing about a different Joy/Pain Connection. The most important thing is not to overthink but to follow the first impulse, memory, or words that come to you from the prompt and the Jump Starter. That is what is being called for.

I chose a line that said "didn't know of the murder," and this is what I wrote:

She didn't know, her grandfather shot his brother, didn't know that her mother had sad eyes when she was a teenager and listened to slow Rolls Royce songs on the hi-fi in the dark and cried.

She didn't know about the time that her uncle who we just buried after a drowning came to me angry one day; a grown man, and I took him to see the ocean for the first time hoping it would leach his childhood pain away. She didn't know that I never thought the ocean would love him so much that it would hold on when he tried to get away.

She didn't know that her mother has not told her all the things about being a woman because she thinks that silence will keep her almost-grown child from the pains and shames of womanhood.

She stood and looked at me for answers that only her mother could give. If I told her, she would not believe me.

There are two poems in Tupac Shakur's *The Rose That Grew from Concrete* that hold the joys and pains dichotomy: "The Tears in Cupid's Eyes" and "Cupid's Smile II." One offers the pain of a lost love, the other, the joy of finding peace of mind again after lost love.

You can use this exercise to create a series of short pieces or poems that center around your joys and pains. When you are done, don't edit your raw material. Write more or write the event more than once, but don't get rid of anything just yet. You may end up editing out or diluting the purity of what will later show up as the connection between pieces of raw material. This could have a negative impact on your ability to successfully get through Chapter 12, The Macrocosmic Plot and Its Planetary Scenes. By editing your raw material before we've gotten to the shaping and arranging stage, you may also end up diluting the response to calls for your writing, and then those who are to receive it, who have called for it, won't recognize the diluted response.

While you are writing, if you start to surface out of the zone, jump-start again to keep you in the deep emotional, psychological, and spiritual space of the writing.

Remember: Write events, not monologues or dialogues. And write in first person, past tense. Engage us with sensory detail (smell, taste, texture, color, images, sounds, the weather, and so on). If you look back at your raw material and realize that you haven't done this, don't take things out of the work, but write these enhancements into the work.

With the Joys and Pains chart, you have a blueprint for some of your own emotional wiring, a way to know yourself and create from that base.

WRITING ABOUT YOU

Let me pause here to talk about the significance of writing from your own emotional and psychological base so that we lay that groundwork a bit more firmly for all of the other exercises in this book, and for the future of your memoir, poetry, or fiction piece.

I think for the memoir and poetry folks, the benefit of writing from your own emotional and psychological base may be more obvious: readers will get a real, authentic look at events that shape you along with your way of surviving and thriving, and therefore relate and connect.

For the fiction folks, the same is true: readers will get a real, authentic look at events that shape your main character along with your character's way of surviving and thriving, and therefore relate and connect. Fiction writers may struggle a bit more with embracing this benefit, because many of us have a tendency to want to use the characters as a way of running away from ourselves rather than as a way to do what writing can do, which is to repatriate the self to the self.

Regardless of genre, we're still talking about character development based on your emotional, psychological, and spiritual base. Yes, we are developing characters based on the only character you truly know: *you.*

Hopes and Fears Exercise

This exercise is designed to help you examine your hopes and fears through a series of writing prompts that offers the opportunity for more digging beneath the surface to find the source of your own personal wellspring of art.

Vocabulary: An **initial wound** is an event that has a long-term, significant impact on your emotional, psychological, and spiritual development. The initial wound results in a significant loss and that loss causes a want, and that want drives and motivates you on a journey to fulfill the want. The initial wound is the primary event of any of our personal plots.

Though an initial wound sounds like a negative place that no one would ever want to revisit, it is the source of art that we want to tap into. A way to get at that wellspring is through your hopes and fears. We all like to talk about hope, write speeches about it, do recitations from famous poets. Fear? Well now, that's like walking into a room of exhausted parents and talking about poopy diapers. Nobody wants to deal with it, look at it, or smell it, especially when you are trying to take a break from it.

We experience fear as the result of some initial wound or negative experience and this fear motivates us to do things or not in this lifetime. Many of us insist on not spending time thinking about the root connections of our current fears to our initial wound. When I express the situation in these terms, it seems a bit silly to ignore our fears, but the fact of the matter is we experience anxiety at the very word. We think that if we spend time examining our fears, then we'll have flashbacks of the initial wound that caused them, and we'll go crazy or we'll get stuck in a perpetual state of grief.

Well, let me tell you, without exploration of your fears, your art will be limited, and in that same way that it's been difficult to have successful relationships because of the apparition of fear creeping around unacknowledged, it will be difficult to write a book with that apparition begging for attention yet being ignored.

So, rather than waiting for your fears to sneak up on you, approach them with a big old flashlight and a tranquilizer gun in hand. Don't wait for them to catch you off guard. Learn their characteristics. Learn about the initial wound that caused your fears. This way, you can use them as tools in your writing or transform them into other gifts. After all, no one wants to read volume after volume of what you hope for as a positive reaction to an initial wound that you refuse to share. Instead, allow readers to connect with your journey of transforming fears into hopes. It's difficult to read a book based on your greatest accomplishments without the compelling information of what your struggles and obstacles were.

The point of delving into your hopes and fears as an artist is to let the things you hope and fear be the connection you make with other humans, which of course is the capacity of art. Someone else has hoped and feared the same and needs the kinship of your story, the medicine of any revelations you had, or the food of your words to nourish and affirm them as they reach for the same positive survival. When we create literature only from our success stories, the world does not learn, find kinship, or find healing.

For that to happen, we must present our failed experiments and foibles as well.

For Example: My story "The Empty Nest" was written when I was scheduled for my first colposcopy (uterine biopsy). My son had left for his own adult life and was at a very aloof emotional age, and my daughter, though only nine years old, had already begun to act like an aloof preteen. I felt alone because my children were being children. I feared that I would be sick without a partner to nurture and hold me. I feared these things because my children are the family I built after my original biological family ostracized me, and as my children (my only family at the time) matured into the phase of their aloof years and I endured my non-partnered years, what would become of me if the prognosis was life-threatening? Though many of the life circumstances of the main character are not mine, so much of the emotional and psychological content of her fears and hopes are mine.

So, it goes without saying that your hopes and fears are the artistic plot stuff that many good novels, memoirs, or collections of poems are built on. What connects your hopes and fears is the tense and often elusive struggle of "Will the initial wounds of my life drag me into the pit of death (fear), or will the fact that I am hell-bent on survival offer new life (hope)?"

HOPES AND FEARS CHART

1. Take a sheet of paper and hold it lengthwise (landscape) and fold in into thirds like a letter, or create a three-column document on your computer. Yes, this format of working with dichotomies is the same as Joys and Pains earlier in this chapter.

2. At the top of one of the outside columns, write the word "Hopes." Think of and bullet at least three things in life that you hope for. Make sure that you keep the hopes specific to your personal and emotional experiences in life. Don't go getting general and saying, "I hope for world peace." For instance, "I hope that I live long enough for my children and their children to enjoy my long life and for me to enjoy theirs." I also "hope that I get the opportunity to be allowed to have a relationship with my granddaughter while she is growing up."

3. At the top of the other outside column, write the word "Fears." Think of and bullet at least three things in life that your fear. Again, make sure that your fears are less universal and of your personal and emotional experiences. For instance, "I have a fear of drowning in a large body of water. Though I love being in water, I'm a sinker and have had more than one near-drowning experience." I also fear "being alone—that I may never find a partner at this stage in my adult life."

4. Look at the two lists. Perhaps there is something on your Hopes list that is a result of something on your Fears list, a cause-and-effect relationship. Perhaps there is an ironic relationship where there is the same thing on your Hopes list as your Fears list, or perhaps there is a connection that you are aware of that I can't fathom or imagine. Certainly, with the examples that I gave you from my hopes and fears, there is a connection between my hope to live and see my children and grands into rich, long lives, and my fear of drowning.

5. At the top of the middle column, write the word "Connections." Look for ways that there is an initial wound that connects something on your Hopes list to something on your Fears list. For instance, the connection of my hope to live long and my fear of drowning is an initial wound from a few years ago. Without any warning, I lost one of

my younger brothers, a former US Marine. He drowned on a pleasure vacation in the rip tides in Cancun. This happened two weeks after my granddaughter was born. He never got to meet her. Literally draw lines between connections that you notice on the two lists.

6. Write the words and thoughts of the initial wound connection on the actual line.

7. Though it's a difficult emotional task to think of the wounds of the past, you'll likely find harmony among your dichotomies. One of the harmonic outcomes to these dichotomies on my lists is that since the day that my brother drowned, I have taken my daughter to swim lessons, and she joined the swim team and is an absolute dolphin in the water. Though I still have lead legs, I get in the shallow end of the pool and she acts as my coach when she is not completely appalled by my ineptitude.

PROMPT 2: HOPES AND FEARS

Your writing prompt is to consider the Hope/Fear Connections that you feel like you have the strongest reaction to, or currently feel is the most present for you. Write about the initial wound event that represents the Hope/Fear Connection or the wounding event that represents either the hope or the fear.

For instance, I jump-started by choosing a few words from a poetry book and listened to some music and ended up writing about the connection between a fear of being alone and a hope that I will get to watch my granddaughter grow up.

After you've done this for one Hope/Fear Connection, prompt again from another Hope/Fear Connection.

Jump Starter: Choose a line, flash on a candid photo, or plug some music in to your ears to jump-start you, and go. Don't worry if you jump-start and end up writing about a different Hope/Fear Connection. The most important thing is not to overthink but to follow the first impulse, memory, or words that come to you from the prompt and the Jump Starter. Whatever you end up with is what is being called for.

HOPES

- Hope that I get the opportunity to be allowed to have a relationship with my granddaughter while she is still growing up.

- I hope that I live long enough for my children & their children to enjoy my long life and for me to enjoy theirs.

- That I get to experience the sweetness of love & companionship that I 'hold cherish & remember.

CONNECTIONS

INITIAL WOUNDS

I lost Kerry in the Atlantic

Estranged from my sd birth family

Lost Kerry & LaVenson

family fibroid from it

Maybe also estranged

failed romances... Lost Kerry & LaVenson

FEARS

- I have a fear of drowning in a large body of water. Though I love being in water, I'm a sinker & have had more than one drowning experience.

- Being alone - that I may never find a partner at this stage in my life, or being estranged from my children too.

- I have a fear of dying while my children are still young. That would just be horrible pain for them, an experience I know from loss of LaVenson.

Remember: When you are done, don't edit your raw material. You may end up editing out or diluting the purity of what will later show up as the connection between pieces of raw material.

If you start to surface out of the zone, jump-start again. And remember to write events, not monologues or dialogues; write in first person, past tense. Engage us with sensory detail (smell, taste, texture, color, images, sounds, the weather, and so on).

Go for it, write, write, for a couple of days on these dichotomy prompts of Joys and Pains and Hopes and Fears.

Some of you may be asking, "Why focus on your fears?" Well, perhaps through your writing, you've revealed the significance for yourself. But also, let's just talk about it a bit here. Your fears are your greatest obstacle to learning, growing, creating, and having the relationships you want (friendships you want, jobs you want, romance you want, published book you want).

I imagine this threshold of fear as also a **threshold of learning**. It is a door with all of the scary faces and memories moving around on it. Whenever we're about to learn, we encounter our worst fears and stand at this door just shivering, but we aren't learning unless we are challenged. Once we open that door, we are on the other side of a new piece of our evolution. The point at which we have the potential to learn in all relationships is this same threshold. Only discernment through self-exploration can help you open that door by revealing the difference between real scary faces on that door and the scary faces of memories and experiences long since passed. So, when we approach and spend time holding our fears up to the light by writing about them, we are working from our emotional and psychological base, and readers will connect with their fears and head toward hope in the same authentic manner that we have. Again, that human connection is art and can only happen when you are expressing from your true joys, pains, hopes, and fears.

While we're on the subject, let me say that this threshold embodies lots of other potential energy. For instance, if you fear that something will happen to you or others again, your motivation might be to desperately prevent it from happening, which could lead you and others out of darkness and into the light. In the movie *The Pursuit of Happyness*, Chris Gardner fears his son will grow up without a father in the way that he did. He desperately wants to prevent this repeated loop, which motivates him to work his way out of homelessness and into a financially prosperous life for him and his son.

It is also the threshold of manifestation. It is where creative imagination as an energy has the potential to become an invention or a story, where the person who has creatively imagined leaves the old platform of "I'm gonna" and steps on the platform of "I did." To think that all that can be manifested from harnessing the energy of fear.

We will revisit this Hopes and Fears Prompt much later in Chapter 16, The Craft of Dramatic Tension – Hope vs. Fear.

Now, step away from this book and the dichotomy writing on joys and pains, hopes and fears so that you can let yourself breathe for a couple of days. Come out of the cave, stretch your legs, let the fresh air flow through your lungs and to your mind. Go out and look at all the ways that in your current life you have manifested riches, gracefulness, and harmony, because you have had fear and pain in your life and from them sprung hope and joy.

Okay—bookmark here and scoot for a week of writing.

(Background elevator music.)

CHAPTER 3

Spelunking

and Internal Saboteurs

Spelunking

Now that we have warmed up our hearts and lungs and are accustomed to breathing and writing at such depths, let's talk about strategies for intentionally going into and coming out of those depths. **Spelunking** is a metaphorical way to help you deal with your fear that you will go crazy or become stuck in some perpetual state by spending time deep in your memories. If you are going into deep caves, you should wear a headlamp and a utility belt. You should bring matches, a torch, a raincoat, and food pellets that can sustain you for days and days if necessary—you get the picture. You get equipped for the mission at hand.

If you are afraid to deal with or write about your memories, then do what I do: tether yourself to something outside of your writing world like any good spelunker should. Ask a friend to meet you for coffee just after you plan to be done writing. Tell your partner or a friend to call at a certain time and check in with you. Plan to share dinner with your roommate. Pick your kid, or for some of us, your parent up from school or day care. Schedule your therapy appointments or appointments to see your spiritual leader just after your writing time. Plan something that will ground you in the present you. If you are writing with a short fifteen-minute break, then jump-start and write for ten minutes and spend the other five minutes walking back to your cubical the long way, via the outdoor garden. If you have to hop in your car after you write, go the scenic route to class or to pick up the kid from sports or the parent from the medical appointment, something to ground and tether you.

This way, before you even jump-start, you get to convince yourself that it's okay to go in deep for the emotional and psychological truth, because you have something you will do immediately afterward that is a reflection of treasured gifts, of friends, nature, your favorite healthy and spiritual rituals outside of the cave. I call this "spelunking" because you are going into the cave and tying one end of the rope to you and the other end to something or someone that grounds you—a yoga class, a trip to a friend's apartment to watch the game, whatever works for you.

In helping you to access your emotional, psychological, and spiritual base, I can offer you guidance on how to use other art to help you get there, and you can employ other folks as part of your spelunking team. If you need to wait and work with this book when you are emotionally and psychologically prepared to do so, then do that. Take care of yourself and make sure you have good emotional, psychological, and spiritual support before you embark on this adventure that will require your endurance.

So, there's anchoring yourself, then there's making excuses to never even put on the spelunking gear.

Internal Saboteurs

In the depths of our creating, we encounter parts of ourselves that may thwart our mission to go into the depths and create something true.

Some of us will pick up a self-help book for writers, learn a bunch of techniques that work, and go right into the mode of finding ways to insist that what was working no longer does, and begin doing things like choosing a line of poetry and pouting, then choosing another line and saying, "Oh, screw it," and then we sit there and read the poetry book instead of writing.

Don't think it's just you. It's the result of your initial wounds. In the introduction of the book, I said that "want" is probably the most utilized word in this book. Well, the most utilized phrase is "initial wound." Every personal plot or individual journey of wants springs from an initial wound or impactful event, which is an event in life that results in a significant **loss**, and that loss causes a want, and that want drives and motivates you on a journey to fulfill the want. The initial wound is the primary event of any of our personal plots, and because this is true, the negative residue of the wound is often digested into our relationship with self.

As a result of having people who exacerbate our wounds—be they our intimate nuclear society of family or the society-at-large—we may become convinced that despite our obvious power to multitask, endure profound trauma, and survive while showing ultimate mental and psychological strength, we are weak. We may become convinced that, despite our ability to puzzle-solve and take one dollar and feed a whole family, we can't take care of ourselves. Or worst of all, we may be convinced that despite the truth of who we are to our societies, we do not deserve to have what we want, and when we are about to get what we want, our internal trip wire resets us at "undeserving."

Over time and as we grow from children into adults, most of us have a tendency to maintain these saboteurish myths regardless of whether the people who instilled the original ill messages are alive or dead. In their absence, we perpetuate the negative messages ourselves. "I never finish anything." "I don't know who's going to want to read this drivel." "I'm a procrastinator." "I'm too selfish to write something useful to others." "I can't sustain a thought long enough to write a memoir or novel or collection of poems."

The **internal saboteur** is the voice that tells you that you can't have kids and write, go to school and write, work a job and write, take care of your elderly parent and write, or write at all. Keep in mind that the voice is just a henchman for the ill messages of the past. Ironically, in the absence of the naysayers, we carry out the activities that lead to the negative outcome where we are left disappointed without having what we want or doing what we want. The lack of worthiness is confirmed, but because we are hell-bent on survival, we sigh and resign ourselves to not getting what we want, then perk up and start the struggle all over again, which is the oscillating behavior that keeps us wanting to write but in a state of inconsistent writing practice. The full-length manuscript or any other tangible goal doesn't materialize with that sort of push and pull and rise and fall in attention.

You may always have these voices with you, but if you want to complete a whole project, you'll need to learn to manage them, to reroute some of the circuitry so that the old message fires in the problem-solving part of the brain rather than in your self-berating little loop of gray matter. Remember these voices are also shape-shifters. As soon as you become aware of one saboteur and find a way to manage that behavior, it pops up again as some other unproductive behavior. For instance, don't be fooled by the **Neat Freak Saboteur**. As soon as you say that you will no longer procrastinate before doing your writing, that little voice will show up as the impulse to get your home clean before writing, when you know darned well that your home will never be cleaned to your imagined standards. We'll work much more in depth with internal saboteurs that shape shift in Chapter 8 when we work to turn the internal saboteurs of our personal plots into the internal character development of our literary plots.

Don't be fooled by the **Sympathy Saboteur,** also known as the **Lethargy Saboteur**. This saboteur says, "I am so tired. Yes, I took the day off work and planned to write during the first half, but now that I'm off, I just want to do nothing, and I deserve that for my day off." So, you turn on your favorite talk show and chill. This sounds so legitimate as sympathetic to the self; after all, you are tired and need rest on your day off to write. The only problem is, if you listen to that voice, at the end of the day you'll be kicking yourself and giving yourself just another reason to feel down about the whole possibility of getting your work done.

Instead of following that voice, when you turn on that TV, remind yourself that the talk show host or whomever you're watching is doing his or her work and you're not doing yours. Another way to think of it is to remember how hard you work, tired or not, when something in life is chasing you (like bill collectors), when your survival is threatened, or when you know a supervisor, teacher, or some higher-up will be checking your work. If you were at work, at school, or working on a contract project at home and got tired, you'd have a cup of coffee or tea or take a brief walk, because you know that you have to do the work to get the money or grade and that if you don't get the money or grade, you'll threaten the survival of yourself and other folks who are counting on you for food today or food tomorrow. Same here.

If you feel tired, don't get yourself in trouble with your internal supervisor by doing nothing; have a cup of tea or coffee or do some crunches and get back to it, because if you don't you'll disappoint yourself and end up just creating another scenario where you wanted the full-length manuscript but didn't get it. We are capable of so much more than we think we are but often don't come to this realization until pushed by villains to survive or perish. When your Lethargy and Sympathy Saboteurs pop up, harness the survival energy that you expend when something is chasing you, and use it with intention toward what you want.

There's the **I Don't Have Time Saboteur**. Let's just list some of the things that make us feel like we don't have writing time. I'll throw my stuff in this basket too: Can't write because the kid broke both feet. Can't write because Mama had hip surgery. Can't write because it's the end of the semester and I have too many papers to write or to grade. Can't write because my client list is getting longer. There are shipments to ship. My sweetie left me. The baby has a cold. My car broke down yesterday. I'm up for review at work.

The stuff of raw material is the stuff of everyday life. For instance, if you are sitting waiting for Mama to finish watching *Wheel of Fortune* and while she's staring at the screen she's motioning for you to bring her more painkillers, say to yourself as a prompt, "The Pain Killers," and write the scenes and events, whatever literal and figurative painkillers come to mind in your relationship with Mama. Jump-start with the prompt and let yourself write until the depths of your heart and soul and all of the inner meaning, connection, and impact of "The Pain Killers" has spewed up from the underground spring onto the surface of your paper like a geyser. In other words, use the activities that appear to be taking up your time as actual inspiration for short writing moments.

I can't say this enough: don't be fooled by the **Innocent Child Saboteur**. Because we have all been children—and all children at some point have an initial wound—this saboteur is the most ever-present distraction. This saboteur is ironically your internal little child who came out into the world clear and discerning but was injured by so much of other people's mess.

It's hard to resist the child's demands because they are so innocent, but your little girl or boy is not wise or discerning enough to direct your journey or drive your evolutionary car. The child inside of us does not have the skillset to do much of what they want to do. Their survival mode comes without wisdom and they just want what they want or in their limited wisdom, to prevent what they want to prevent. "I don't want to write today because . . ." or "I don't want to take a writing workshop because I hate people telling me when I should try and write or if I should try to write," or "I don't want anybody to read my work, because I hate being criticized." If this child saboteur gets their hands on the keys to your little journey car, they will innocently steer your creative journey off a bridge with victim-child reasoning.

Of course, if you really think it through, you will find the victim-child and their poor reasoning popping up in other relationship management moments in life where children aren't supposed to be running the show. I'm just saying, manage that kid; let the grown-up, who has things to accomplish in this grown-up lifetime, show up and steer the path of the adult you.

There's the ever-sympathetic **Philanthropic Saboteur**. This is present when you are so busy doing for others that you can't do for yourself and you are actually just finding a socially agreeable way to sabotage your work. No one in our society is going to criticize a person who sacrifices themself for others; as a matter of fact, they give awards for it. When we are sick in the hospital with one thing or another because we give to others, we are praised, and we eat that attention up, unless of course we're being praised for our good works posthumously. You tell the tale of how you threw out your back, pulled an all-nighter, took your sick neighbor to all of their appointments. And others nod and say, "You are a good person."

Philanthropy seems like such a socially acceptable way to sabotage ourselves, but sharing is only sharing when we have something in surplus to share. It doesn't count if you are giving away time, yet you haven't done what you need for yourself. When I find myself resorting to this behavior, I know that it's little Zelda—who got attention for doing the dishes but not for doing her homework—steering the situation.

In the endless list of shape-shifting saboteurs, there is a quite famous player, the **Unworthy Saboteur**.

The Unworthy Saboteur is almost as famous as the victim-child with the arguments: "I've been writing about myself my whole life; it's time I cut this out and did something more meaningful than write this drivel." This saboteur is also likely to carry messages like "You don't get to sit around and write. You don't deserve that after causing so much trouble in other people's lives." And one of its most famous sayings, "It's too late in my life to write. That time has passed and I should have done it when I was younger." These messages translate to "I am not worthy of even a third of the time that I have offered everyone else in my life."

One way to keep this unworthy form of the saboteur quiet is to remember that who will find your work worthwhile is none of your business, and to trust that your writing is an organic response to some call out there for connection and your job is to write the emotional, psychological, and spiritual truth—no matter how much or little time you believe you have on a daily basis, what wrong you have done that didn't go punished, or how much time you have remaining on this planet.

Another way to quiet the unworthy voice is to continuously remind yourself that you deserve to reserve for yourself a minimum of one-third of what you offer others, that you may have done some wrong, but telling the truth about the root of your pains is redemption, and that you deserve to leave behind your account of how this life is constructed. You are as deserving as Confucius, Shakespeare, Toni Morrison, Dante, Virginia Woolf, Stephen King, Amy Tan; you get the picture.

Now, I've saved the most powerful two saboteurs for last, the **Shame Saboteur** and the **Mortal Fear Saboteur.**

The Shame Saboteur says, "What if my mother reads this?" "I don't want to hurt my family by telling of my experiences," or "I don't want people to know what awful thing happened to me and how it wrecked my world. I just want them to see the me who rose from the ashes." All the while, you swing back and forth with the effort to tell the truth because you see how free it has made others to do so, or you remember the value of reading someone else's journey of surviving then thriving. You know that someone who needs your stories is calling for them.

Think of it this way: if your writing is food, medicine, or kinship—in other words, connection—for some unknown audience, and you starve that audience of your work just because a handful of people might not like the taste of it, you have done the universe a disservice. You have pulled yourself out of the ecology of creating in order to alleviate some sense of shame that was planted in your relationship strand probably long before you were born. Instead of progressing that strand, you can break it by living an authentic life where your experience of this thing called life is left behind as bread crumbs for someone else who is trying to walk a similar journey.

Last and most powerful is the Mortal Fear Saboteur; this is the fear of death or not surviving that I spoke of briefly during the Joys and Pains

Exercise. It is the mother of all fears, the root of all fear, the alpha and omega fear; and all other fears are descendants of it. It is our internalization of this saboteur that makes all forms of oppression possible.

If a person or group of people wants another person to do what they say, even if what they say goes against the individual's desire for a good life, they threaten the individual with images, smells, sounds, tastes, textures, or memories of death and of their own or a loved one's potential demise. Then, they can be off in the Caribbean enjoying a yearlong vacation, and when they return, the individual will not have moved because they have lost discernment over what is harmful or dangerous and what is simply challenging and difficult. Rather than having discernment for the instinctual value of fear, the individual then just lives in constant mortal fear, stuck, accomplishing little in life. Most of us walk around in circles with certain desires in our lives, because we bought into the invisible fencing that our internal saboteur of mortal fear has constructed.

Deep breath. What to do about that mortal fear internal saboteur? How do you get your discernment back?

I can only offer you my method. First, identify what forms the internal saboteur of mortal fear takes in your life. One of mine for years was "If I write my truth, something awful might happen, like my mother will kill herself, or I'll lose my job, or my siblings will further ostracize me." How did I come up with such notions? Well, as a child, I was told and sometimes shown all of the things that could happen if I didn't keep my mouth shut.

After identifying this mother of all saboteurs, you can run litmus tests to see if you are in danger or if your internal saboteur is creating illusions of danger and is therefore running the show. Remember, in almost every adventure, someone throws a rock at what they think might be a booby trap to see if the landmines explode or if the snare is set off. Throw a few rocks; publish some small excerpts of your work and see what happens, because the question is not "Will the land mines go off?" but "Do I have the capacity to survive a journey of my desires whether land mines go off or not?"

We could go on naming internal saboteurs, because they shape-shift and take new form, but here are some things to remember:

1. These saboteurs or self-defeating behaviors aren't random. They are the result of some initial wound or series of initial wounds, physical and verbal messages that you internalized after doing the best you could at the time to make sense out of what was happening in your family or society-at-large.

2. Those who are calling for your work will recognize the authenticity of the pure response, and those who don't respond or have a negative response didn't call for it; it's not their sustenance; it isn't medicine meant for their consumption. A bit of caution here: I'm not saying that you should resist the constructive criticism of those who can help you make your writing clearer and more authentic. You need these folks and their honesty. We'll address that more in Chapter 19, which addresses what you should do after you've finished the first draft of your manuscript.

3. Most importantly, you must allow for the main ingredients of art to be present—your vulnerability and the courage to be vulnerable—and then you must follow the impulse to create, not regardless of the saboteurs but regarding them and integrating them into your work.

PROMPT 3: THE SABOTEUR

You have probably remembered and engaged with your own internal saboteurs. Pick one, the one that seems to be running amuck, the one that you feel is currently steering your writing journey and possibly your relationship journey all over the place, or the one that you feel to be present in this very moment. Write an event/scene from your life where this saboteur was present. Do this several times with each saboteur that is active in your life. After you have written about your internal saboteurs, save the writing as you will with all of your raw material from your writing prompts. We will use the saboteur writings in later chapters. You will see how our internal saboteurs are an integral part of our personal plots and therefore should be utilized in our literary plots.

I'll close this chapter with a passage written by Clarissa Pinkola Estés from her book *Women Who Run with the Wolves*:

> If you feel you have lost your mission, your oomph, if you feel confused, slightly off, then look for the Devil, the ambusher of the soul within your own psyche. If you cannot see, hear, catch it in the act, assume it is at work, and above all stay awake—no matter how tired you become, no matter how sleepy, no matter how much you want to shut your eyes to your true work. (439)

CHAPTER 4

Warm-Up Prompts

to Create Raw Material from Your Relationships

Using the Life You Live:
Your Authentic Relationships to Build Authentic Art

Remember, without vulnerability there is no art. It is the vulnerable truth revealed within a painting, a dance performance, a movie scene, a story well told that makes us say, "Oh, I loved that." It is the shared truth that we connect with in a piece of art when we say, "That was good," and it is the failed attempt at authenticity when we say, "That was awful."

As consumers of art, we don't spend a lot of time saying why we didn't like something; we are simply turned off, but nine times out of ten, it's because we didn't recognize anything emotionally or psychologically true that we can connect with in what we were consuming. In other words, the artist forgot the main ingredient, the vulnerability of self, the ingredient that does what art is meant to do: connect with other humans over shared experiences and relationships. After all, you can't connect with someone if you don't reveal enough of yourself for the traction of connection.

Many of us fear that we may go crazy if we open up that box of our emotional relationships, because inside of that box are tattered dolls and GI Joes with the heads nervously chewed off, all reminding us of the bad memories of childhood. But also in that box is the ring from the box of Cracker Jacks that reminds us of the joy of surprises, or the dried-out seed pod that reminds us of how much we love nature.

To keep the status quo and keep everybody around us happy and pleased with us, we attempt to exist in and exhibit just the happy hemisphere in our relationships. We say, "Why would I choose to remember bad things about bad people and make myself miserable?" But that isn't authentic, sustainable, or even organic to the reality of life, and it certainly isn't conducive to creating art. The things that hurt us are as much a part of our potential wisdom and growth as the things that make us feel good.

If you go back and look at your Joys and Pains and Hopes and Fears charts, your responses were all about relationships with people, places, things, creatures, yourself. Our reactions to our relationships bring about our daily lives. These past experiences have as much to do with who we love as they do with who we loathe. We end up finding the treasures of our personalities and the treasures of our enemies' personalities in the same tattered chest. The Pandora's Box of emotions is a museum of "us-ness." So many of us have held on to the total essence of someone who was an **agent** in helping us to heal from one of our initial wounds, and also held on to the total essence of a person who exacerbated our wounds or became an **obstacle** on our journey of healing. The folks who are agents and obstacles to our healing are in some of the most significant relationships in our personal plots.

The Relationship Museum Exercise

In your mind of places (your house, previous places you have lived or traveled to, your job, your car), search for three objects that represent each of the following relationships:

- Myself
- The person I feel most responsible for
- The person who helps me out in this world (agent)
- The person who gets in my way (obstacle)
- My belief system

Make five columns and three rows for this, or more if you need a bigger chart/museum. In the boxes below each column, write the objects that you own that represent that relationship. These objects are precious to you or emotionally precarious for you and represent memories, emotional moments in your relationship with other people that no one else would know the significance of by looking at the object alone. For instance, in these two short excerpts from *Fifth Born II: The Hundredth Turtle*, the black, waist-length leather jacket (from my museum) is the object of significance in my relationship with my brother LaVenson, who is represented in my museum as my agent. By just seeing it there in the museum, it means something to me but nothing to you until I offer you the significance scene in *Fifth Born II*, where I simply loaned the emotional significance of

Relationship Museum				
MYSELF	THE PERSON I FEEL MOST RESPONSIBLE FOR	THE PERSON WHO HELPS ME OUT IN THIS WORLD (AGENT)	THE PERSON WHO GETS IN MY WAY (OBSTACLE)	MY BELIEF SYSTEM
Laptop	Shark's tooth	Waist-length leather jacket	Sewing box	Bamboo
Guitar	Handmade doll	Red seeds from unknown plant	Stickers	Rock and pebbles
Compost	Paint brushes	Two novels	Lollipops	Garden
Bamboo	Cell Phone			My writing tools—Jump Starters, etc.

my relationship with the jacket and my brother to Odessa's relationship with the jacket and her brother Lamont:

> That night I went with you to your choir rehearsal. I sat in the pews and looked at your back in the black waist-length jacket. You were a deity blending the voices that rose in a swell of breath and body heat into the high rafters. The top of my head tingled like a hand or foot fallen asleep; my soul not able to stay in my body. Your arms flailed the musical commands, a translation of the harmony, the melody. All the voices from single open mouths, a swell of one forceful wave, and I wanted to swallow that sea. . . .
>
> Three men, and I believe, one woman, dressed in lovely evening reds and blacks, smooth brown faces, beautiful people. They are your friends and I want to move hand-to-glass with the same grace and freedom from self-conscious staccato that you and they possess. You are in the waist-length jacket again and look like John Travolta in your handsome swagger that shows you believe in the movement of all the muscles inside your tight jeans. You disappear into the smoky dark toward the bathrooms. Your friends call behind you, "Give it to em baby," and "We love you, Song Bird," kisses blown to where you vanished behind a curtain. Glasses clink above laughter and cigarette smoke inside the warm belly of this club. I cross my legs, uncomfortable without you there, the sudden awareness of stale air around me.

PROMPT 4: RELATIONSHIP MUSEUM

This will produce several raw material writings. Choose one of the objects in your museum. Jump-start and write an event that offers the significance of the object. In other words, tell the story associated with the object. Do this for each of the objects.

Make sure that you offer not just an external description of the object, but the events that tell us the emotional significance of the object. In other words, the object is external to you or to the character but represents an emotional/psychological response in your relationship with another person. For example, under my relationship with myself, I have "bamboo," because it is such a blessing and a curse as it sways green and stands up even after an ice storm, which inspires strength and resilience but also creates runners, and no matter what I do they threaten to overtake my home. I wrote a poem using the object "bamboo" from my museum:

My mother did not know that by leaving her home in St. Louis and running away from my father, home to her mother in Mississippi and giving birth to me in her origin and her mother's origin and her mother's origin that after the doctor said she could travel, she would be taking me from my home to St. Louis, to a home that would never be mine. She did not know that for 18 years, I would be looking South until I could return myself to that warm salt water, and breeze that sways tall green things like crib mobile for the reaching.

My mother did not know that five years after giving birth to me, two years after her mother's death, that on summer vacation, in Mississippi, while she was still mourning the loss of her mother, my father would molest his own daughter right there on the sandy floor behind the coke chest where the smell of sweat and salt and ancestor's bone meal mingles in the dust. She did not know that I would be a talker, and even through the tears and trauma that I would run to her, like she'd run to her mother and I would tell.

My mother did not know that the twist of grief in her gut, the twist of her own hidden woman-traumas, and her motherless-loneliness would leave her backed against her own wall, maybe behind the coke chest or Granmama's upright piano, and that she would scream and yell, and lash out with fists and that in her blind survival her own child would be hit as many times as necessary until the pain could subside. My mother did not know that the pain would be indelible and with each beating the vibration would carry through to her mother and her mother's mother and her mother's mother's mother, and that in that house the gift of my birth and the sin of the birther against the daughter would stand up like bamboo on some hidden runners. My mother did not know that no matter how many times I take my machete to new shoots and old stalks, the runners will run and spring up green and gorgeous from the ground in St. Louis, Mississippi, Ghana, breaking through pipelines, pushing up crops, pushing up whole houses and breaking walls into splinter.

My mother does not know, that I have sat myself down, in the middle of my own bamboo forest, and like a short-muzzled lemur drink the poison from the shoots and turn it into fresh water. I have married myself to the runners and that I am in the potted philodendron in her dusty St. Louis living room. I am dormant in the wormy wood soil beneath the Mississippi house waiting for rot to bring sunlight, that I am nourished by the bone meal of red clay mothers that rest in the Mississippi earth, that I run beneath the brine of the ocean, and am waiting for the rain beneath the stirred clouds of Ghanaian skin,

hair,

bone meal,

salt, and dust.

The museum can literally be your Pandora's Box of objects that represents your Pandora's Box of emotions. Some things in this box bring up strong positive emotions and some strong negative emotions, but everything in the box certainly stirs emotions around your relationships. I think about Tupac Shakur's poem "U R Ripping Us Apart!!!" which he dedicates to an object, "crack," an object in his relationship museum that might fall under a column that represents his relationship with his mother.

The Relationship Museum can help you create a whole series of expressions based on the emotional significance they hold. There are also other ways to use these objects in your writing. Later in Chapter 18, The Craft of Scene Arranging, we will talk about plants and character tags and how the objects in the Relationship Museum can be used for those purposes.

Keep filling in the Relationship Museum and let the objects be your prompts, but do use a Jump Starter with them if need be. This will keep you from telling the dry, surface-level terrain of the events of your life when you could be telling the emotional and psychological truth of the gorgeous, mysterious underground streams. Sometimes, the prompt itself will land you in a deep place, but you know the difference in your surface mind and your "in the zone" mind by now, so jump-start if you need to.

The Mirror Exercise

This exercise is designed to help you look at yourself and your relationships from a new angle by responding to a series of prompts that will leave you with the raw material of a short manuscript: a short story, a personal essay, or a small collection of poems. (The short manuscript is always a nice pilot writing for what in the later chapters can become your full-length manuscript.)

The visual for this prompt is a drawing of the inside of a car, where you are in control at the steering wheel with all of the traditional mirrors and glass surfaces in your vision.

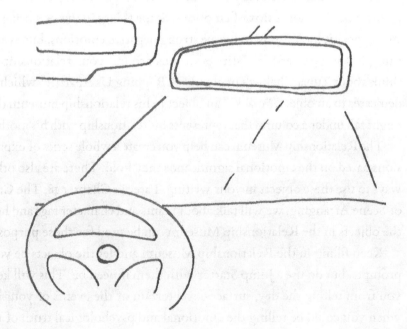

VANITY MIRROR

1. Take a blank sheet of paper, document, or note on your phone, and consider this a vanity mirror. If you are a visual learner like me, you can write your responses in the vanity view mirror in the drawing provided on the left.

2. Now, hold it in your hand and look at yourself. On the page or area where the vanity mirror might go, write or type positive characteristics of yourself. I call these **gifts** (or internal agents, but we'll talk more about them later).

3. Be sure to write the positive characteristics of how you see yourself, not how others see you. These may be physical, spiritual, intellectual, social: any internal and external descriptions.

Here is what I wrote in my mirror: "Gift: Great mom. Humor. Puzzle Solver." (Every time I do this exercise, I come up with a different set of characteristics for myself.)

PROMPT 5: VANITY MIRROR

Write an event from your life where the most prominent of these characteristics of self was present. Use time, place, and sensory detail. I jump-started with a line from a poetry book, "broken-hearted mornings," to write about one of my characteristics, "puzzle solver."

Here is the raw, unedited version of what I wrote:

I have asked if you will join me in therapy to try and fix our brokenness. I am listening to you in the session, seeing your face on the screen, trying to wait my turn, trying to keep in my head that I want to talk about our botched visit, but I am loosing focus because of what I see. You in the framed box of the screen in a work shirt.

I tell myself to concentrate on our session, to listen to you pour out your side of what we are in therapy for, but there you are dressed up the way you loved dressing up as a little boy, "Mom can I wear a tuxedo to your graduation?" I see behind your head a row of your dress shirts, dresses and coats of your partner, little shirts of my granddaughter caught up short between the sleeves of her parents. You are in the closet on your laptop for this session and I try to make meaning of your secret location, but it is my turn, and just before I speak, I remember the threat that you and your partner have collectively formulated.

I say I want to pass. "I need more time to think."

WINDSHIELD

1. Take another blank sheet of paper, document, or note on your phone, and consider this a windshield.

2. Think about someone you're currently having an issue with. On the right side of the road, write what they are doing to get on your nerves.

3. On the left side, write what you do in response, how you feel, and what you want.

Many of you have been conditioned to say that you don't have issues with anybody. Throw that thinking out. Consider the person who has gotten in your way, gotten on your nerves, stopped up the works for you, taken things that didn't belong to them, argued you down, made a mess. You may find that you have been writing about this person in other prompts. This is normal, because when something has gone awry in one of our relationships, it is on our minds every time we go to take a deep breath and offer a deep expression.

Here is what I wrote on the right side of the road: "My son wants to be closer, but won't make himself vulnerable. Begs for me to share, then when I do, he points out what I am doing wrong and how that keeps us apart." And here is what I wrote on the left side: "In response, I try to solve the emotional puzzle of us (therapy, visit, don't visit) always doing something. I feel ensnared. I want to watch my granddaughter grow up."

PROMPT 6: WINDSHIELD

Use a Jump Starter to write an event from your life where you and the person in the windshield are having one of your conflicts. Remember, let us smell, hear, taste, touch, and see. Use time, place, and sensory detail to bring us into an actual moment with this person.

Here is the raw, unedited version of what I wrote:

This is the 27th year, the one where my son and I both learn that I will not teach him everything that he is to learn. 6am, I stand in the arid cold morning of Denver, Colorado, the sun still beneath the covers of mountains; shades of pink reminding me of the flesh of my womb where he kept himself warm and alive for 8 months.

It is the morning I will get on the plane and love him by not talking to him. It is the morning after he has done what his misguided heart has commanded, whispered that if I do not do what he and his partner say, I will not get to have a relationship with my granddaughter. It is our old game of belonging, and I watch his eyes. I am trying not to show the sea sickness from the cycles, trying not to let him see that his birth, saved my life, helped me belong, but any card shown these days turns against me.

REARVIEW MIRROR

1. Take another blank sheet of paper, document, or note on your phone, and consider this a rearview mirror.

2. Remembering what you wrote in the windshield, adjust the rearview mirror and look into the past. Jot down another time (or many) with some other significant relationship where you felt and wanted something similar.

Here is what I wrote, "Me and any of my adult siblings. How I used to try visiting, calling, emotional puzzle solving only to end up ensnared in old dynamics and pushed out."

PROMPT 7: REARVIEW MIRROR

Choose the event that feels most related to your feelings and wants in the windshield and write the event. Use a Jump Starter if need be to get in the zone.

Here is the raw, unedited version of what I wrote:

Either side of the tread on both of my tires was just beginning to show wear, but I calculated the distance between Virginia and Missouri. Round-trip

would put me just at the limit of wear with no blow out. It was three months after the last time I'd been to St. Louis. That time I drove in but flew out, because my partner took the car to visit holiday family in Pennsylvania and I could not move myself from staring at solitaire cards on my sister's kitchen table. She and I had buried our brother. He was like a twin to her. He was like a parent to me, and there I sat at her kitchen table. Happy Holidays vacated by our mourning family.

That visit was not a visit, everything like double exposure of past and present. But, this visit I am grounded. I know what I want, to see my sister's baby, just born who survived the mourning in utero, and I want to see my two nephews and put them side by side with my son and see the connected puzzle pieces of broken family united in their same smiles.

When I arrive my sister answers the door, holding the bundle in her arms. No hug. No good to see you, and she vanishes into her bedroom. I go to the park with the boys, where we fly kites and giggle and make a new memory that I do not know will be our last memory until fifteen years later when my sister will let me back in saying that it was her ex-husband's fault.

You might find revelations of connection between the feeling and want. You may see reasons why you feel and want the way you do in your current relationships.

For instance, in writing the scene from the past where I wanted and felt the same, it is clear to me that I feared that my son's threat might mean not seeing my granddaughter for years. After all, I did not see my sister's daughter for the first fifteen years of her life.

PASSENGER'S SIDE VIEW MIRROR

1. Take another blank sheet of paper, document, or note on your phone and consider this your passenger's side view mirror.

2. Consider the obstacle person's gifts and positive characteristics. Write them down.

This might not be easy, because these gifts have always been there but might be in your blind spot. They might exist just outside of the range of what you are willing to acknowledge, or outside of what you have been able to see while the obstacle person's negative characteristics blocked your view. But that's what side view mirrors are for.

Here's what I wrote: "Funny. Likes smiling. Politically astute. A keen sense of social justice."

PROMPT 8: PASSENGER'S SIDE VIEW MIRROR

Now, look at the gifts of the obstacle person in the side view and write an event where that person's gifts were present. Use a Jump Starter if need be to get in the zone.

Here is my raw version:

I had been called more than once by the director of your day care. That day, it was nap time. Lunch time was over and I could hear your four-year-old

voice in the background holding church with the other four-year-olds who only wanted their nap time. She asked, "Can you talk to him. A boy said to him at lunch time that boys don't wear pink and he hasn't stopped schooling them."

They were the pink converses that you insisted on wearing every day, there is a photograph of you and me, our feet side by side on a fall day, my white running shoes, your pink Converses.

DRIVER'S SIDE VIEW MIRROR

1. Take another blank sheet of paper, document, or note on your phone, and consider this your driver's side view mirror.

2. Consider a combination of what you want and your gifts. Write them down here. Keep in mind that your gifts are things you already have.

Acceptance, and finding some of what we want in what is in our control, is a hard, harsh thing to consider, because we want what we want without compromise. But right there next to us, in our blind spot, is the ability to get some of what we want (sometimes all of what we want) by relying on what's in our control, our gifts.

Here is what I wrote: "Humor. I want to watch my granddaughter grow up."

PROMPT 9: DRIVER'S SIDE VIEW MIRROR

Write an event from your future, one where you fulfill what you want by relying on your gifts. This will require you to take a look back in the vanity mirror at what you wrote down as your gifts. I thought this time about my sense of humor.

How will you get what you want? Not by shaking down the obstacle person and making them change their ways, but by using your gifts. In this scene, allow yourself to get what you want from yourself, not from them.

Yes, strange to write a **revelation** when you haven't fully had one yet. Revelation in this book is defined as a moment in your life when you understand an initial wound or an impactful event, understand what

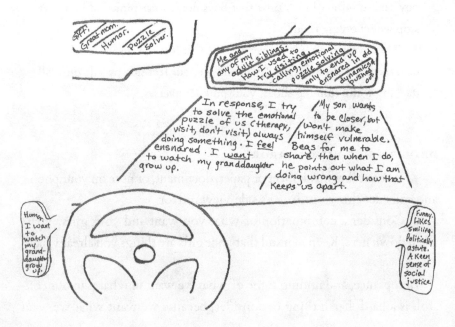

helps with the healing, understand what gets in the way, or understand how to self fulfill the want caused by the impact. Art is so fabulous a tool for our self-expression and self-discovery.

As always with your writing, bring us into an event. Though it is an imagined event, still let us smell, hear, taste, touch, and see. Use sensory details to bring us in to a moment in your imagined future. So to get started, use a Jump Starter and go.

Here is my raw, unedited writing with additions for detail:

I have not seen my granddaughter since she was four and she is eight now.

I secretly pray, the way that I did when I saw the Lockhart forehead in her ultrasound, that she will still look like me, undeniable connection, that her mother and father cannot control, molecules shifting in her DNA chain like tectonic plates moving to make this FaceTime frame of her look like the frame of me in the long mirror this morning.

When I see her, I will make that silly face that I made at her father every night when he was a little boy—eyes squeezed tight, lips touching my nose.

My son appears on the screen, speaks to me polite, but stern in the FaceTime frame. My granddaughter still has not emerged, but I say something silly to my son and find myself in a guttural laugh despite my grief, and she appears at the side of the frame, a perfect amalgam of her parents' faces. As I am studying her, she sticks her face in front of my son's, her eyes bulging, tongue stuck out. She pulls her face at the sides of her mouth with her long index fingers. And I laugh from my gut, the sound like reckless water falls and then she is laughing at my laughing until it is time to hang up.

In any relationship, we are attracted to people because they have something that we want—we are jealous or we are angry that they have it and won't give it to us or they don't have it but we want it anyway, setting ourselves up to have unrealistic expectations of people. Or we are just plain passive-aggressive because what we want is some old dynamic in our lives that they represent, and we intend to shake them down until we get what we want.

What does this have to do with poetry, memoir, or fiction? The main character in fiction and the voice in memoir and poetry are driven and motivated psychologically by a series of relationships that represent attraction based on want.

Almost always, there is conflict that the main voice or character has with someone because they want things that they can't get from the person they are in relationship with and can only get from themselves.

In Viramontes's "The Moths," the main character wants to belong and to participate in the give-and-take of relationships. She is unrelenting in her attempts to get this from her parents, and unrelenting in her anger, and they do not offer a place in the family for a girl like her. The abuelita offers belonging, offers a different look at how a woman can survive, and offers the character the opportunity to practice doing for others so that she can fulfill her want of connection through action.

In Ta-Nehisi Coates's *Between the World and Me*, Coates goes through his college years at an HBCU (Historically Black College/University) wanting answers about Black love, Black freedom, and the American abuse against the Black body. He wants his professors and the books of his Black mentors to offer him answers, but he only feels spun around with more questions. A girl who loves differently, lives differently, and whom young Coates holds prejudices against, shows him ways of loving and living in freedom that do not involve violence.

In Grey Brown's *What It Takes*, there are poems of want and regret for the father's absence and later want and regret for the daughter's absence. Almost always, the main voice or character clashes with someone because they want things that they can't get from that person but can only get from themselves, often by looking at their own shortcomings and gifts.

If you put all of the raw material from the Mirror Exercise together, and clean it up for tense and pronoun shifts and take out any repetition, you actually have a whole short memoir piece, small collection of poems, or the character and plot development for a work of short fiction.

Here is the my first unedited rough draft with all of my raw material:

This is the 27th year, the one where my son and I both learn that I will not teach him everything that he is to learn. 6am, I stand in the arid cold morning of Denver, Colorado, the sun still beneath the covers of mountains; shades of pink reminding me of the flesh of my womb where he kept himself warm and alive for 9 months.

It is the morning I will get on the plane and love him by not talking to him. It is the morning after he has done what his misguided heart has commanded, whispered that if I do not do what he and his partner say, I will not get to have a relationship with my granddaughter. It is our old game of belonging, and I watch his eyes. I am trying not to show the sea sickness from the cycles, trying not to let him see that his birth saved my life, helped me belong, but any card shown these days turns against me.

I have asked if you will join me in therapy to try and fix our broken-ness. I am listening to you in the session, seeing your face on the screen, trying to wait my turn, trying to keep in my head that I want to talk about our botched visit, but I am loosing focus because of what I see. You in the framed box of the screen in a work shirt.

I tell myself to concentrate on our session, to listen to you pour out your side of what we are in therapy for, but there you are dressed up the way you loved dressing up as a little boy, "Mom can I wear a tuxedo to your graduation?" I see behind your head a row of your dress shirts, dresses and coats of your partner, little shirts of my granddaughter caught up short between the sleeves of her parents. You are in the closet on your laptop for this session and I try to make meaning of your secret location, but it is my turn, and just before I speak, I remember the threat that you and your partner have collectively formulated.

I say I want to pass. "I need more time to think."

~

I remembered the day that I calculated the distance between Virginia and Missouri. Round trip would put me just at the limit of wear with no blow out. It was three months after the last time I'd been to St. Louis, that time I drove in but flew out, because my partner took the car to visit holiday family in Pennsylvania and I could not move myself from staring at solitaire cards on my sister's kitchen table. Her and I had buried our brother. He was like a twin to her. He was like a parent to me, and there I sat at her kitchen table. Happy Holidays vacated by our mourning family.

That visit was not a visit, everything like double exposure of past and present. But, this visit I was grounded. I knew what I wanted, to see my sister's baby, just born who survived the mourning in utero, and I wanted to see my two nephews and put them side by side with you and see the connected puzzle pieces of broken family united in the same smiles of my son and my nephews.

When I arrived my sister answered the door, holding the bundle in her arms. No hug. No good to see you, and she vanished into her bedroom. I went to the park with you boys, where we flew kites and giggled and made a new memory that we did not know would be our last memory with them until fifteen years later when my sister let me back in saying that it was her ex-husband's fault.

~

When you were a toddler, the director of your day care called me more than once. That day, it was nap time. Lunch time was over and I could hear your four-year-old voice in the background holding church with the other four-year-olds who only wanted their nap. She asked, "Can you talk to him. A boy said to him at lunch time that boys don't wear pink and he hasn't stopped schooling them."

They were the pink converses that you insisted on wearing every day, there is a photograph of you and me, our feet side by side holding their ground on a fall day, my white running shoes, your pink Converses.

~

I have not seen my granddaughter since she was four and she is eight now.

I secretly pray that she will still look like me, an undeniable connection, that you and your partner cannot control, molecules shifting in her DNA chain like tectonic plates moving to make this FaceTime frame of her look like the frame of me in the long mirror this morning.

When I see her, I will make that silly face that I made at you every night when you were a little boy—eyes squeezed tight, lips touching my nose.

You appear on the screen, speak to me polite, but stern in the Face-Time frame. My granddaughter still has not emerged, but I say something silly to you and find myself in a guttural laugh despite my grief, and she appears at the side of the frame, a perfect amalgam of her parents' faces. As I am studying her, she sticks her face in front of yours, her eyes bulging, tongue stuck out. She pulls her face at the sides of her mouth with her long index fingers. And I laugh from my gut, the sound like reckless water falls, and then she is laughing at my laughing until it is time to hang up.

Now, if you made it through the Mirror Exercise, all I can say is you can't put the genie back in the bottle. For me, it feels like that when I embark on the emotional and psychological journey of writing; once I've started a piece and have embarked on discovering and having personal revelations that will allow me to make art, there's no going back to my innocent ignorance.

Remember: When you are done, any edits to your raw material should be to authenticate the voice in the story, not to delete things you find too personal to share. Also, by deleting parts of your raw material, you may end up diluting the response to the call for your writing, and then those who have called for it won't recognize the diluted response.

PART 2

The Stepping Stones
of the Full-Length Manuscript

The following terms are used heavily in these chapters. Having a definition of their meaning within the context of this book will prove helpful.

Initial Wound: An event that has a long-term, significant impact on your emotional, psychological, and spiritual development.

Loss: Emotional, psychological, or spiritual depletion as a result of an initial wound.

Want: A desperate motivation to gain something lost in an initial wound event or to prevent some similar event or similar initial wound feelings from occurring.

Agent: A person, place, or thing that helps you out in this world, particularly in your healing from an initial wound.

Obstacle: A person, place, or thing that gets in your way, particularly obstructing your path to healing from an initial wound. This may also be a person, place, or thing that exacerbates an initial wound.

Revelation: A moment in your life when you come to understand an initial wound, understand what helps with the healing, understand what gets in the way, or understand how to fulfill the want caused by the initial wound.

Outcome: The moment when you turn the awareness of revelation into action for change and evolution.

Outcome Action: After you have had revelation and outcome, the outcome action is the plan of action by which you sustain your new way of being.

Scene/Event or *Event/Scene*: A fully rendered internal and external moment in fiction or memoir where this moment and its temporary outcome mirror the overall plot. In poetry, scene often translates into a whole poem where there is temporary outcome. For instance, in Sharon Olds's poem "The Race," there is the outcome of her making the flight and seeing her father again before he passes away. We will explore this concept further in coming chapters.

CHAPTER 5

From the Horizon

to the Shore of Your Personal Plot

We come to this world naked and alone, and many of us will leave all dressed up but still alone. Everything that happens in between is a series of major initial wound events, and from them we spring forth on several emotional and psychological journeys—some that meet with a form of revelation and outcome and many that we take with us straight to that ceremonial exit.

These personal plots we collect like river pebbles that weigh us down, but we can make art with them, turn the heavy mess into collage, dance, song, poetry, fiction, memoir, and some good living.

We all have so many life plots that began because something profound happened (an initial wound) and as a result, we suffered a loss. That loss left us wanting or needing something, and as we tried to fulfill that want or need we were met with many obstacles, yet had many agents aiding us in achieving our want. We all walk around with several personal plots: unresolved wants and needs, each the result of some initial wound.

The Stepping Stones Exercise

Much like the Mirror Exercise from Chapter 4, this is a series of prompts that will work to bring out one of those personal plots and help you write through to some resolution utilizing your journey of personal plot to construct the literary plot. Whereas the Mirror Exercise left you with the raw material for a full-length manuscript of a short work, the Stepping Stones Exercise will leave you with the raw material of a full-length manuscript of a novel or memoir, or poetry collection.

You will be writing some of the plot from prompts designed to get you to reflect on past experiences as with the previous exercise. But with this exercise you will engage in character development research, write additional scenes that advance the plot, and take actions in your life so that you live experiences that will inspire you to write yourself to revelation and outcome.

This real-life plot stuff is the stuff of good fiction, as well as good poetry and memoir. Creating with your real-life plots offers you something that you can do with those experiences outside of simply carrying them around; by writing them, you can grow with them and so can others. Your plots are your truth—the things you have lived—and there are only two things you can do with the truth: affirm or deny it. Affirming it gives you creative license to let the experience live outside of your psyche and potentially become food, medicine, or kinship for some other being, while clearing your head and heart for the other inevitable personal plots that will be accumulating for as long as you are living. Denying the truth only leaves you with a pileup that could lead to any number of ailments of the mind, body, and spirit.

Before we even start the work of this chapter, let me beat you to the punch by saying, "It's hard, and it hurts."

Yes, as with the previous chapter, you will need to refer often to Chapter 3, Spelunking and Internal Saboteurs, because there isn't anything easy about working up the courage to be vulnerable for the sake of making meaningful art. You will need to spend countless hours here, standing in your own underground cave, staring at the vague silhouette of yourself in the reflecting pond.

But the consolation for this difficult internal excavation is that afterward, we can utilize all of those discoveries in our artwork, and with those brilliant gems make magical connections with others. And that feels quite good.

On that note, suit up with your spelunking gear with whatever tools you possess for fabulous artistic adventures, and let's get going.

HORIZON

1. At the top of a blank sheet of paper, draw a circle about the size of an orange.

2. Through the middle of the circle draw a wavy line, which represents water. Now, you have an interesting drawing of a horizon.

3. Think of an issue that you currently have with someone that you care about. Some of you will have to take a minute for your internal goody two-shoes to be quiet so that you can be honest about this question, while others will be able to think of the issue immediately, maybe because you just finished having an argument in your head with this person, or because you wrote about them so much in Chapter 4, or perhaps they were the subject of the windshield in the Mirror Exercise.

4. Around the bottom of the circle, below the waterline, write what this person is doing that is upsetting you. For instance, when I first did this exercise I wrote for the other person's issue, "She wants to help people who she thinks need money, especially if they are Black, because she loves Black culture. Problem is, she can't tell you a thing about her own culture, and she doesn't want Black people who have risen above their social circumstances in her intimate circle." Whew! That was a lot. How about you?

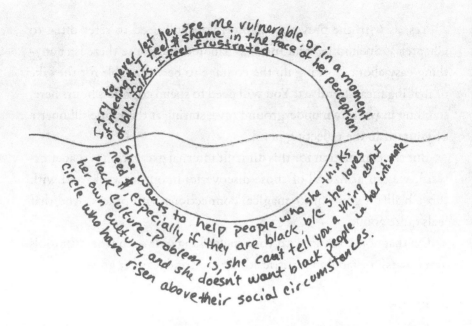

5. Now, around the top of the circle above the water, write your reaction to the other person's behavior. Be sure to write the action you take in response to their behavior (your external behavior) and how you feel in response to their behavior (your internal reaction).

For instance, I wrote around the top of the circle, "I try never to let her see me vulnerable or in a moment of needing money. I feel money shame in the face of her perception of Black folks. I feel frustrated."

PROMPT 10: HORIZON

Write a scene or event that represents the issue between you and this person. Try not to be self-conscious about telling all or self-conscious about fairness in your telling. It is okay to vent; there will be plenty of prompts to help you make emotional clarity out of what must be told. Right now, tell it like that two-year-old would after being pushed off the swings.

Use sensory detail. Write about the sounds, smells, sights, taste, and textures of things rather than just philosophizing. Also, make sure that you include your internal world of emotional responses to what is happening around you. What flashbacks, memories, or fantasies were taking place inside of your head while the actions were being taken and words were being spoken? Your scenes/events will be engaging if you offer the external and internal experiences simultaneously.

As always, write in first person, past tense, with little or no dialogue. This keeps you and the reader close to the emotional, psychological, and spiritual base of the voice. To get you into it, use a Jump Starter from Chapter 1.

Keep in mind that sometimes you will write the scene out and notice afterward that you need to put it in first person, past tense; or that you will have to go back and add sensory details or internal details of feelings, fantasies, and memories; or that you need to take out and minimalize the dialogue.

That's fine. If necessary, come back and include these essential details at a later time. But for now, grab a Jump Starter, get in the zone, and just write.

Here is the raw, unedited version of what I wrote:

"Class," she explained and identified herself as middle class, but she forgot to say out loud that she is a woman, which places her outside the benefits of any of the millions of white, moneyed, male, heterosexual constructs of the word.

She crossed the street in shades, leather jacket, leather boots, dyed red hair, politically correct only in label, but not in the reality of what makes her comfortable. A Black woman cleans her house, but she works for Black women's rights. There is a country club inside her mind.

When I was reeling in pain about my day or dealing with the white privileged world outside of our home, she told me to "be careful…" not to mix my tone of anger against the people in my day—that she is one of them. She told me that she will never know poverty because her grandparents left her all the petroleum stock to assure this and I marveled at her choice to tell me this.

STEPPING STONES

1. Below the horizon of the issue, draw smaller circles down to the bottom of your page, leaving room at the bottom that is untouched. But see if you can get at least five circles in there, like stepping stones in the water.

2. Now, for each stepping stone, briefly jot down other times in the past where you felt the same way that you feel in the issue at the horizon. Begin with the stepping stone nearest the horizon (most recent past) and proceed by writing only events where your feeling or reaction in the stepping stone event is the same or similar to your feeling or reaction in the event at the horizon. Go as far back in time as you can remember and write a brief reference to the relationship.

3. You can also jot down about other times in other relationships you felt this way, like with a coworker, community member, family member, lover, friend, and so on. For me, this would mean other relationships where I felt socioeconomic shame and frustration in the face of someone's view of me.

4. On these stepping stones, you only need to place a brief reference that you know represents the issue. For instance, on my next stepping stone I wrote "Me and Mary W" to represent my relationship with a previous supervisor that occurred sixteen years ago.

Note: It's going to be important to skip huge chunks of time so you can go as far back as you can remember feeling or reacting this way. So, if you have, for instance, ten similar stories about different people you dated but each event presents the same issue, you can just choose the one that feels most relevant to you. The only time that I would say to include stepping stones with similar events is if you leap back five or ten years into a different stage of your life and the events are still similar. If this is the case, let it be, because you changed over such a long span of time, and in each of those relationships you were a different you.

The most important thing is to take significant leaps back in time. This way, within the five stepping stones, you can end up as close as possible to your earliest memory of feeling this way.

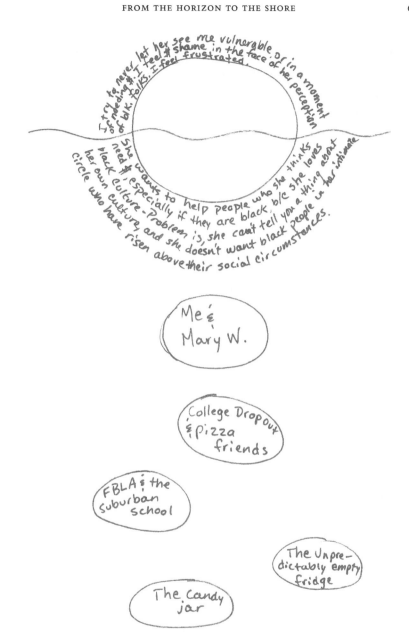

She wants to help people who she thinks b/c she loves a thing about her intimate circle who have risen above their social circumstances.

She needs #, especially if they are black, b/c she can't tell you a thing about black people. I try to never let her see me vulnerable. Or in a moment of shame, in the face of her perception of blk. folks. I feel frustrated. black culture. Problem is, she doesn't want black people her own culture, and she

Me & Mary W.

College Dropout & Pizza friends

FBLA & the Suburban school

The Unpredictably empty fridge

The Candy jar

PROMPT II: STEPPING STONES

Spend the week writing each scene or event from your life that represents the issue that is on each stepping stone. Be sure to write the entire scene/

event, not just the action that holds the specific incident. Write what led up to and away from the incident, and by all means include the relationship. In the past, people have done the writing for these scenes and not even mentioned the other person or entity that they were in relationship with. In other words, tell the whole story of each stepping stone.

Make sure that you use sensory details rather than just philosophizing. Also, make sure that you include your internal emotional responses to what is happening around you. What makes it an event/scene that others can engage in is the parallel of the external and internal experiences.

Don't forget to write in first person, past tense, with little or no dialogue, and use Jump Starters to get you into the zone. *Do not* spend time thinking about how to say it. These are likely stories that you have told over and over to other people in exposé format, or you have told the stories to yourself in your head over and over. Jump-starting will help you to have a fresh way to tell an old story from your personal plot.

Do this prompt for all five or more stepping stones.

Here are my stepping stones: "Me and Mary W., College Dropout & Pizza Friends, FBLA and the Suburban School, The Unpredictably Empty Fridge, The Candy Jar."

Caution: Try not to use too many stepping stones, because this will blur your process of later choosing which raw material suits the plot when you arrive at Chapter 12, The Macrocosmic Plot and Its Planetary Scenes.

The Initial Wound

Keep stepping back until you reach the issue that you feel is the initial wound event that is the outcropping, the shore from which all of the stepping stones sprung. When I kept going back in time, I reached the first time I felt ashamed for not having what others had. It was the time my family was running away from my father and my mother took the family to spend the night at my uncle's house and I saw the difference in

how my uncle lived and how we lived. I asked for a candy from my uncle's beautiful candy jar. My uncle thought it was cute, but my mother was ashamed and upset with me for displaying my need. I call this the Candy

Jar Event; I was hungry, but I was scolded and made to feel ashamed for asking so blatantly for what I needed.

As we discussed in the Mirror Exercise from Chapter 4, some initial wounds may be more pinpointed as a wounding, like the initial wound that is the base of my novel *Fifth Born*. Odessa Blackburn, like myself, was molested by her father, which caused a chain of ostracizing behavior from her mother. In James Baldwin's "Sonny's Blues," the mother's death was a concentrated wound that sent both brothers off in different directions to fulfill their wants.

Other initial wounds may be less isolated as events but happen over a period of time, like the slow, insidious build of events that occur in Ta-Nehisi Coates's *Between the World and Me*. Throughout his life, the main voice experiences a slow series of wounds that the American Dream inflicts on Black bodies, human bodies, even the earth as body. Even still, there may be wounding events that are pinpointed, but the trauma is due to others agitating the wound, like the teasing from classmates about the scar on young Alice Walker's eye in "Beauty: When the Other Dancer Is the Self." Like water dripping on a rock, the wound is deepened by the pressure of others pounding on the tender spot.

So, now you go for it. Continue to single out the reoccurring feeling or emotion that you have in each stepping stone, and see how far back in time that feeling goes. See if you can locate the initial wound, which is the event that caused you to feel this way for the first time.

For instance, my financial shame is the reoccurring feeling that I singled out, and the first time that I felt this was the Candy Jar Event, which is my initial wound in this of my several personal plots.

If you can't seem to locate that initial wound event, or if you find yourself landing close to the present and not able to peel back the layers and revisit the moment that caused the hurt, here are some strategies to help you to see beneath the surface:

1. What is the feeling that you have in the horizon event? Remember the scene that you wrote as the first prompt in the stepping stones exercise?

You currently have an issue with someone, and when they do whatever they are doing to get on your nerves, certain feelings come up for you. What are these feelings? When was the first time you felt this way, not when was the first time you encountered a similar person.

2. Look back in your life at who or what has consistently helped you to survive difficult times, like with the issue you are currently having at the horizon. What is the earliest memory you have with this very positive agent? When was the first time this or a similar agent helped you survive something in life? What was that moment you survived?

3. Sometimes it's easier to focus on other people's issues. We philosophize and psychoanalyze them with ease but have trouble doing this for ourselves. Here is a trick that will utilize your natural propensity to dissect others as a tool to get at your own initial wound: name someone you hated, were afraid of, or seriously didn't like early in life. Ask yourself why you didn't like them. It's likely that you didn't like this person or were afraid of them because they were in some way inflicting wounds, and you were one of the wounded.

You may find that you have stray stepping stones here and there that aren't associated with the horizon feeling or the initial wound feeling. It's fine to leave those be for now, because they are either from other personal plots in your life, or they are associated with the same issue, but you haven't yet put your finger on the connection.

You'll need courage to keep running backward into your past to find those events that represent the wound, and to use those events as prompts to write. Remember, the goal is to end up on the shore of the initial wound.

PROMPT 12: INITIAL WOUND EVENT/SCENE

1. Write the event, or one of the events, that was the catalyst for the issue or feeling. Take along your spelunking gear from Chapter 3, and you will likely need to have a conversation or two with your internal saboteurs in order to keep them quiet.

2. Like any scene/event you are prompted to write, jump-start and

write again and again until you feel you have written down the emotional, psychological, and spiritual truth devoid of intellectualizing or attempts to craft. Remember to stay in first person, past tense, with little or no dialogue. Tell not just the event but also what led up to the event and what happened afterward. This keeps you and the reader close to the voice and to their growth and reaction to moments in their life.

3. Remember, the initial wound may have been a series of cumulative events that occurred with one person as the perpetrator or initiator of the wound as we see in Virginia Holman's memoir, *Rescuing Patty Hearst*, where the initial wound happens over a period of time. The main voice has her mother's psychiatric state as the wound, but the severity of the wound is a series of events that cause an impact over time.

4. In this case, it's best to write the first event where you became aware of the wounding nature of the events as your initial wound. In *Rescuing Patty Hearst* then, the initial wound event is the day the main voice, Virginia, realizes that her mother cannot focus well enough to remember how to get home, and it is Virginia's eight-year-old attention to detail that gets them there. Holman also offers a good example for times when the perpetrator of the wounds (her mother) isn't a bad person; she is just taken over by bad circumstances. The perpetrator of the wound may be a parent who abandons by death or other circumstances beyond their control. Don't feel guilty about writing them in as the conduit for the wounds.

Here is the raw, unedited version of what I wrote:

Metal sits cold in our sunken carport, urban driveway inside a chain link fence, where a chained pet beloved family dog sits near his doghouse guarding, but not thinking to bark at my father in the moonlight. The drunk man who I always want to go fishing with is leaning over in the car, because he knows that when he turns into the werewolf and goes after my mother that she will snatch up her five children and bundle the new baby and head to the nearest relative.

I didn't know anything about cars and carburetors when I was five, but

I knew that mothers don't hide in closets at night, but when I woke up, there she was; nightmarish at first to see the house dress, the silhouette of arms strong enough to cart six children to the store at the same time, see those arms flexed around her own body. "Shhhh," she whispered, the whites of her eyes the only thing fully visible. Then I could hear the drunken scary version of my father stumbling into walls, laughing at himself, cursing her and I kept her secret, watched her leave the closet cave and return over and over with another child, socks, shoes coats, with only, "Shhh" as the command that we knew to follow.

When we stepped out into the cold night ten legs of kids, one wrapped baby and Mama, "alternator" was the missing thing I remember that meant we'd be walking in the cold, in the dark, in the alley that in the day time was red bricks and marbles and skipping rope and tire races, but at night seemed forbidden and dangerous. "I'm cold," I said, wanting her to pick me up and make me warm, but "keep walking" was what she said. I must have sleep walked, because the next thing I remember was walking past Uncle Tip's legs, into his dark living room where the plastic covered furniture forced us to the pallets Mama laid quickly on the floor.

In the morning, my belly made a tight fist; there were whispered phone calls, and lots of moments of Mama talking in her listen-to-me voice. Uncle Tip offered some of the breakfast that streamed in from the white and green kitchen, clean. My two boy-cousins sat clean cut, their eyes inviting, where Aunt Annie Laura moved around sweetly to place sausage and pancakes in front of them.

"They'll eat when we get home," Mama said, giving us each the whites of her eyes that said, "Agree by not talking," but it would not be asking for breakfast if I asked for the candies from the jar inside the glass china cabinet just above my head. "May I have some of those candies," I heard the small timber of my little voice and thought how much I sounded like my sister, how much I wished she'd asked the question instead of me.

"No," was all I heard my mother say. My uncle laughed, "She asked so politely," then he made his face and fingers petite on a big man the way the lion on *The Wizard of Oz* did and repeated, "May I have some of those candies?" My mother laughed with him, me and the candies a diversion from my father bent over in the night removing her escape, a diversion from her arms wrapped around her body in the closet, and I felt it for the first time, shame, crept up my spine, bent my soft bones over to make me small again, fetus again, not yet born again.

GROUND ZERO

I call this initial wound event "ground zero." It's the thing that happened that set these stepping stones in motion and has you standing at the horizon in your current life still grappling with the same issue, the debris of the initial wound event all around you.

This can feel daunting and even depressing to think about, but there's hope—life plot is the stuff of literary plot, and where there is literary plot, there is revelation and outcome. Let's stay vulnerable and courageous and walk through the other prompts of the Stepping Stones Exercise to see if we can pull ourselves toward personal revelation and to the stuff that brings applause from an audience: outcome.

Though this messy art making is hard, don't let your internal saboteurs lose your Stepping Stones Exercise; accidentally throw it away; leave it on the bus; or let the baby, your elderly parent, the cat, or the dog get a hold of it.

Instead, just breathe and step away for a while. Take a couple days off from your work with this book, then come back to it all ready to have the courage to be vulnerable and to know yourself well enough to construct literary plots from your personal plots in such a way that you create meaningful art.

Best of all, remember the spelunking advice from Chapter 3. If you are afraid to deal with or write about your memories, then do what I do: tether yourself to something outside of your writing world like any good spelunker should. Ask a friend to meet you for coffee just after you plan to be done writing. Tell your partner, or a friend, to call you at a certain time and check in with you. Plan to share dinner with your neighbors. Pick your kids up from school or day care, or for some of us, pick your parent up from school or day care. Schedule your therapy appointments or appointments to see your spiritual leader just after your writing time.

Note: Once you locate the initial wound, you may find yourself realizing that you were being safe in offering a current horizon event. Maybe you said the horizon was about you and a coworker, when in fact your big current issue is between you and your son, or you and your mother or father, or you and your partner. If that's the case, no problem—save the less authentic horizon event in an outtake file and write the new one.

Vocabulary: An **outtake file** (digital or hard copy) contains writing that you don't currently need, but you don't want to delete just in case the writing is valuable later. Create an outtake file and title and date it, for example, "OuttakesToday'sDate." This will alleviate any panic you have about tossing writing. We rarely use any of the writing that was just a practice run, but there may come a time when the scene you have put aside that didn't seem relevant is later an important scene.

Remember: Rewrites are always to increase the authenticity of the scene, never to pull back and write from an emotionally less vulnerable place. As well, while creating raw material, let any additional writing or outtakes be for the purpose of increasing the emotional and psychological truth. Right now, you are not editing for your audience, because you will need all of the material, no matter how messy, to help you recognize the true organic plot. You may end up editing out the very clue to your true plot or editing out the thematic glue for your story.

CHAPTER 6

Write-Ins:

How Do I Get What I Want?

Write-ins are writing moments when you produce events or scenes with
some intentional prompting that you think may advance your plot and
get at more of the want for your character, or in the case of poetry or
memoir, get at more of the want for the voice. Sometimes, these are
also writing moments where you will write what you believe to be the
missing scenes or the missing element of the scene.

Vocabulary: For the sake of shared vocabulary, I will begin to refer to your
first-person "I" as the **main voice** or **main character** of your writing.
This is so that as you write your truth, you will begin to see the ways in
which the personal plots in your life parallel and are one and the same
with literary plot. The deeper we get into the remaining chapters of this
book, the more the terms main character and main voice will be used. I

also use these terms to distinguish between the "I" in memoir and poetry (main voice) and the "I" in fiction (main character).

If you are writing fiction, there is the main character—with memoir and poetry, the main voice—that is being propelled through the book by their relationships with other people:

1. In the movie *The Pursuit of Happyness*, it is Chris Gardner's relationship with his son that fuels his want to work his way out of homelessness.

2. The short story "The Moths" by Helena María Viramontes gives us a female main character whose sense of family belonging changes through her reactions to her abuela's way of living and way of dying.

3. In Alice Walker's essay "Beauty: When the Other Dancer Is the Self," we have a main voice whose reactions and revelations are based on her perception and society's perception of her injured eye.

4. In Sharon Olds's poetry collection *The Father*, the main voice evolves through the journey of her father's dying.

Stepping Stones Write-In:
The Want

Like any voice or character driven by want in a literary plot, *you* are driven by want in your personal plot. The initial wound event left you wanting or desperately wanting to prevent things in a relationship. When you think about it, it makes perfect sense. In the wound event, you lost something—skin, blood, a person, your self-esteem, your freedom—which left you wanting to replace that lost thing. The wound then created a want.

PROMPT 13: WRITE-IN THE WANT AND INITIAL WOUND

1. Read your initial wound event and ask yourself, "What did I lose and what did that loss leave me wanting or desperately wanting to prevent?"

2. Write that loss and the want down at the top of the document where you are keeping all of your scenes.

3. Go back to your initial wound event; jump-start and write an extension of the event now that you are aware of the loss that was created by the wound and the want that remains.

4. Make sure that the event that you wrote holds the essence and some reflections of this want.

Caution: You are just adding onto the scene knowing what you now know, but there is no need to stiffen the writing of the scene by philosophizing about what you know, or to write your awareness of the want into the scene as some omniscient voice. Stay in first person, past tense, and write the event where the reader gets to be present for the internal and external occurrences.

Think of it this way: you are writing the same emotional and psychological truth, but with your new awareness of the loss and the want, you remember and now know the significance of things that were happening inside and outside of you.

For Example: In my initial wound event, I lost a sense of financial security and the gracefulness of asking for what I needed. This left me *wanting consistent financial security* and left me feeling *shame* for even wanting or needing this financial consistency. In my childhood household, it was unpredictable when there would and wouldn't be provisions, yet we were told not to tell our business outside of the house, so there wasn't any taking handouts or showing that we occasionally needed a hand. Confusing messages that left me feeling shame whenever I was in a situation where someone had financial stability compared to my own. Like most children of working-class families from my era, I wanted my family to be like the Brady Bunch. Yes, the Brady family had issues, but none of those issues were financial. So, writing in the want could be as simple in my case as allowing my child self to notice the neatness of my uncle and aunt's kitchen compared to our own, noticing the difference more money makes in the appearance of a household.

Here is the raw, unedited version of what I wrote:

Our kitchen table turned from full to empty to full. I saw the scene before we walked out in the night to get to Uncle Tip's house, my mother hiding in the closet, my father like an angry bear in the house seeking out the intruder in his drunken stupor, then him outside the house in the back yard taking away the alternator in the car so that an escape could not be something that my mother could afford. On the way there she told us not to tell. Her shame over not being able to control whether or not her children were safe or when they were or were not fed; her own safety was the wager. "I stayed for y'all," she would say every time.

The jar was right there and the only thing that stood between me and it were polite, obedient words. Next time, I decided that I would not ask, but take, like my mother should have done when my father was at work—pack slow, taking the time to plan transportation that would not include her youngest daughter walking with numb, cold toes in last year's too small shoes. Don't tell; I didn't, nor would I ask for what I needed; I'd take, I'd plan, I'd run without waking the sleeping bear. I turned my mind back to my siblings standing in the kitchen ready to walk out into the daylight, back where we belonged while my mother assured my aunt that we didn't need breakfast, could eat when we returned home.

PROMPT 14: WRITE-IN THE WANT AND THE HORIZON

Now, go back to the horizon where you have the current issue with a person. Ask yourself what you want from this person. Likely the want in this relationship is similar to the want on the shore of the initial wound and each of the stepping stones. For instance, my want at the horizon is "I want her to see me as financially competent and equal," which is very much linked to my childhood want for financial consistency, except at the horizon I am focusing the fulfillment of the want on a particular person.

In your personal plots, this want drives the journeys and represents at least one of the desires you hope to fulfill in some relationships. The ironic thing is, you may likely want from a person (or are attracted to them) yet despise them for the things they possess that you want. For example, there I was hating on the woman at the horizon for her financial status and her way of viewing Black folks, when it was some of that financial certainty I lacked. I wanted the financial confidence she had. No, I don't want the racist or classist notions, but I wanted some of the confidence and self-assuredness around finances. So, not that I enjoy admitting this, but I was attracted to being in a relationship with the woman at the horizon because some part of me was wanting for myself her financial confidence, and at the same time I loathed the byproducts of her financial confidence. Jealousy is a great spotlight for revealing your unfulfilled wants and helping you to make a list of what you want to achieve.

Here's another example: in the movie *Frozen River*, Ray's initial wound is that her husband took the money. Because of this, she lost the money for the double wide and that left her wanting the money for the double wide. Sounds simple, but look at how it drives all of her stepping stones. Ray has major issues with Lila for stealing her car, for cheating her out of money (something that triggers the initial wound). She is jealous of Lila for being Mohawk and living where the laws are designed to protect its citizens, but what she doesn't yet realize is that, were she not attempting to fulfill the want left by the wound, she would never have met Lila. Sometimes, we have adversaries and obstacles because of the paths we take to get what we want. Ray is trying to get from Lila something that she lost because of her husband, and each is jealous of the other for the ways they are racially privileged in their separate societies.

1. Prompt your writing by reading through the current issue at the horizon and ask yourself, "What do I want from this person?"
2. Then, make sure that the event that you wrote holds the essence and some reflections of this want.

When you look at each of your stepping stones, you are likely to have the revelation that each of the relationships you wrote about are your attempts to fulfill the want in some manner with people, when the want existed long before you ever met them.

You may notice that in some of these scenes/events/stepping stones, the relationship temporarily fulfilled your want, and in some relationships your major frustration was that the person didn't or couldn't fulfill your want. Ironic how we seek out people who don't have what we want, but we shake them down for it. We get obsessed with them even years after they make it clear that they don't have what we want. Our fantasy of getting what we want from them keeps us psychologically engaged.

In the short story "Sonny's Blues," the main voice does not admit that what he wants is family, and he is afraid of losing Sonny again. He lets this want manifest in a series of obsessive actions and reflections that suggest Sonny change who he is in order to become who the brother wants and needs as family.

In this excerpt from Amy Tan's short story "Rules of the Game," Waverly wants to win at chess, but more so she wants to win against her mother to outwit her mother as a show of her own individuality. In this short scene, she gets what she wants:

> A man who watched me play in the park suggested that my mother allow me to play in local chess tournaments. My mother smiled graciously, an answer that meant nothing. I desperately wanted to go, but I bit back my tongue. I knew she would not let me play among strangers. So as we walked home I said in a small voice that I didn't want to play in the local tournament. They would have American rules. If I lost, I would bring shame on my family.
>
> "Is shame you fall down nobody push you," said my mother.
>
> During my first tournament, my mother sat with me in the front row as I waited for my turn. (96)

Here, Waverly wants to win at the use of invisible strength and does; for just a moment, her mother is none the wiser that her daughter has defeated her and used reverse psychology to get what she wants. I used to be obsessed with getting what I wanted from my parents and in various relationships afterward as well.

Note: Like Waverly in "Rules of the Game," you may have a situation where the person who you have an issue with in the horizon event is the same person in the initial wound event who you consider the perpetrator of your wounds. If this is the case, still consider the want as something that the person at the horizon cannot fulfill for you, though your relationship with them is driven by your obsession with having them fulfill this want. This is often the case with this exercise when folks have living parents who were present during an initial wound.

PROMPT 15: WRITE-IN THE WANT AND THE STEPPING STONES

Now, go through your stepping stones and ask yourself what you wanted from these people you are (or were) in relationship with. Don't go to these people in your life and literally ask them about having or not having what you want. This is a question that you are asking yourself.

In the same way that you did with your horizon scene, go back to each of your stepping stones scenes; jump-start and write from this new perspective of knowing the loss that was created by the wound and the want that has manifested itself in several relationships. You will likely find that with this new perspective of knowing what you wanted during past events, there are things that you now remember that didn't seem relevant or associated before.

Stop Here: If you have not yet done so, take time to identify the want because it will drive the personal plot, which will inform your literary plot. We will refer to it over and over throughout the rest of this book, and the want will be our guide, which will give literary form to each of your stepping stone writings and shed light on the plot of your full-length manuscript.

The want is the most significant component of the plot, but it must be organically born out of the initial wound, not contrived.

Remember that the components of this book are cumulative, one exercise building on the next. You'll have to do each component to end up with the first draft of a full-length manuscript.

Note: In each of the scenes/events—the horizon, the stepping stones, and even the initial wound—the focus is on what happened to *you*, what it left *you* wanting, and what relationships *you* pursued to fulfill that want. Notice that we aren't building the exercise on what motivated other people. Their motivations will come into play in Chapter 13, Secondary Characters and Their Impact on Character and Plot, but their wounds and wants aren't the driving force of your personal plot. In literary plot, the story is driven by the main voice's or character's wounds and wants. This is also true with the personal plots that literary plots are derived from.

This is also a good time to stop and ask yourself, "Have I written a scene/event for the horizon, each of my five or more stepping stones, and the initial wound event?" If not, stop here and do so in order to make sure that you have built enough scenes/events to understand the exercises and prompts that are to come.

Stepping Stones Write-In:
The Language of Joy

We know the language of pain. We speak it so often as humans that we develop a complex and beautiful structure of words to express it. But the language of joy? Many of us, myself included, have to practice the language of joy, of how to express our most profound joy using external and internal details that bring full connection with others who experience similar joy (complacency, satisfaction, and so on).

Go to all of your stepping stones, the ones where you got what you wanted however temporarily, and do write-ins for the joy. The idea is to practice using our poetics and extensions of internal and external sensory detail to express joy, complacency, or satisfaction with as much fervor as we have learned in our lives to express pain. Without the language of joy, the language of pain becomes unrealistic, overbearing, and imbalanced. We know pain, because it is in such opposition to some joy that we know as well. The two exist as elements of one sea and your life is the container.

This would be a good time to go back to Chapter 2's Joys and Pains Exercise and look at the things you wrote that bring you profound joy. Reflecting on these may help you to write with an authentic sense of joy, complacency, or satisfaction.

It's ever so important then to offer the language of joy about a situation as well as offering the utmost pain. For example, in "The Moths" by Helena María Viramontes, the main character is told that she will need to help her abuelita and it brings a joyful memory of what it has meant to help her abuelita in the past. This is given to us just before the passages of helping Abuelita to die. The language of joy helps us to have context for the main voice's pain:

> Abuelita would wait for me at the top step of her porch holding a hammer and a nail and empty coffee cans. And although we hardly spoke, hardly looked at each other as we worked over root transplants, I always felt her gray eye on me. It made me feel, in a strange sort of way, safe and guarded and not alone. Like God was supposed to make you feel. (28)

Another example is the poem "Play Ball" in Grey Brown's collection *What It Takes*, which offers the language of joy, complacency, and satisfaction with the gifts-of-play that her daughter offers. The poem is an event cradled in the midst of the voice's struggles with her child's autism. This offers the life balance of joys and pains in the collection.

> No one else here has any idea
> how far you have come
> but from here in the field
> I spy the occupational therapist
> molding your hands to the ball,
> catch our physical therapist
> adjusting your stance,
> hear the speech pathologist
> cheering from the stands.

I nod to our pediatrician, a calm,
but attentive referee,
the whole afternoon rolling out
perfectly conceived,
the sun and sky
brilliant visual cues
lighting you
there in the center
setting us all
into play.

PROMPT 16: WRITE-IN THE LANGUAGE OF JOY

To help *you* to find these opportunities for the language of joy in your manuscript, go to the sections where you have written things like "I was happy," "I felt joy," or "I was glad." Write the section of the scene that conveys your joy, complacency, or satisfaction. Similarly, find the sections where you have written at length about a horrible pain or injury, like Viramontes, and offer us a moment of joy with that person before offering us a moment of pain. Jump-start and write while avoiding the vague words (happy, joy, content, complacent).

PROMPT 17: THE WANT BEFORE THE WOUND

Sometimes, we can feel so miserable about our wounds that we swear there was never joy. One way to help you find the happy, joyful, contented, complacent time is to write the scene when you had what you wanted, not as a want after the wound but before the wound and the want even occurred. Think of what you are walking around with as your want. When was this part of you not lost from you? For instance, in *Bastard Out of Carolina*, Chapter 2 offers the scene of Bone's safety inside of the details of her family with all of their odd characteristics—her uncle, who was considered dangerous by others, and her grandmother, who dipped snuff—but they loved her and she felt it. In Alice Walker's essay "Beauty: When the Other Dancer Is the Self," we see baby Alice in the first scene calling herself the prettiest one, before the physical wound that changes her perspective on her beauty.

Jump-start and write that scene. Be sure as usual to land the writing in time and place with sensory details, no philosophizing. Do it as a ten-minute write initially so that you don't stress over what to say or how to say it. Then add to it as part of your daily writing.

Here are the ways that this may help you with the language of joy.

1. Sometimes, the time before the wound and want is part of the initial wound scene. It offers the dichotomy of light and dark, the contrast that is the wholeness of the events in our lives, the joy and pain, hope and fear, and so on. It offers the calm that contrasts the tension and makes it all the more dramatic. (More about dramatic tension in Chapter 16.)

2. Similarly, sometimes writing this scene of you having the thing before you lost it in the wound can give you insight into the other scenes where the want was temporarily fulfilled.

3. It can also help you to write in the agent (what helped) to your initial wound scene and of other scenes. (More about scene shaping in Chapter 12.)

CHAPTER 7

Keeping
Your Raw Material Organized

Remember, it is of utmost importance to our work and to the development of your full-length manuscript that you actually do all of the writing assignments and keep them as raw, honest events. If there are writing assignments that you have skipped, you'll need to go back and work on those.

This book works as a cumulative learning tool. It is like a cross-country journey, and you can't skip ahead five states and expect to have the experience of the folks who drove through each state and wrote about their experiences and all the experiences that they were reminded of.

If you haven't already done so, type what you have into a document. For now, begin with the initial wound scene and step forward in time with the stepping stone scenes until you arrive at typing in the horizon scene/event, and then include what you have recently written. Yes, this arrangement is the reverse of the order in which you created the raw material scenes.

With each of these scenes, make sure that you are typing in the version that has the write-ins and that you are typing in the most authentic and emotionally honest of your rewrites. If you have several rewrites, you will need to select the scenes that you believe

- Offer the internal and external sensory details of the scene.
- Offer the emotional and psychological truth.
- Offer the complexity of dramatic tension with your agents and obstacles.

Name and Date Your File: The reason you are dating your file is because you are likely to do different versions of this manuscript and the date will help you to identify the most recent version. For instance, if it's a Word document, you might title it something like "MyMemoirToday'sDate."

Create an Outtake File: As mentioned in Chapter 5, for the rewritten scenes that you have decided not to keep, create a separate file and date it: "OuttakesToday'sDate." This will alleviate any panic you have about tossing writing. We rarely use any of the writing that was just a practice run, but there may come a time when the scene you have put aside that didn't seem relevant is later an important scene.

Caution: Do not take the old writing of some novel or memoir you were working on before this process and simply drop the new writing in. That's just going to leave you with a raggedy mess, and when your work with this book is over, you'll wonder how your writing partner was able to do a full content edit on their manuscript and win a competition while yours is coming loose at the seams. On another precautionary note, don't try and economize with thoughts like, "But I wrote five hundred pages already. I'm sure I can use them somehow." Those five hundred pages were training for all of the writing you are doing and will do, but they won't necessarily become part of the finished product.

CHAPTER 8

Research Your Psyche

and Write It In

Let me start off with restating something that is very important. You may have noticed that we are focusing on *you* through the stages of your life, not on the other person at the horizon or the other people in your stepping stones. Unless we are looking at them in order to stimulate what was going on with you, we are leaving them dormant for now. For the sake of personal and literary plot, it's the main voice's or main character's behaviors and motivations of behavior that drive the plot, not the behaviors of each person they encounter. Again, the behaviors of others become secondary and only necessary to look at as they inform us about how to evolve the main voice or character out of the old cycle of want. After all, when we have a want in life that is the result of some profound event, we are attracted to people who we feel can fulfill that want, and we don't change from that course unless we have new awareness or unless we have cause to change. Let's do some research work to inspire awareness and revelation and perhaps to cause a change.

Internal Character Development Research

Whether you are writing memoir or fiction, or poetry, one of the overwhelmingly deficient areas of most folks' writing is the **internal character development**. Most of us have become very efficient at describing through our writing what happened around us or a character during an event, but then we don't show the internal scene that is happening inside of our mind or the character's mind that parallels and is a response to the external stimuli. In short, we forget to write the feelings in some way other than by creating an internal monologue that we put in italics.

Instead, it is important to show what someone is feeling by showing us the scene that is happening in their heads, which is their psychological and emotional response to what is happening around them. The italics then should represent an internal scene, not the telling of an internal scene that we never in fact experience. Yes, sometimes this is a flashback or memory, but other times it is the writing of a negative or positive fantasy stimulated by what's being said or what the voice is experiencing in their external environment.

For Example: In the movie *Smoke Signals,* several of Victor's internal scenes of his initial wound are offered through flashbacks that are triggered by sensory details in the external setting. For instance, when he is running to get help for the woman after the car accident, he flashes to running to catch up with his father, running to get away from the pain of his father leaving, and to the general reality that his father ran away.

In my novel *Fifth Born II: The Hundredth Turtle,* Odessa is trying to communicate with her brother about his being gay, but she only has her teenage wisdom, childhood experiences, and stereotypes that come with demonized notions. In this scene, she is remembering her father's poor treatment of Lamont, and at the same time remembering a bus driver who she thought was gay and was afraid of because her homophobic upbringing equated gay with child molester.

Here, we see how she is observing things outside of herself but also feeling and thinking things internally that in fact cause distance from the person she wants to be close to.

Lamont looked away and left me there staring into the remembered moment.

The bus driver looked in the rearview at the passenger in the back of the bus and said, "Hold on. Shhh." I sat back watching his feminine gestures, the way he pursed his lips in irritation with passengers who didn't signal when they wanted off the bus. I heard Deddy's voice again: Faggot! *I remembered the child molestation movie they had shown us at school, the indelible black and white image of the little boy found face down, white dress shirt and black patent leather shoes turned out awkwardly. I looked out the window trying to remember the names of street signs, all the while singing to the boys; the undercurrent in my head a chatter of reasons why this was not my fault, why I shouldn't have been left all summer with three boys, while Lamont, Tawanda, Roscoe, and LaVern had been set free from the house by one excuse or the other. I remembered how the pink and purple of dusk fell over the sky that day while the fear rose in a hard knot in my throat. . . .*

Lamont grinned, waiting for me to snap out of it. "Well, you just gonna stop the story there? You bought the boys ice cream; then what?" He fiddled with the sequins on his belled pants, and I did not know I was frowning until he looked up and rolled his neck in response. I had not realized that in remembering this, I had paused long enough to skip time, long enough to feel estranged from him just before having to leave. The light at the corner had gone green, yellow, red, two times, and I'd almost mended a circuit between the flip of the bus driver's hand, the memory of the child molestation movies, and Lamont's fancy jeans.

"Girl, I don't know who you think you lookin at like something stink." He was standing now, ready to fight, as if I was one of the mean girls on the playground.

I answered with a question I had not intended to ask. "Did you turn gay because you were molested by a man?" (84-89)

It is by experiencing the internal scene in response to the external scene that allows us as the readers to understand the struggles of her character in this scene, which is much more engaging than being told by the author, "Odessa has internalized homophobia." Offering the internal scene will prevent you from needing the old craft lesson of Show Don't Tell.

Researching the Wound and Want

One way to authentically render the internal development of your own character (yourself) is through research.

Now for the fun part: go to the library, to the bookstore, or online and look for self-help for someone with an initial wound and a want like yours or self-help for the issue that you have as a result of the initial wound. Okay, so you may be laughing or crying about this idea, but I'm for real.

For instance, I looked for resources associated with shame and finances and found an article online at creditcards.com titled *Financial Rejection: When Wealth is Uncomfortable*. That article led me to a book titled *Mind over Money: Overcoming the Money Disorders That Threaten Our Financial Health* by Brad Klontz.

This research on yourself can spark a lot of latent emotions. You may find yourself staring off into space like a deer in the headlights. You might even try to run like hell or ask yourself what this has to do with a manuscript. Remember, research has everything to do with character development and plot. *You* are the only character you have ever really developed. Researching yourself may cause a lot of fear as you stare at your own reflection, and it may be difficult under these circumstances of fear to hold on to the logic of what you know makes good, authentic writing. But this research is crucial to creating authentic art.

My philosophy on the *why* of researching your wounds and wants is this: to wield power in an external written universe—be it poetry, memoir or fiction—one must be willing to explore one's own internal universe.

Remember: In basic plot structure, something profound happens that creates a loss, which leaves us wanting something. In the movie and memoir *The Pursuit of Happyness*, Chris grows up without his father present and this motivates him to be present in his own son's life. Later in the story, Chris experiences financial devastation that leads to homelessness, and this secondary wounding event leaves him wanting financial prosperity, which he finds, ironically, by working with the finances of people who are affluent.

In our example from the movie *Frozen River*, Ray's gambling husband takes the money for the new home, leaving her without money and without an adult family member. She finds herself in yet again a moment of desperate survival where she wants to save her children from homelessness. That want drives the plot.

In your case, your want drives your personal plot and has led you on many successful and unsuccessful journeys, which are your stepping stones or scenes. Heaven forbid you skip the research on the emotional nuances of the issues born of your wound. What makes *Frozen River* and *The Pursuit of Happyness* work is that the creators offer the devastating emotional nuances of what it is like to be financially broke while experiencing the pressure of being a solid provider and protector for one's children. The state of being broke is not compelling enough without the psychological nuances of parental pressure that both Ray and Chris experience.

If not researched well, you risk that readers with a similar experience will consider you ill-informed about your main character or main voice (who is based on you). Or, knowing that all of our artistic creations are semi-autobiographical, your audience will assume that you were not courageous enough to make yourself fully vulnerable about your connection to the voice or character, and may associate your shame as the author as shame regarding people like them. In this case, you go from intending to connect to pushing people away.

If in your own research, you are spending a lot of money on tissues, that's normal. It can be sad to think about your internal little boy or girl not getting what they need and want, or sad to think about the scenarios that led to them having particular needs and wants. It's okay to cry for them; they deserved the best, as we all do, and yet, shit happened. It's good to know what's bothering them so that you can write a new outcome to the plot that the child has walked in for so long without resolution. You will inspire others when you write through to the outcome of the issue in this child's literary story.

The research on self is incredibly difficult, but incredibly important, because you are researching the emotional and psychological nuances of the main voice's or character's wounds, wants, and both the consequences and benefits of those wounds and wants. Done in depth, the research helps make for masterful art.

Here is a list of research resources on frequent wounds and issues put together by individuals who have taken my workshops:

- *Mind over Money: Overcoming the Money Disorders That Threaten Our Financial Health* by Brad Klontz
- *In an Unspoken Voice: How the Body Releases Trauma and Restores Goodness* by Peter A. Levine, PhD
- *The Working Poor: Invisible in America* by David K. Shipler
- *Mom Still Likes You Best: Overcoming the Past and Reconnecting With Your Siblings* by Jane Isay
- *Bringing up Girls: Practical Advice and Encouragement for Those Shaping the Next Generation of Women* by James C. Dobson, PhD
- *Walking on Eggshells: Navigating the Delicate Relationship Between Adult Children and Parents* by Jane Isay
- *Motherless Daughters: The Legacy of Loss* by Hope Edelman
- *Getting to Commitment: Overcoming the 8 Greatest Obstacles to Lasting Connection* by Steven Carter with Julia Sokol
- *Men Like Women Who Like Themselves (and Other Secrets That the Smartest Women Know)* by Steven Carter with Julia Sokol

- *What Children Learn From Their Parents' Marriage* by Judith P. Siegel, PhD
- *Will I Ever Be Good Enough? Healing the Daughters of Narcissistic Mothers* by Karyl McBride, PhD
- *What You're Really Meant to Do: A Road Map to Reaching Your Unique Potential* by Robert Steven Kaplan

This is to mention just some of the self-help literature that has been helpful to others writing from these exercises. There are many, many more to explore and so much room for you to add to this list. Any of the authors mentioned here likely have other works or online videos and articles you can experience as well.

Know that this self-help research can also lead you to valuable personal accounts of healing in fiction, memoir, poetry, movies, documentaries, and even in other art forms. The most important thing is to look for books or resources that don't just talk about the wound or the pain of the wound, but instead to look for resources that will help with the healing (agents) as well as inform about those things that have gotten in the way of healing (obstacles).

PROMPT 18: CHARACTER VOICE RESEARCH

Create a file titled "CharacterVoiceResearch" or another memorable title. Find at least three resources for self-help research for a wound and a want like yours. For each source

- Write down the title and author.
- Write a paragraph or two (or however much you need to write) on what you learned about your wounds, wants, and issues from this source.
- Write down what you learned about your agents from this source.
- Write down what you learned about your obstacles from this source.

This file can serve as your resource library on your wound, and may become a resource that you offer to other writers in research mode. For those of you who are academically inclined, this is a whole new twist on an annotated bibliography.

Pinpointing Your Issue

If you can't seem to put your finger on your issue, here is a strategy that may help. Many of us have an easier time identifying other people's issues. Research the wound, wants, or issues of the perpetrator of your initial wound and their issue's impact on you.

Caution: Only engage in the perpetrator's self-help research as a means of identifying your own issue. The wounds and issues of your secondary characters will come into full play in Chapter 13, Secondary Characters and Their Impact on Character and Plot. Extend your research beyond written material to interviewing other people in the life of your perpetrator. Tread lightly though, and try not to use words like "wound" and "issue" if you want to get good information as opposed to a defensive response.

For instance, through researching your mother's issues and looking for a better understanding of why your mother was narcissistic, you may find that you have picked up on and embodied some of her harmful survival tactics (internal saboteurs), or may notice that you have embodied some of her gifts (**internal agents**). Think of internal agents as synonymous with gifts. These are the survival tools that you embody that are of some long-term good for you and perhaps to others. Research of your mother's issues may reveal an understanding of your own issues. My mother is an artist who was not able to continue practicing her art into adulthood. Doing a bit of research and finding this out about her helped me pay attention to the fact that I embody that artistic gift and offer it to others.

Finding these connections between your issues and your perpetrators' issues can help you to put a finger on and label your own issues well enough that you can research them as subject headings. With this backdoor way of getting at your own issue, you are likely to find ironies similar to those in the Joys and Pains Exercise in Chapter 2, where your gifts, much like your joys, are the result of pains inflicted by someone else. For instance, I am a protective mother because my mother didn't have the capacity to be protective under the circumstances of her relationship with my father.

Another strategy for pinpointing your wound, want, or issues is through parallel setting and internal character development research. In Chapter 14, we will fully explore setting and its impact on character development, but for now a wee bit of setting research can jar the issue associated with your wounds and wants.

This strategy isn't emotionally easier, but it can jar you loose from that place of not understanding the issue. Think of the place where the initial wound event occurred and do research on that place, picking up any of the images or sensory details of place, or take a well-anchored and grounded loved one with you and go visit this place. Parallel setting and internal character development research make good sense, especially since good writing calls for the external details of setting paralleled with the internal details of one's reaction to place. In writing *Fifth Born II: The Hundredth Turtle*, going to Harlem and seeing the places where I visited my brother and going to the church that was his church helped to jar loose my emotions, which helped to open me up to some of the issues of internalized homophobia that I was grappling with at the time.

Here is another method to getting at internal character development when you don't know what you were feeling at that time in your life. When going back and asking how you can add your current awareness to the character's or voice's emotional reality, here are some questions to ask:

1. What did you feel? Infuse that into the voice or character.

2. What did you do when you felt that way, even if you didn't have words for it? How did the feelings manifest themselves? Show the reader.

3. What did you notice in your environment when you felt this way, and why did you notice it? Let the reader see, hear, smell, taste, touch these things in the character's or voice's external setting.

Write-In the Obstacle (Internal Saboteurs)
and the Agents (Gifts)

Organically embedded in each of the events that you have already written is the obstacle. For instance, in the initial wound event, there was the perpetrator of the wound as a profound obstacle. Then, likely in other stepping stones, there are representatives or phantom images of that same or another obstacle manifested either externally as other people or internally as your unwanted or unwieldy saboteur-behaviors. Yes, the same saboteurs in your relationship to your writing that you unmasked in Chapter 3 lurk in other relationships where you want something just as desperately as you want to complete a full-length manuscript.

In your research, as you read personal accounts of other folks' obstacles, you will be reminded of both internal and external obstacles at the shore of the initial wound and in each of your stepping stones.

Remember: I want you to write in first person, past tense, no dialogue. Make sure you give us the event/scene with sensory detail of time and place.

PROMPT 19: WRITE-IN THE EXTERNAL OBSTACLES

Though it is likely that the obstacles are organically present in each event, there may be times when this is not true. In those cases, go back and read and notice sections where there is no manifestation externally of the obstacles within the particular scene/event. These scenes include the initial wound, stepping stones, and horizon. Do write-ins or rewrites for those scenes/events. You may be wondering how it can even be possible to leave out the obstacle, but when we have wound stories that we haven't shared outside of our own heads, we tend to offer one tiny part, assuming that the audience can feel what we felt, saw, heard, smelled, tasted, and touched in the remembered event.

For example, on pages 12–13 in Part One of *Cold Running Creek*, the army men that threaten the freedom of the small band of Choctaw are the external obstacles in the section and are described with sensory details that will help the reader to experience them: "The man's eyes were small blue shadows beneath his hat. Raven had never seen eyes like the sky. . . . Then Raven looked up to see their bearded faces, which showed copper in the light of the setting sun. . . . The blue eyes, the dirty suit coat too high up his arm, the fermented smell of corn whisky in the oil of his skin and the sweaty hair."

Again, write-in external obstacle extensions of the initial wound, the stepping stone, and the horizon scene/event or do full rewrites of scenes/events. You may need to do this several times over the course of a week. You can do this in tandem with doing your internal character development research, which may help you to be inspired by what others have had as obstacles and peel back the layers of your own obstacles. Don't forget to take breaks to go play in the joys of your life so that you don't get stuck in the yuck of obstacle memories.

PROMPT 20: WRITE-IN THE INTERNAL SABOTEURS

In looking for the places where you did not write-in the internal obstacles in scenes, you are likely to realize that internal obstacles are just another name for internal saboteurs from Chapter 3. One of the ways that you can present your internal saboteurs in your scenes/events is in the form of **flashbacks**. A flashback is a memory, fantasy, or musing from a character's past that is triggered from things in the character's present external environment. These memories, fantasies, or musings are embedded as short scenes directly into the outer scene where the memory is triggered. This offers the reader internal character development information about an internal saboteur that is preventing a voice or character from getting what they want, as seen in my example of pages 84–89 in *Fifth Born II: The Hundredth Turtle*, where Odessa's internal saboteur is her internalized homophobia.

Now, write-in or do rewrites to include the internal saboteurs in each scene/event. Though some scenes will not have internal obstacles, be sure to consider all scenes for this write-in. These scenes/events include the initial wound, stepping stones, and horizon. Again, you may need to do this several times over the course of a week or so in tandem with your internal character development research in order to be inspired by others' internal saboteurs and peel back the layers of your fears. Writing in your internal saboteurs can bring up lots of embarrassment and shame because we have a tendency to have these internal obstacles getting in our way at the same time that we are trying to keep these internal obstacles a secret from others. That type of emotional subterfuge can only be inverted by vulnerability and awareness. Use a Jump Starter if need be to help you get into the writing.

Don't forget to take joyful breaks so that you don't consistently walk in the hardship of saboteur-memories.

PROMPT 21: WRITE-IN THE EXTERNAL AGENTS

What is also present in each of the events that you have already written, but likely not on the page or less illuminated, are the agents. You survived each event in order to be able to get here to write about it all. But what or who helped you survive the initial wound event? What or who helped you survive each of the stepping stones?

If the answer to these questions doesn't readily come to mind, know that your research should remind you, once you read what helped others who have similar wounds and wants as yours to survive.

Write the external agents that helped you to survive each scene/event. These can be extensions to each scene/event or full rewrites of those scenes/events. You may need to do this several times over the course of a week. Again, it may help to do these writings in tandem with your internal character development research in order to be inspired by others' agents and to quiet your victim voice long enough to remember that you had help.

This is a great opportunity to appreciate the people and things in life that have helped you get through hard times. This is also a great time to acknowledge your trial-and-error process for survival—those times when you tried something or someone new as an agent and some of them worked, so you put that part in your survival kit. Some agents that you tried on for size, however, didn't work at all and you moved on. Use a Jump Starter if need be to help you get into the writing.

For example, in Part Two of *Cold Running Creek*, Old Raymond is the external agent for Lilly, who has recently been thrust into slavery. He becomes an integral part of her survival of plantation life. Here, the reader is offered a description of Old Raymond with sensory details that will help the reader to sense his nature as an agent:

> I screamed a scream that dredged up the full memory of my capture. . . .
> The cabin door was the only sound above my noise. It squeaked on its hinges as a Negro man entered; broad chest, yellowing hair; his face was soft, old, and assuring. He came toward me, opened his giant hand, which smelled like biscuits and coffee, and covered my mouth; uncovered and covered it again until my screaming was over. (112)

PROMPT 22: WRITE-IN THE INTERNAL GIFT

The gift is what you possess internally that helped you to healthily survive events/scenes of your want. The gifts are your internal agents: your tenacity, your belief in a higher power, and so on.

Notice that I am not including here negative agents. That might sound oxymoronic, but many times in life we survive a moment by resorting to something that is a quick fix and unhealthy, because it soothes the pain of wanting. These are actually internal saboteurs masquerading as gifts. They helped you get out of the darkness but were of short-term benefit and of long-term disadvantage to your well-being. Many of our addictions mingle under this umbrella. These saboteurs masquerade as gifts but are indeed rackets. We'll talk more about rackets soon.

Through your internal character development research, you will likely be reminded of inherent gifts that you were born with or gifts that you inherited from someone. For instance, in the memoir *Rescuing Patty Hearst*, Virginia seems to be born to both a desire to understand what she does not and an ability to remember details and later use them to get out of tight situations. She also has the gifts of patience and loyalty toward her mother. As the story progresses, it's evident that these are also gifts that her father possesses that she likely inherited. These survival traits are her internal agents, inherent gifts that helped her survive.

The internal gifts are healthy go-to mechanisms when you are in a pinch, as opposed to unhealthy go-to mechanisms when you are in a pinch. Think of the internal gifts as the opposite of internal saboteurs.

In order to figure out the gift inside of your wound or issue, you can ask yourself the following:

- What gifts did I discover in my internal character development research that others like me possess that I may possess as well?
- What gifts did my obstacle people possess that I absorbed or inherited?
- What gifts did my agents possess that I absorbed or inherited?
- What is the gift I possess inside that is born out of my wound?

What helped you to survive each event/scene? Extend or rewrite the initial wound, the stepping stone, the current event at the horizon. You may need to do this several times over the course of a week. Again, get inspired by others' internal gifts to peel back the layers of your internal gifts. This is a great opportunity to feel the power of your own heroism, which has helped you get through hard times. Use a Jump Starter if need be to help you get into the writing.

Ironies of Your Obstacles and Gifts
The Racket

You may find in your writing this week there are times when you can't distinguish the internal gifts from the internal saboteurs. Or in some circumstances, the internal saboteurs acted as internal gifts and saved your butt from harm. Or even stranger, perhaps what helped you survive wasn't always of long-term good, but nonetheless—in the emotional and psychological reality of it all—helped you survive in the moment.

Vocabulary: A **racket** is when you attempt to turn some self-defeating behavior, which may have benefitted you in the short term and infrequently, into a long-term, stable solution for getting what you want. Though it may have worked as a short-term, fast-action (often lacking in common sense) way to get you out of the heat of the survival moment, it isn't something that can sustain you long term.

The difference between internal saboteurs and rackets is duration. Think of an internal saboteur as a lapse in common sense where you momentarily defer to the ill messages of the past. On the other hand, think of a racket as you embracing the internal saboteur and attempting to turn that annoying internal voice into the new common sense way of getting what you want. A racket then is when you sign up your internal saboteurs (which are usually short-term survival methods) to do the work of agents (which are long-term fixes).

And it's just what it sounds like: a fraud, a deception, a period of time where you pretend that you have what you want when in reality, you do not.

Rackets can cause a great deal of emotional confusion because you are simply trying to get what you want and have some relief from the struggle. You find yourself thinking that you've arrived and that it wasn't so hard to get what you want after all, and you later realize that you did it again, tried to get what you want by circumventing your fears. In reality, you will likely need to spend a lot of emotional and psychological time recalibrating and practicing daily, healthy survival methods so that you can get what you want by facing your fears on a daily, then weekly basis, until the fear is less in control and you are getting what you want on a regular basis.

After we've had some revelations and amazing outcomes, we'll talk more about getting yourself a daily practice to sustain your outcome. We will get to this in Chapter 10, Write the Outcome Then Step into It. In the meantime, know that we grow and change by consuming the stories of others (real or fictionalized) who have self fulfilled their wants through the process of understanding their own internal obstacles.

Remember, your saboteurs aren't just some evil part of you. They have helped you temporarily survive outrageous struggles. The problem is they don't serve you well anymore, especially when you want to grow out of the patterns of an issue as you do with this personal plot, which requires long-term fixes.

So here you are, working on one of your personal plots and not wanting to cast anymore stepping stones out from the shore of the initial wound. You've read a bunch of self-help books, have looked at yourself in the reflecting pond deep inside of a cave where your headlamp is the only light. You are scared and want to feel good now, so you run one of the same rackets with your writing relationship that you run in other relationships. Your racket may be that you tell people that the way you get things done is by changing your mind. Therefore, with writing the full-length manuscript, you decide that the overall want in the story is something different every week; that way, you stay away from the difficulty of sustaining thoughts about your initial wounds and can shift to something else that doesn't hurt. This long-term racket helps you avoid hurt, but like with all rackets, you don't get what you want long term.

When I read my stepping stones, I recognized a racket that I ran in my personal plot. One of the internal saboteur messages that was activated if things got too hard was "run," like I did at eighteen years old. I believe that running prevented my father from doing irreparable damage to my mind and body, and I also believe that it saved me from murdering him, as my disturbing dreams of defending myself to the point of physically disabling him were increasing.

The problem? Well, running saved me once and was an excellent survival strategy, but running continued to come into play in situations that were difficult but not harmful, and I lacked the ability to discern the difference. So as a young adult, my run-away racket was engaged as my daily survival.

I wrote about this of my rackets in *Fifth Born II: The Hundredth Turtle*, when Odessa emotionally abandons her brother for a couple of years of their young adult lives when she finds out he has HIV/AIDS. She doesn't know if she can handle the devastation of it all, so she runs. As the story progresses, she denounces her racket and deals with the pain in real time.

The tricky thing about rackets is they screw up your discernment. If your racket is in place to protect you from feeling pain, after a while, you don't know what pain you're being protected from. With my old racket, my sense of self-preservation said, "Don't wait to find out if things will improve or become harmful, just get the hell out of there." When the dust settled, most of the time I had been right to go, but other times there had been no need to leave, only a need to grieve or allow myself to feel sad. The trouble was, my racket had me operating at a luck-of-the-draw success rate, where I could only discern if running away was the right thing to do after the fact. The danged racket wasn't serving my forward movement.

Remember, rackets are unsustainable go-tos that you employ when you are in emotional or psychological distress, and you attempt to continue to employ them at the same success rate. They make you look and feel sane, but they break down, and then you're in your shit again. Rackets then are just what they sound like.

If you need to make money quick to feed your family, you might have a financial racket that doesn't offer long-term solutions, isn't sustainable, and isn't good for you. Some people may gamble or play the lottery. The problem is, they may continue to gamble or play the lottery, hoping for that one win like they had before.

Addiction sets in when a series of rackets become the norm for survival, leaving you always in emergency mode. Think of Ray in *Frozen River*. She felt she needed a racket and Lila had one in place. They both ran the smuggling racket well past its sustainability, hoping that it would be beneficial in the long term, but it left them in a situation they almost did not recover from.

You're probably wondering why the hell you need to get this vulnerable and give yourself up. Well, literary irony is born of real life irony, and that's what rackets are when they pose as agents.

PROMPT 23: WRITE-IN EXPOSING YOUR RACKET

Hopefully, you have had revelations about your racket. If not, go to your internal character development research and see if you identify with other people's temporary-remedy behaviors that spun wild into rackets and addictions. Jump-start if need be, then write the scenes/events where you ran your racket. Do this with each stepping stone and with the horizon.

Extend the scene/event by doing a write-in, but keep in mind that this may require you to rewrite the scene/event entirely. You are likely to remember things that you did, things others did, and things that happened in your environment that you didn't notice before becoming aware of your rackets. Write those in. It is also likely that you will find a really strong, true racket that shows up for most of the events/scenes of this personal plot, or that the racket shifted, disguising herself each time.

The Shape-Shifter

Internal saboteurs and rackets that shift when the characters or voices shift are **shape-shifters**. They are the internal saboteurs that elude your intelligence and good instincts, and like the bamboo chopped from the garden, they pop up again, having run underground undetected by your common sense. You recognize a behavior that doesn't serve you well, so you stop, only to find that you are practicing that same behavior under an even more agent-like cloak.

PROMPT 24: WRITE-IN UNMASKING THE INTERNAL SABOTEUR SHAPE-SHIFTERS

Again, you may not have a case where this shape-shifting is true of your rackets or internal saboteurs, but if you do, write into your scenes/events those moments of irony where what has been cured surfaces as a new saboteur. Insert them where they fit best among your stepping stones and horizon event. It is likely that these are whole new scenes that you will be writing.

The Ironic Origins of Some Internal Gifts

The internal gift is the antidote for the internal saboteurs. Where the internal saboteurs insidiously trail underneath the emotional, psychological self and surface over and over again, the internal gifts offer a long-term base in the long-term identity of your spiritual self, like an underground spring that never runs dry. When the work of weeding out your internal saboteurs wears you out, you can reach down in the wellspring of your gifts and be restored, you can build your home above the spring knowing you will always be replenished, and you can offer the internal gift over and over and be restored, not depleted by the giving.

The first step of this write-in is to answer some questions that are an extension of the above discussion. Write down and keep your answers so that you can refer to them in the coming chapters.

1. What gifts did the perpetrator (obstacle) of your initial wound give you? You've written about the wound that was inflicted, but in what way is your strength, resilience, patience, compassion, tenacity, and so on a result of the perpetrator (obstacle)? It may take some time to answer this question, because it's difficult to think of a perpetrator of a wound as the intentional or unintentional giver of gifts or of this person as the initiator of gifts that you possess. For example, in the novel *The Whale Rider*, Kahu's stubbornness is inherited from Koro Apirana, her great-grandfather. In my current personal plot, my father never bought anything on credit. He said, "If you can't afford it, you can't have it." This was one of his financial survival tools. The fact that I possess forms of this philosophy for myself kept me out of the worst part of America's bank crises. It's a gift from the perpetrator. There is also the gift of my mother's endurance and of her ability to make something to wear or something to eat out of seemingly nothing. This can feel emotionally destabilizing to think of the perpetrator of a wound in a different light, but it's often when we are slightly off balance that we discover whole new ways of walking, thinking, writing.

2. What gifts did your agents give you? These are probably a lot easier to identify in your psyche than gifts of your obstacles. For example, in *The Whale Rider*, Kahu's patience is inherited from her father, Porourangi, and her uncle, Rawiri, who have had to put up with her great-grandfather's stubbornness for much longer than she has. In my current personal plot, my seventh-grade teacher told me to walk with my head up. It's been the prideful way that I walk since then, and even when I'm not feeling confident, I feel the confidence of my walk and my psyche follows suit.

3. What innate, internal gifts did you use in each or any of the stepping stones or scenes of your writing to help you survive? For example, in *The Whale Rider*, Kahu's wisdom and sense of knowing who she is helps her survive each stepping stone. She is never in doubt about who she is but is struggling with Koro Apirana, who resists. In my current personal plot during the events of the Mary W. stepping stone, I used my intellect and my ability to create to get out of being potentially fired for racist reasons. It is the gift of my parents' entrepreneurialism combined with my intellect and creativity. Think of these internal gifts as the strengths you came to this life in possession of.

PROMPT 25: WRITE-IN THE IRONIC ORIGINS OF SOME INTERNAL GIFTS
Jump-start if necessary and write a scene that offers one or more of the following:

- A look at the perpetrator operating with the gift.
- You operating with the gift bestowed upon you by the perpetrator.
- A look at the agent operating with the gift.
- You operating with the gift bestowed upon you by the agent.
- A scene or scenes of you operating with your innate gifts.

What may very well happen is that you fulfill more than one of the above writing prompts in one scene or that you jump-start and each of the above prompts calls for its own scene. Exploring the origins of your gifts will likely cause you to have revelations about your entire journey with your want. It will likely send you back to write-ins or rewrites of some of your stepping stones so that you bring out the ironies of your gifts.

It's too easy to sit around measuring your disparities and looking at the people in your life who you want gifts from but who won't give them or don't have them to give. (Yes, I'm talking tangible and intangible gifts that you want.) This prompting and journaling will keep you busy writing about what you do have—not just what you have from the people who complied with your wishes and gave you what you wanted in life, but also what you have from the people who you imagined to be deficient or stingy.

Here's my write-in about the ironies of the gift:

Light is coming in the sky.

The clothes are drying here in the living room where the woodstove has kept us so warm inside this house though it is in the 20s outside.

Split and haul the wood and for the first year, my daughter helps with the hauling of the wood from the shed.

Last weekend, we cut down a small cedar growing in an awkward place on the land, brought it in and decorated it because she so wanted a tree.

My ability to get what I need from my surroundings when I don't have the cash to get it from the store is a gift from both of my abusers, my parents.

Before closing out this chapter, let me recap what raw material you should have if you have done all of the prompts from each exercise.

- *Jump Starter Writing*, ten-minute writes to get you used to jump starters
- *Joys and Pains Exercise*, Prompt **1**
- *Hopes and Fears Exercise*, Prompt **2**
- *The Saboteur*, Prompt **3**
- *The Relationship Museum Exercise*, Prompts **4**
- *The Mirror Exercise*, Prompts **5–9**
- *The Stepping Stones Exercise* (in progress), Prompts **10–25**

CHAPTER 9

Bringing Back

the Chief's Stone Necklace, and Other Risky Tasks

Likely, the people in your stepping stones and the person at the horizon who you currently have an issue with—though they might have their own complex issues and flaws—are also the victims of your wants. You have gone from relationship to relationship, holding people up and patting their pockets to try to get them to give you something that was lost at ground zero of your initial wound. These folks don't have what you want, or they do but they simply don't have the capacity to give it to you. Yet, you hold them accountable for not having it or not being capable of accessing it within themselves. Or, from the perspective of someone with your insistent want, these people have what you want yet refuse to give it to you. This can make for some tense relationships, fraught with drama and misunderstanding, which, fortunately, can be used for the dramatic tension of literary plot.

So, beyond acknowledging and writing about the want, beyond writing about how the want has manifested itself in relationships with other people, there is revelation. Beyond revelation, there is the opportunity to change and have new outcomes where you stop wreaking havoc on the world with your insatiable want and start getting the want by seeking to self fulfill.

The work you have done up to this point is only a portion of a personal plot. In real life, you are still in cycles of creating stepping stones from the initial wound event. In other words, you are still active in the misdirected longing to fulfill your want. Even your horizon issue, if not tended to with some new awareness, will become yet another stepping stone. When we see this in a literary character, we know that the story isn't over, because they haven't had a revelation or change that will shift them out of the pattern and bring some closure and outcome to the current plot.

Your personal plot begins to complete itself when you take the current issue at the horizon and require of yourself more than just the temporary, raggedy survival tactics of the moment.

When you stand bravely—with new awareness—looking at the horizon and insisting on taking new action, you can have revelation.

This chapter sheds light on the places in your personal plot where your misguided efforts at getting what you want have now led to this place where you stand at the horizon, exhausted with your behavior and ready to take positive *actions* that will result in you doing something new and healthy and therefore living and *writing* beyond your personal plot. The idea is for new action to bring about revelation so that you can healthily land in a new way of being: outcome.

Until now, most of the writing you have done has been on events that you already lived. But in order to change the repetition of creating new stepping stones, you'll need to live something new in order to write something new. This is where your horizon event steers away from becoming another stepping stone event in your life and steers toward new, solid ground.

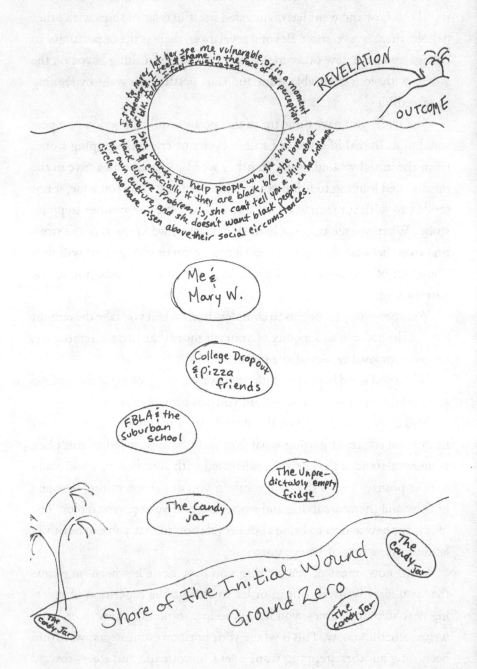

REVELATION

OUTCOME

I try to never let her see me vulnerable, or in a moment of weakness. I feel a shame in the face of her perception of lak. folks. I feel frustrated

She wants to help people who she thinks need it, especially if they are black, b/c she loves black culture. Problem is, she can't tell you a thing about her own culture, and she doesn't want black people in her intimate circle who have risen above their social circumstances.

Me &
Mary W.

College Dropout
& pizza
friends

FBLA & the
suburban
school

The Unpre-
dictably empty
fridge

The candy
jar

The
candy
jar

Shore of the Initial Wound
Ground Zero

The
candy jar

The
candy jar

Action and Write, Write and Action

Let me explain the meaning of **Action and Write**, which can be flipped as **Write and Action**.

There are experiences that we intentionally step out and take, and we can then write because we have lived them; and there are experiences that we want to have in order to bring resolution to our current personal plots, so we write them first and then step out to take the action we have written. We *fear* that we won't ever get what we want but *hope* that we will, and the only way to dissolve that dramatic tension is with the action of living the new experience.

Yes, dramatic tension has been driving your personal plot journey. The question is, what action can you take in order to have a different outcome and not let the current horizon event in your life become another stepping stone where you fail at getting what you want, or where you end up getting some temporary racketed version of what you want?

With all of your new awareness of your personal plot, you have to have new experiences and actions and write about them. In essence, it's the common sense of doing something different in order to have a different outcome. You must first do the action, then write about the emotional journey of doing the action as the first steps toward writing outcome. In other cases, you must first imagine and write the next step in the journey, then take action and live it.

Caution: This is not the opportunity to say, "I'll just fantasize how things would be better if it was a perfect world and write that." You won't be satisfied; you will have run a shortcut racket. The Write and Action prompts in this chapter will serve the purpose of having you imagine something then stepping into that imagined place with your actions, bringing about a situation that you will live and write—or of vice versa, but always the writing and the action. If you shortcut and choose the writing without the action, you'll be pouting when you get to the end of this cumulative process and wonder why it didn't work.

These exercises won't be easy, but they will be of long-term good in getting you what you want: an authentic full-length manuscript that is art.

Action and Write:
Bringing Back the Chief's Stone Necklace

In *The Whale Rider*, Kahu wants Koro Apirana—her great-grandfather, the chief—to acknowledge her courage, strength, and connection to the ancient ones, to acknowledge that she—a girl—will be the new chief. She tried on several occasions to prove this to him, like preparing the speech about her ancestry and dedicating it to him. On this occasion, he did not come to hear her.

One day, Koro Apirana takes the boys out on the boat and throws his stone necklace overboard in hopes that the boy chief will reveal himself by retrieving it. None of the boys can stay in the water long enough to dive to the depths of the reef where the stone has floated into the darkness.

On another day, when Kahu is out on the boat with her uncle and great-grandmother, Nanny Flowers, she finds out they are fishing where Koro Apirana lost his necklace. She does not ask permission but rather jumps overboard to retrieve it. Though this was a test for the boys, she wants to please him and prove worthy of his attention. She retrieves not only the necklace but also a lobster for her great-grandfather's tea. This action, like the others, falls flat, because Nanny Flowers is determined not to anger Koro with the news of Kahu's success.

It is the journey to prove herself by retrieving the stone that offers Kahu connection with the dolphins, who guide her to the stone and bring her back to the surface. In many ways, it does not matter that Koro Apirana does not know that she has retrieved the stone. The stone is merely a tangible manifestation of her courage, strength, and connection with the ancient ones. The action of bringing back the tangible manifestation of her want leaves Kahu with the revelation that the stone is hers in the lineage of chiefs and when the time comes, she will fulfill the outcome of the story.

Action: Bring back the tangible manifestation of your intangible want. Bring back proof that you have sought a healthy, not-harmful-to-others way to self fulfill your own want, as opposed to seeking others to do that for you. Offer an object as evidence that you have done this (like the chief's stone necklace), and let the effort to attain it be fierce. There are a million obstacles that you could immediately throw in your path, like "Well, I can't do that because I can't afford it," "No one is going to let me have time off work to do that," "I'm so young, no one will take me seriously if I say I want to do that" or "Yes, I'm still breathing, but I'm too old to do that."

Keep in mind that you should allow yourself to go with whatever healthy, not-harmful-to-others tangible proof that will help progress you toward fulfilling your want. If that is a plane ticket to Germany or a confirmation of receipt for a job you applied for, bring back proof that you have begun a no-turning-back means of self fulfilling the want, regardless of the messages of your internal saboteur.

For Example: In January 2013, while living in an apartment before starting LaVenson Press Studios, I went to the planning department in the county where my house and land are located and spent $90 on an in-home business license. I wanted financial consistency and intended to fulfill that want on my own. I got it in the mail a few weeks later. The business license was my chief's necklace: a tangible manifestation and proof to myself that I possessed the strength and courage to fulfill my want, and the financial commitment was proof that I intended a healthy way of self fulfilling that want of financial consistency.

In *Frozen River*, Ray goes to the trailer office and puts down the next huge payment for the double wide as commitment and tangible proof that she is on a no-turning back journey of self fulfilling her want. Thankfully, she doesn't fulfill the want by continuing to run her racket. It is the tangible proof that helps her have a revelation about a new way to get what she wants.

PROMPT 26: WRITE THE JOURNEY TO RETRIEVE THE CHIEF'S STONE
Journal each day about the journey. Do this writing until you have brought back the chief's stone, the tangible proof that you are in fact the chief, ready to guide your life in a positive direction. This is a great exercise to do with a group of folks using this book. This way, you all hold each other accountable and have a show and tell of sorts. If you are at a loss for an object that represents your wants, look at the Relationship Museum under the column "Myself" that represents your relationship with yourself.

Remember: Don't forget to utilize your Jump Starters from Chapter 1. They will keep you from sitting there, trying to figure out what to write, and instead keep you inspired.

Write and Action:
Releasing the Blame and Taking the Responsibility, The Bridge between Revelation and Outcome

The revelation scene is an opportunity for the main voice or character to take responsibility for fulfilling their own wants, and it's also an opportunity for the main voice or character to release blame and take responsibility for their rackets and internal saboteurs. Up until now in the stepping stones exercise of personal plot, the internal saboteurs have been excused as the best the main voice or character can do to survive.

For instance, Ray is breaking the law in *Frozen River*, lying to bill collectors, and racially setting herself above the Mohawks, all to get what she wants. In the short revelation scene where she pauses at the lake after letting Lila take the blame, she stops blaming others for her plight and takes responsibility for the crime she has committed, and gets what she wants the long, slow way.

My short story "The Empty Nest" is one long revelation scene. Hazel (the main character) takes responsibility by acknowledging her racket. For years, she tells herself that everyone around her is inept and that's why she is alone. She eventually stops blaming the world for her solitude and allows for the revelation that her solitude is the result of her fear of commitment—a threshold she must cross before she can get what she wants. In *Fifth Born II: The Hundredth Turtle*, Odessa stops making Lamont and Ella Mae responsible for her connection with her siblings and pursues this responsibility on her own. In the movie *The Pursuit of Happyness*, Chris pursues the American Dream by taking it into his own hands to rise above homelessness. In the memoir *Between the World and Me*, Ta-Nehisi pursues the contents and consequences of the American Dream and takes responsibility for helping his son with that same pursuit by writing his memoir. These two authors chase the same tornado (the American Dream) for different reasons, but they release others from responsibility of attaining the goal for them.

Releasing blame is the bridge between the revelation and the outcome. Once the voice or character has revelations about what they need to do to change, they will hopefully take some responsible action. Releasing blame of others is the first step in this responsibility.

Caution: Keep in mind that you are working with personal plot in order to build literary plot. Don't use this exercise as an opportunity for the self-berating saboteur to say, "I blame myself." The idea here is to realize that an event occurred (the initial wound). In that event, you lost something, which left you wanting something, and you pursued that want by sometimes illegitimate (internal saboteur/obstacle) and other times legitimate (gifts/ internal agents) means. What happened in the initial wound wasn't your fault, but if you want change and outcome, it's your responsibility to do something new.

If you are blaming yourself, turn that into taking responsibility for your actions in order to have a new outcome. This personal plot awareness and revelation makes for good literary plot awareness and revelation. If you are blaming yourself, then release that blame in this exercise in the same way that you would release the blame you have placed on another person or entity.

PROMPT 27: WRITE — RELEASING THE BLAME

Look at your stepping stone scenes. Who or what have you blamed for not having what you want? Imagine and write a scene/event in a realistic future where you take responsibility for your own saboteurs and release the people and things you've been blaming for not having what you want. Jump-start and write.

PROMPT 28: ACTION — RELEASING THE BLAME

Now that you've written about it, use the writing as your courage to take the action of actually releasing the blame where you call, write, or get in touch with someone in some way and take an action that lets them know, and more importantly lets you know, that you are releasing the blame. If the person has passed away or is emotionally not available (like an abuser who is still active), still take the action since the exercise is about your revelations, not about theirs. Be sure that you are not setting the person up and wanting from them a response. This wouldn't be releasing the blame but just shifting the ways in which you hold them hostage. Write about this experience too.

One of the ways to take action and release the blame from someone who has passed away or is emotionally not available is to write a letter, knowing that you cannot send it but considering that you are relaying the message in a psychic way, where messages can cross the boundaries of death and psychological damage.

The Threshold of Learning

These revelation prompts might bring to the surface specific remnants of memories and of revelatory connections between the behavior you have had in relationships and your responsibility to make change. At the same time that this awareness can feel liberating, it can feel scary, overwhelming, and daunting. Some folks find themselves standing at a threshold of learning. At this point, you are aware of all the things you have wanted to do differently with your personal plot, and all of the ways that you can take it to a new, soulful level. At the same time, you are aware now of the new relationships you'll need to have with all of your deepest joys and pains in order to fulfill the want.

The dilemma is this: "Now I'm aware of what I can do to get what I want, but it's just too frightening to leave the comfort of the stepping stones. If I go back to my old ways of trying to get what I want, it's gonna hurt like hell to have awareness of something yet not reach for it. If I go forward into the unknown of my growth, I'm not sure if there will be anything there to support me. Maybe I'll go nuts like Picasso, Ernest Hemingway, Sylvia Plath, or that relative of mine who people use as a symbol of why to avoid self-exploration—'She went crazy after going to therapy.'"

It's good to laugh about the extremes of our thoughts, because there are some human truths in those fears. At this threshold of learning, there seems to be the inevitability of pain: there is certain pain in going backward when you have new awareness, and temporary pain in stepping forward into your own evolution. It must hurt like hell to turn from a tadpole into a frog, but oh, the joys of newfound mobility and the power of a prehensile tongue.

But how do you step across a threshold or open a door to your own changes when only your instincts tell you what's on the other side and you have no experience that lets you know that it will be okay? Remember our discussion in the introduction about this writing being an emotional, psychological, and spiritual journey? This is the spiritual part, which always reminds me of the movie *The Pursuit of Happyness*. Chris has seemingly insurmountable odds in his life, having grown up experiencing separation from his father and his mother, and then surviving an abusive stepfather and ending up a homeless single parent. But he is driven by a grit and determination to provide for his family and takes a risk on a non-paying internship because he believes he can succeed even though everything around him is telling him that he is a statistic. He is driven by faith in his own abilities.

All you know is that you are compelled to finally tell some life experience and determined to have revelation and outcome for that life experience through writing, but you don't know what the outcome will be.

Intellectually, you know that this is the stuff that's at the base of the type of literature you love and the type of writer you want to become. You can extend and hypothesize on that thought by supposing that, since you are a living being inside of ecology with other living beings, your evolution is being called for. You feel compelled to write the experiences and seek out resolution for them, because someone must be calling for the food, medicine, and kinship that your work will bring. That's all you know, and now you must act, which is the hard part. And there's always putting this process down until you feel more prepared to take the journey, or relying on the advice of spelunking in Chapter 3 to help you traverse the space between revelation (awareness) and outcome.

Yes, the saboteur can be loud when we are doing something new. Keep in mind that our saboteurs are just trying to protect us from the unknown. Also keep in mind that they aren't likely going away, so walking through that gate and showing them that everything is just fine in this new way of being and that they can transform and be part of it is a great thing.

Yes, no matter where you go, that part of you will come with you, but be careful not to let the saboteur voice come with you while speaking in the same old voice. Insist that this voice evolve and mature with you. Saboteurs must be given a new job suited for their skills; the bad attitude saboteur can become the gift of self-determination, the hide-for-solitude saboteur can become the gift of the artists who writes or creates for four straight hours per day. Give them a suitable, positive position in your new life. Otherwise, their way of being will hold you back at one step, and that failure will feel like proof that you can't do what you want to do at the next step and the next.

At the threshold of learning, you have already written most everything in your personal plot that deals with what you remember (which of course shifts), and you are about to take actions that will offer revelation, change, a different way of seeing things. This step into a new way of acting in order to spur a new response is like a door with scary faces of the past on it. Most of you reading this book will dream about ferocious animals and alien invasions during this time, because what exists on the other side of the threshold are new ways of being that you don't have context for.

For every person wanting to change, evolve, or get something, there comes a time where all else will fail you and faith and your inherent strength is all you have. You can create or utilize pre-existing tools that can help you to manage these inevitable fears as you walk through that door. Bring with you into the chaotic unknown of change some familiar, healthy, comforting artifacts that can help you step off into the unknown void where your wants exist.

1. Suit up with your faith, whatever that faith is.

2. Also suit up with your strengths. Go back to write-in Prompt 22 and remember how you survived, remember what inherent gifts you possess that helped you survive. Bring them with you.

3. Go back to the Relationship Museum in Chapter 4 and look at the objects and artifacts that you entered under "Myself," your relationship with yourself. What objects there can serve as a security blanket or talisman as you cross the threshold? Literally, put them in your pocket or on your desk as you write every day.

Know that, well equipped, every step you take into the unknown, dark void is a step that will then be illuminated.

CHAPTER 10

Write the Outcome

Then Step into It

One way to get at the outcome is through the actions that occur as a result of the revelation. After the main voice or character in your story has realized that there are new, positive ways to self fulfill the want, you can offer the action of the voice or character seeking new, positive ways of fulfilling that want.

Or you might choose to have the main voice or character have a saboteur-like response to the revelation, something along the lines of revenge or self-annihilation.

Or you may choose to leave the world in suspense.

In this book, we're going to only focus on the type of outcome where a new, positive action is the result of the outcome. Why? Because we are building literary plot from personal plot, and the positive outcome action is a marvelous opportunity to evolve our readers and ourselves.

Outcome Action

The **outcome action** in a story comes after the revelation, and is the part of the outcome where readers are left satisfied that things will be okay because the main character's or voice's change is sustained through their new plan. As I said, not all stories offer an outcome action moment as part of the outcome of the story. Some may end in a cliff-hanger, which leads you to believe that perhaps the main voice or character will revert back to the stepping stones of their plot and that their outcome will not be sustained, or some may end offering that the main voice or character had a negative reaction to the revelation and outcome.

The outcome action prompts are crucial for you to do with your personal plot regardless of whether you choose to write-in an outcome action to your literary plot. These writings become the litmus test to detect rackets. Sometimes, we have an outcome and when we put together the plan to sustain the outcome, we realize that the outcome is not sustainable—it is a racket disguised as a sustainable outcome that in fact becomes the shore of other people's initial wounds rather than becoming the shore of others' initial joys.

Up until this point in our personal plots, other people's behavior and setting have had such an impact on us that we shifted when they shifted. But with the outcome action, you will intentionally take actions that will shift and change you and by default others. The outcome action is the second most impactful time in your personal plot (the initial wound being the most impactful). But the outcome action differs, because you are not being acted upon. This time, you are choosing to act upon your own life. As in the image, you are creating a new shore of solid ground from which positive stepping stones can be cast. You are standing on the outcome action shore. How awesome is that?

You can prompt the writing of the outcome action by

1. Imagining an outcome and creating a timeline of action.
2. Creating and living a new practice that will sustain an outcome by

sharing the gift of the positive outcome with someone else so the reader knows that the positive outcome will carry on.

3. Writing in the plan to manage the internal saboteurs who may seek to thwart the outcome.

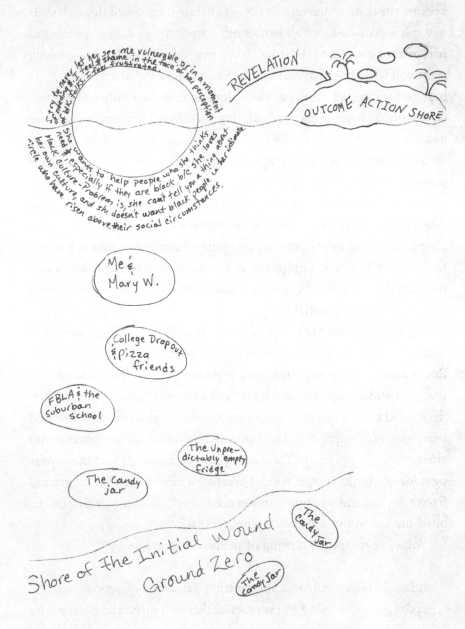

Outcome Action
through the Imagined Outcome and Timeline

Sometimes, you have to write the outcome and then walk into it and make it real. This is because the frightening threshold of learning that stands between the revelation and the outcome can be energized by your attention to the wants and wounds of other people in your life, or by your attention to the wants and wounds of people in your past, or even by the mandates and social strictures of your society. This can make it feel impossible to get beyond this last wall of action and to step to the outcome side, because you are connected to many of these people through marriage, parenting, sibling bonds, or cultural identity, and you know that if you shift or change, they will shift and change in ways you can't know.

If you find yourself having trouble living an outcome because you can't stop imagining the worst, consider my philosophy: since you are going to be imagining things about the future anyway, you might as well make the choice to imagine something positive as opposed to imagining something negative. It sucks not being able to know the future, so imagine the best outcome scene and then step into that positive future.

Similar to the exercise of Releasing the Blame and Taking the Responsibility, you will write first and then take action based on what you have written.

A marvelous poetic example of writing the outcome and then stepping into it is Forogh Farrokhzad's poem "The Wall." I interpret it as a story about the men and the society that restrict her, and how she commits to a future of seeping out, above, through the wall and someday turning back to erect a wall to contain the type of oppression she has endured.

PROMPT 29: WRITE THE LIST OF WANTS

Write a list of wants that will sustain your outcome and are disconnected from other people's wants and wounds—not "I want to leave my oppressive town, but I feel they will never let me leave," or "I want to start a new business, but I feel like people on my job will not be able to function without me," or "I want to get a new job or get a degree, but my family won't be able to function with me out of the house full-time," and certainly not, "I want to stop gambling, drinking, complaining, gossiping, but I can't because my friends and family will think I'm no longer one of them." Though these are all real and legitimate fears of the wall of obstacles around you, the idea is to use your writing to do like Forogh Farrokhzad and "set off to the banks of the sun" (13).

Here's my short list of wants from my Stepping Stones Exercise:

- I want financial consistency in my life.
- I want to merge my workshop businesses.
- I want to start buying the things I need for myself.

You can usually find your core, root wants as the wants you've sought to fulfill all along in this personal plot. And you can usually find your fear of acting on your wants hiding behind your fear of what someone will say or do to you or has said or done in the past.

What internal gifts have helped you survive over the years and have been of long-term good for you? These can become the means by which you seek resolution in your imagined outcome. (Mind you, I'm not talking about the short-term actions to survive, which are mostly saboteurish and don't do you long-term good.)

This focusing on imagining a life where you have what you want separate from others' wounds and wants is where you let what's of long-term good for you step up and be in the foreground of your personal plot.

Before I give you this prompt of writing an imagined outcome, let me tell you that the goal of writing an imagined outcome is to remain authentic by utilizing your true wants in order to imagine a future that can make you feel more light and less heavy, more joyful and less a victim of painful, unrequited wants, and able to create a life that you can walk into.

In writing *Fifth Born*, I felt stuck and was having trouble writing an outcome because of my real emotional and psychological reality with my mother. I didn't know how to get beyond the frightening threshold of learning. Stuck in the mortar of that wall was the fact that I wanted my mother to value and acknowledge me. Also stuck in that wall was the fact that I was so disconnected from my siblings because of the dynamics of my mother's emotional negotiations in our abusive household. She needed to protect her husband's name at the expense of the only one who was doing the tattling, me.

At the time of writing *Fifth Born*, I hadn't come to many of the psychological understandings I have now. So, I didn't know how to write an outcome when so much was unresolved in my heart. Moreover, I didn't know how to stop going round and round creating more stepping stone events by trying to get from my biological family something they didn't possess at the time.

The last third of the novel is created from an imagined outcome where Odessa steps beyond the metaphorical threshold, the eleventh tree on her grandfather's property. Led by her internal gift to observe, she spends the day watching her family and stays away from them long enough that her options shift when she chooses to step beyond her fearful threshold of learning and into the unknown future. This happens to be her best-case scenario, where she finds her true biological mother, who is based on the best qualities of my biological mother. In short, I separated my own mother into two characters, a mother who raises Odessa and an imagined, surrogate mother who has the capacity to embrace Odessa.

Writing that fictional outcome helped me to step into the lived actions of a similar outcome. In my real life, after writing *Fifth Born*, I was able to focus less on what my mother doesn't possess of my long list of wants and more on what gifts I possess, and I became a much better surrogate mother for myself. I based the character Ella Mae on the qualities of a good mother who possesses the best qualities distilled from my mother and myself. In this case, writing good fiction can be a matter of telling a lie to expose the truth, imagining an outcome to expose the best personal outcome. The imagined outcome then, makes a nice bookend to Prompt 17: The Want before the Wound in Chapter 6, where you wrote a time in your life before the initial wound, where you did not want for what you want in this plot because you had not yet lost. Here, you imagine what it will be like to again have what you want of your own volition.

PROMPT 30: WRITE THE IMAGINED OUTCOME

What does your ideal life of having what you want look like, without blame or responsibility being put on others for you to have what you want, but an imagined outcome where you seek to self fulfill your want? Jump-start several times if you have to and write scenes of this imagined positive future. Make sure these are events—even though they are imagined—that feel real because you have imagined a future where you fulfill your wants from your own emotional and psychological base. In other words, don't write that you won the lottery and that your issues with money were resolved. That means that your issues weren't resolved, and they certainly weren't resolved through your internal gifts. Instead, it means that the quick-fix addiction of one of your rackets paid off, yet you didn't change, evolve, or have resolution.

Readers shouldn't be able to tell the difference between these scenes and the ones that you wrote from your true personal plot. They should feel the natural progression of your or your character's or voice's evolution. These future scenes/events should be as filled with external setting and internal setting as your other scenes. They should be in first person, past tense, no dialogue, with good sensory details in order to ensure a stripped-down version of good storytelling. This should be a positive outcome that you can go and live tomorrow, because your internal gifts are guiding the way, as opposed to your worries about how others will be impacted guiding the way.

Caution: It can't just be another time where you are involving someone else in getting what you want. If so, you just made another stepping stone by attempting to fulfill your wants in the same old misguided way. So, if you craft an outcome where you get what you want, let it be one where you are not simply still demanding that others provide, but where you self fulfill the want.

Now, with that said, self fulfilling the want doesn't mean living autonomously without others, but it means having an awareness and discernment to fulfill with responsibility. This means involving others who want to be involved in filling gaps that wounds left in your life. It means allowing them to come and go as their growth guides them, knowing that you hold the substance of self-love that fills the gap when others cannot. Remember, take no hostages.

Timeline of Action

Perhaps now that you have made your positive outcome real through writing, you can step into the action of living it, which then will enhance the writing because you will have firsthand experience.

PROMPT 31: ACTION — CREATE A TIMELINE

Draw a timeline, much like a number line.

- At the far left end, insert a tick mark, and above the mark write down what you want. Below the mark, write "Now" or "Current."
- At the far right end, insert a tick mark, and above the mark write down the imagined outcome you wrote. Below the mark, write the date you imagine reaching your outcome.
- Make evenly spaced tick marks between the current and the future, and jot down actions you have to take to make this occur and the dates you imagine taking each action. Progress from left to right chronologically, beginning with where you are currently.

Here is an example of my timeline for the personal plot of my Stepping Stones Exercise. The current far left reads, "I want to use my intellectual and artistic gifts to secure financial consistency." At the far right, I jotted down the imagined outcome, "Use what I have to build my dreams. Use my land to start a writing studio and combine my two businesses."

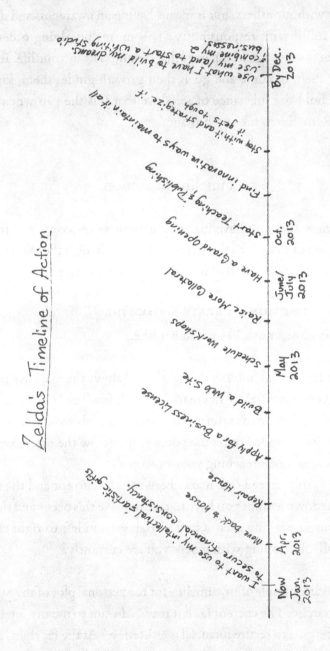

Zelda's Timeline of Action

Now/
Jan.
2013 — I want to use my intellectual, artistic gifts to secure financial consistency.

Apr.
2013 — Repair House / Move back a house

— Apply for a Business License

— Build a Web Site

May
2013 — Schedule Workshops

— Raise More Collateral

June/
July
2013 — Have a Grand Opening

Oct.
2013 — Start Teaching & Publishing

— Find innovative ways to monetize it all

— Stay with it and strategize it if it gets tough

By Dec.
2013 — Use what I have to build my dreams; combine my 3 businesses?

My additional tick marks from left to right chronologically read, "Move back to house, Repair House, Apply for a Business License, Build a Web Site, Schedule Workshops, Raise More Collateral, Have a Grand Opening, Start Teaching & Publishing, Find innovative ways to maintain it all, Stay with it and strategize if it gets tough."

I'm currently working on those next-to-last two tick marks, since I have had some revelations about some of my internal saboteurs showing up as I work hard to take these actions.

Make sure that each action on your timeline begins with a verb so you keep in mind that you have a plan to do things that will merge your present life with your imagined future life ("use," "call," "send," "repair," and so on). Devising a timeline will help you to write an outcome action scene.

PROMPT 32: WRITE THE OUTCOME ACTION THROUGH THE IMAGINED OUTCOME AND TIMELINE

As you accomplish the things in your timeline, write a scene/event that represents each item in the timeline. Yes, this may take several months, but one of these scenes may feel authentic for the outcome action of your manuscript.

Outcome Action through the Practice of Sharing the Internal Gifts

The outcome action scene of your plot can be written by living the new **practice** that will sustain your outcome. Getting a practice means coming up with a consistent repeated action that will help you to sustain the change that you've had through your outcome. For instance, you may begin jogging every day as a practice to sustain your outcome of weight loss.

So, you have had a revelation and a change, but we know that changing any rooted behavior requires maintenance for the change to keep it steady. Change is more like a swinging pendulum: you're doing better, then you're practicing old habits. Wait, now you're doing better again.

At least you are not practicing poor habits consistently. The way to bring the pendulum to rest at consistently doing better is to have a practice to sustain your outcome, something that you do every day to hold the change steady until it becomes your new way of being.

For instance, eight years ago my back went out. I wasn't doing anything particularly more strenuous than usual (of course, at the time my normal physical activity was other people's boot camp), but with the cumulative stress on those lower back muscles and the spine, suddenly I was laid up, consistently in pain. Through chiropractic and acupuncture treatments, I was in pain sometimes and better sometimes, but I added the daily morning practice of yoga to the mix, and eventually I was better consistently. When I don't do my yoga, my back feels achy, so for the last eight years, even when I travel I do my yoga. Sometimes, that means using my gift of creativity to make a yoga mat out of hotel towels, or it means overcoming criticism from a family member who finds yoga as yet another crazy thing that Zelda does. Every day, regardless of what else is going on, I engage the consistent practice that has sustained my outcome of a healthy back.

Another example is my daily writing practice of a minimum of four hours a day. It is the only way that I know to bring forth enough raw material to produce what I want, which are full-length manuscripts. It is also the only way that I know to keep my writing tools sharp. The characteristics of a good writing practice are the same as any practice devised to sustain your outcome; all of the same elements apply.

With my current personal plot, I have started a practice of doing the same financially progressive routine for my family and my business each week. Regardless of how I feel, I know that I have to devote half a day on Mondays to marketing and money, and half a day on Tuesdays to writing or following up on new proposals.

So, many of us will take to the types of practices mentioned above that don't involve any other people or accountability so that if we stop practicing, no one else ever knows. A way to place accountability into your practice is to practice your outcome by offering your internal gifts.

(See Chapter 8, under the subheading The Ironic Origins of Some Internal Gifts.)

Sharing your internal gifts helps you to sustain your outcome because you involve other people who become your accountability, and you change the cycle of creating stepping stone after stepping stone in your personal plot. It's an opportunity to notice that you have and appreciate those internal gifts in the same way that you have become aware of your obstacles and saboteurs. It's a wonderful thing altogether to use the gifts as a way to settle the long-term, restless pains of your initial wound, and to create useful sustained outcome for your plot. What truly satisfies a loss and fulfills a want is a gift. By giving the gift, you get what you want and simultaneously become someone else's external agent. This is the opportunity to stand on that outcome action shore and cast stepping stones of positivity that become someone else's initial joy.

A scene of the practice in place makes great closure for the main voice or character in your manuscript. But you can't write it until you have lived it. Keep in mind that many stories do not have an outcome action. Once the main voice or character completes the journey of seeking to fulfill their want, they have changed and the story is over. But, in many stories, it is satisfying for the reader to know that the outcome will be sustained.

For instance, in *The Whale Rider*, Koro Apirana and Nanny Flowers practice part of the outcome action by uniting and embracing, just like the people uniting and embracing their sense of both reality and faith in the supernatural. This is the closing scene where the whole tribe comes into the hospital room to witness the harmony of Koro the chief and Kahu the chief-to-be, and simultaneously the ancient bull whale and the old mother whale have stopped their arguing beneath the sea. Interestingly enough, Kahu was trying to offer this gift of harmony throughout most of the novel with her actions of singing to the whales, retrieving the stone from the depths of the ocean, and telling everyone that everything will be okay for their people. But no one was accepting her gift at the time, because this would go against Koro, the chief, the bull whale of the people. Know that for the personal plot, writing an outcome action is of great value regardless of your later literary usage of those scenes. It helps to let you know if you have truly had an outcome that is sustainable through a practice, or if you have begun to run a racket disguised as an outcome, which as you know is not sustainable and doesn't have healthy, non-saboteurish gifts attached.

PROMPT 33: WRITE THE LIST OF POTENTIAL PRACTICES

Make a list of potential practices that would sustain your outcome and the change you have had. Remember, the goal is to find both a practice that is positive and involves the giving of your internal gifts, and one that does not involve your saboteurs, who will land you right back in the repetitive stepping stones cycle again.

PROMPT 34: ACTION AND WRITE — OUTCOME ACTION THROUGH IMPLEMENTING THE PRACTICE

Now, choose a potential practice from your written list and take a month to work on implementing this practice with a component of gift giving and accountability. For instance, I set the workshop schedule for LaVenson Press Studios for the next two years and published them on the website so that I consistently offer my gift as a teacher yet maintain my outcome without my run-away racket interfering. I'm involving my whole clientele on the accountability for my practice. If people don't see a workshop listed in the newsletter, for instance, they will e-mail, wondering if it is soon to be posted. After all, my whole clientele will be expecting those workshops.

You may need to pick a potential practice and employ some trial and error of fits and starts to come up with a practice where you can sustain the outcome while managing internal saboteurs.

Once you settle into a practice, it's important to commit to the daily practice for at least a month. If your outcome, for instance, was human connection, you'll have to do something like perhaps offer your gift of being a good helper and volunteer on a schedule of accountable hours at your local community center, school or day care, or community organization so that you give your gift, sustain your outcome, and keep your saboteurs at bay with others holding you accountable.

As you select and employ your daily practices, and as you struggle through a month of staying committed to them, write each day about your feelings. Write a journal or travelogue of what happens each day. The writing itself is a daily practice.

Single out scenes from your journaling (and write more experiences if so moved) that you feel are the outcome action of your personal plot. You will recognize it as the piece where you have chosen a practice to settle into that has an element of accountability; feels most long term, fulfilling, and soothing to the pains of your overall want; and at the same time offers some positive gift to others. Many of you may get hung up on offering the gift in a way that does not simply play in to your saboteurs, so here's another Action and Write to help you to specifically get clear about the gift-giving aspect of your practice.

Action and Write – The Field Trip

How can you re-gift so you are reacting to what you want by giving rather than holding others accountable and insisting they give to you?

Action: Identify a person or entity that has the same want that you have been walking around with as a result of your initial wound. Now that you have identified your internal gifts, written about them in the stepping stones, and answered some questions about their origins, devise an action (field trip) through which you will offer this very positive gift to a person or entity.

Caution: Do not attempt to offer someone something that *you* perceive that they want but they have not agreed to as their want. For instance, don't roll up at a homeless shelter with a hundred toothbrushes because your parents denied you dental care and you want to use your generosity as a way to make sure that others have clean teeth. First, call the homeless shelter and see if dental care is something that they need and want as a donation, and then if the answer is yes, offer them what they say they want for their clients in the way of dental care. This way, you are matching up your gifts with others' wants rather than using your gifts again toward what you want without regard for what others want.

Also—and of great importance—do not take this as an opportunity to revert gifts into more wants. What do I mean? Do not decide that, for instance, you will offer your loving attention to someone who you feel is the perpetrator of denying you love and attention. If you try to give gifts to the folks who have been shunning or denying you, what you are really doing is trying new ways to get them to fulfill the want. Careful, examine your motives.

If you choose to offer the gift to someone else as part of your revelation, outcome, and outcome action process, the gift-giving process itself can help you to do something outside of surviving the wound and reaching for the want. Remember, the gift can be tangible or intangible. Perhaps you need to give someone the praise you never received yet the praise someone else has been craving. This action has the ability to transform the want into a form of nourishment. Instead of just inhaling, inhaling, inhaling oxygen in an attempt to get what you want, you rhythmically exhale and give the byproduct of your experiences to those needing your gifts. This takes you out of the old loops of your stepping stones and offers you the opportunity to have more revelations through your new actions that can lead to change and outcome.

PROMPT 35: ACTION AND WRITE — THE FIELD TRIP

On a daily basis, write about every aspect of planning this field trip, of taking the field trip and of the feelings that come up after the field trip. Think of it as a travelogue or journal for this part of your journey with your personal plot.

This exercise of sharing my gift led me to the writing of this book. Rather than combining my intellect and creativity to get away from someone doing harm (my old run-away racket), I decided to gift my teaching and writing processes to others who are working to bring forth the emotional, psychological, and spiritual authenticity in their art.

You may need to offer the gift several times in the course of a month in order to settle on something that feels true and authentic. Hold on to the journal writing that you do, ponder how you feel, write some more, talk with others you know intimately and trust with your vulnerability, and allow an idea of offering your gift to emerge.

Caution: If you walk around with an altruistic saboteur like myself, make sure that the gift you are offering is also a gift to yourself. Make sure there is mutual benefit. It's always of huge benefit to me and to others for me to write a book or teach, which creates long-term income, but it isn't a gift to me to offer writing workshops for free when I need income.

PROMPT 36: WRITE THE OUTCOME ACTION THROUGH THE PRACTICE OF SHARING THE INTERNAL GIFTS

Single out a scene from your field trip journaling (and write more scenes if so moved) that you feel is the outcome action of your personal plot. You will recognize this event/scene as the piece where you felt that your actions were most tied to your feelings of want but where you realized that you could fulfill the want through offering your own gifts (internal agents).

For example, in the short story "The Moths" by Helena María Viramontes, the outcome action is the main voice offering her abuelita the same kind of nurturing (gift) that the grandmother has always offered her. In the beginning of the story, the grandmother "made a balm out of dried moth wings and Vicks" and soothed the girl's angry hands, and at the end of the story the girl is a woman. When her abuelita dies, she picks the grandmother up and takes her to the tub for soothing and bathing, offering Abuelita the same gift of nurturing. "There, there, Abuelita, I said, cradling her, smoothing her as we descended, I hear you. Her hair fell back and spread across the water like eagles' wings. The water in the tub overflowed and poured onto the tile of the floor. Then the moths came."

When we are able to accept the gifts of our perpetrators, agents, and our own internal gifts and then offer them to others, each of us becomes an agent in someone else's personal plot. Again, you are on the outcome action shore, where the impactful event is not a negative event that causes stepping stones of want, but where the impactful event is the actions you choose to take that will cause stepping stones of fulfilled want and initial joy, not initial wounds.

Remember, there is also the big gift that you offer through writing the authentic truth of your journey as a full-length manuscript. It is the food, medicine, or kinship that someone else needs along a similarly perilous journey.

Action and Write:
Managing the Internal Saboteurs to Maintain Outcome

We are using personal plot to create literary plot, but with literary plot we don't have an opportunity to spend more time with the voice or the character after the art is done. In real life, we just keep on living with ourselves, and though we write a revelation and an outcome to our personal plot, we must keep on living with our tendencies. So, there's the outcome of "They lived happily ever after," and there is the more realistic outcome of "They learned to manage their saboteurs and found some daily practices to help them sustain their outcome."

With the latter, when you find yourself returning to the old ways of fulfilling your wants, you'll have a plan to quickly correct yourself and get on a forward-moving course.

Action: Bring back proof that you will manage your internal saboteurs, the ones that you recognize may become obstacles to you self fulfilling the want and reaching your goal. Keep in mind that you will also need to manage the shape-shifters, those internal saboteurs that mutate like a nasty virus in order to elude the effects of antibiotics.

After bringing back the Chief's Necklace of the business license as proof that I am committed to self fulfilling my want, it was necessary for me to bring back proof that I am committed to managing my internal saboteurs so that I can continue to reach for my goal. This time, I brought back the e-mail where my intern accepted the position and the e-mail where I got a referral from a friend for a bookkeeper.

Let me explain how I came to realize that I needed these two external agents to help me manage my internal saboteurs.

Six months into working at the studio, I felt isolated and like there was no way that I could singlehandedly pull off what I wanted to pull off. I also felt like I just couldn't get enough folks to register to satisfy my monthly expenses. "What went wrong?" I asked myself.

Then I examined a host of saboteurs that needed to be managed. I was offering trade and barter, discounts. And worst of all, the entire business model was designed to keep me at home where I'd be safe and sound and in control, but I was the only one running the business, so there was no one to keep me from running if I decided to. I didn't realize that parts of the business operation were designed to accommodate my saboteurs, those temporary survival measures of the past that didn't serve my long-term goals.

I had to change this and fast, so I got an intern to come in a couple of times a week, and I am in the process of seeking a bookkeeper to come in twice a month to keep the money organized and keep money management in the analytical zone and out of the emotional zone.

What has since become clear is that I can do this endeavor but not on my own. Remember, internal saboteurs aren't all bad. After all, they saved you, if ever so temporarily; they employ quick-fix actions without discernment. The journaling about my saboteurs helped me see that I have to employ some folks with discernment—make good, sound decisions about finding someone trustworthy to handle marketing and publicity and someone else to handle my money. I'll have to manage my shame saboteur and my trust saboteur so that I can meet my goal of financial consistency without being tripped up by my emotional triggers.

PROMPT 37: OUTCOME ACTION THROUGH MANAGING THE SABOTEURS

Journal each day about the journey of managing the saboteurs that may stand in the way of you self fulfilling your want. Do this writing until you have brought back the tangible proof that you will manage them, and even journal about that tangible object, which may be a want ad for an accountability agent. Much like the Chief's Necklace Exercise, this is a great exercise to do with a group of others who are doing the work of this book. You all can hold each other accountable and hold each other in good kinship. Allow your journaling to prompt you to write the scene/event of outcome action that offers the reader the story of you putting the management plan for your saboteurs into practice.

While you take new outcome actions, you'll have to consistently manage your saboteurs. They are a part of you and likely won't be going anywhere soon, but you can manage them and keep them out of your attempts at self fulfilling the want. If you don't, your outcome will just become another stepping stone, which is what almost happened with the venture of opening LaVenson Press Studios as the outcome to my personal plot. If I create it but then can't manage my internal saboteurs, I won't be able to sustain it, and the whole venture turns into an elaborate racket. This writing exercise is another means of creating a daily practice to sustain your outcome.

In Summary: The outcome action is the second-most impactful event in the plot; the most impactful is the initial wound. In the initial wound event, and in all of the events of *you* (main voice or character) seeking to fulfill the want, you are being impacted by other people's actions. In this event, you are choosing a positive action to sustain your outcome, and that action has a positive impact on others and alters the course of their personal plot in a positive way. You are not standing around doubting yourself and being acted upon; you are the positive action and impacting others.

For instance, in the movie *Frozen River*, when Ray sacrifices and offers her gift of endurance so that both she and Lila can get what they need, this action has a positive impact on every other character in the story. This is in contrast to her husband's action causing an initial wound and having a negative impact that causes a loss and a want and sets the series of Ray's stepping stones in motion.

It's nice to know that we can change the negative impact of events by offering the positive practices and the gifts that are born from those events. When you think of the entire Stepping Stones Exercise, it's clear that with lots of intention and awareness, wounds can be transformed into gifts.

Note: Now that you have rewritten many of your scenes, before moving on to the next section, arrange your scenes chronologically with the initial wound, then each of the stepping stones scenes as they occurred in time, then the horizon, then the revelation, outcome, and outcome action.

PART 3

Shaping
Your Personal Plot

For the sake of easy reading, each time that I refer to "scene," from this point forward, I am referring to "scene" or "event," or "poem."

And for the sake of developing personal plot into literary plot, from this point forward I will no longer refer to "you" as the subject of the scenes, but I will refer to the main voice or character.

CHAPTER 11

7 Pivotal Scenes

to Anchor the Overall Plot

Before we begin to add the more intentional and intellectual aspects of this process, let's stop here for just a moment and remind ourselves of some things that we know but might find difficult to remember under the circumstances of feeling quite naked in this emotional and psychological writing.

Art is the combination of vulnerability and skill. At no point in this process will you get what you want with a full-length manuscript if you chuck the emotional, psychological, and spiritual process for the more intellectual processes of structure and craft. They all go hand in hand.

In order to proceed with part three of this process, you will need not only lots of raw material (you should have accumulated a great deal through the several writing prompts so far), but you will also need raw material that is authentic in its emotional and psychological truth, devoid of philosophizing or other emotionally evasive tactics, like third-person narrative. Not that other perspectives in writing aren't valuable, but in writing your first manuscript you are teaching yourself to write the emotional truth. For that task to be clean and unencumbered, there needs to be as few additional distracting elements as possible. This is comparable to the first-year film student who learns to tell a visual story well without sound so the visuals carry the tale. In this case, the unencumbered first-person narrator carries the personal emotions rather than those emotions being conveyed vicariously. Crafting a third-person or omniscient narrative well requires an additional level of introspection on the author's part. You don't want to attempt this and end up bringing the craft quality of the narrative down because you weren't prepared to utilize a technique that required both great vulnerability and a high level of craft combined.

Now, if you already know that you didn't tell the whole of your emotional truth about how something made you feel, or what memories or fantasies occurred in your mind or body when you experienced something, then go back to those prompts, get in the zone with some Jump Starters, and turn off your analytical brain and write.

One way to recognize moments where you offered the reader something without giving its emotional significance is to read through your work for key phrases, words, people, or occurrences that had a profound impact on your life but that you didn't write about. Or look for places where you have alluded to secrets but didn't let the reader in on the secrets. These are like sinkholes; they appear surface level, but if you put your foot there, you will end up far beneath the surface.

For Example: If you go on and on in a scene, mentioning or reacting to the absence of an individual who has passed away but never offering the scene of that passing (so that the reader is emotionally privy to everything that the voice or character is privy to and the impact it had on the voice or character), then you need to rewrite or write-in. It's likely that this missing, untold thing is outrageously significant to the main voice's or character's behavior and therefore to the plot.

So, the reminder is that this book offers you a writing process where all of you must come along. Even with shaping the personal plot into literary plot, you can no more leave your emotional and psychological truth sitting on a bench waiting for you to return from this journey than you can leave your intellect. You'll need all of you.

This can be scary, because the world we live in requires that we have multiple social filters, and almost always our emotions and psyche are told to stay home. Don't be afraid that your emotions and psyche will misbehave on the public page, cuss and embarrass you, or demand what they want out loud and make a fool of you. Don't be afraid that you have come out of the house looking ugly with your mascara running or with your hair in rollers or in knotted-up, serious bed head. Don't be afraid, because we are taking you out in public just as you are, no matter what you look like, smell like, or act like.

This is your true self, and the world has been denied your remedies, recipes, and good company for far too long.

The Overall Plot

When I refer to the **overall plot**, I am referring to the following:

- Who is the story about? (main voice or character)
- What pivotal, difficult, life-changing event happened? (initial wound)
- What was lost, and what did the loss leave the voice wanting? (loss + want = emotional/psychological motivation)
- What helped fulfill the want? (agents and gifts)
- What got in the way of fulfilling the want? (obstacles and internal saboteurs)
- What revelation changed the course of the voice and their wants?
- What was the outcome to this journey?
- What was the outcome action that shows that the outcome will be sustained?

All of the prompts so far, including those in the Stepping Stones Exercise, have led you to a place of having all of the raw material you need for discovering the overall plot.

Within the confines of this book, these eight elements constitute your overall plot and seven warrant their own scenes within any story in order to anchor the plot. The plot element of who the story is about is disbursed without needing a scene devoted specifically to that description. We learn who the story is about through the focus on their experiences.

PROMPT 38: WRITE THE OVERALL PLOT

Following the definition of overall plot above, write a short paragraph of three to four sentences that offers most of your overall plot. You will not include revelation, outcome, and outcome action because as we rewrite, write additional scenes, and live in the practice of our new outcomes, we may discover new revelations that bring about new outcome actions. The second reason that you will eliminate revelation, outcome, and outcome action from your overall plot description for now is because those are spoilers. You don't want to give away your ending. If you can, sprinkle in a little about the setting.

For Example: *Fifth Born II: The Hundredth Turtle* tells the story of Odessa and LaMont, young adult siblings ostracized from their larger family because Odessa threatens the family secret of incest and LaMont is gay (who and initial wound). Desperate for family connection (want), the two look to one family member (agent) to shift their propagandized notions of each other in order to handle the hardships of single parenting and an HIV diagnosis (obstacles). Set in rural Mississippi and Harlem in the 1980s, the two encourage and encumber each other's journeys to adulthood (setting).

As you have guessed, this will inspire you to come up with a holding title for your manuscript. Please consider it a holding title, just to hold space until you or someone, like a really smart editor, comes up with a permanent title. Create a new blank document and title it "Manuscript-7Pivotal" or some such designating title. Place your overall plot as the first paragraph of your **7 Pivotal Scenes** version of your manuscript. The overall plot and the next organizational tool, 7 Pivotal Scenes, will help to keep your writing anchored to your plot.

From this point forward, each time that I refer to your overall plot, I am referring to this statement that you have just written and that you will certainly rewrite as you enhance the story. This discovered plot is much better than having an outline, yes?

So far, you have organized your scenes chronologically with the initial wound, then each of the stepping stone scenes as they occurred in time, followed by the horizon, the revelation, outcome, and outcome action. Yes, you may feel that there are gaps or missing transitions or scenes. Hold that reality for now.

For shaping your personal plot into literary plot, we will identify the 7 Pivotal Scenes that anchor the plot, then move on to developing the setting and secondary characters as they relate to the advancement of the plot.

7 Pivotal Scenes

Seeking out the most pivotal scenes will help to keep your plot anchored, help you know which scenes to take out, and help you know if additional scenes need to be written in order to both advance and enhance the plot.

PROMPT 39: LIST THE 7 PIVOTAL SCENES
Begin by opening your document titled "Manuscript7Pivotal." Just after your overall plot paragraph, which is the first paragraph of this document, create a short bulleted note for each of your scenes that matches the following criteria.

1. Initial wound scene(s). One or a series of initial wound scenes that caused a loss and therefore a want or need.

2. Increase of obstacle scene(s). In the series of events that are the journey to obtain the want or need, some external things or beings got in the way (obstacles), and some internal beliefs and behaviors got in the way (internal saboteurs). Choose the obstacle scene(s) from your raw material that had the strongest influence on the main voice's or character's journey. You may also think of this as a persistent obstacle that shows up consistently through the main voice's or main character's journey. For now, place them in chronological order.

3. *Intro agent scene(s).* In the series of events that are the journey to obtain the want or need, some external things or beings helped (agents), and some internal beliefs and behaviors helped (gifts). Choose the agent scene(s) from your raw material that had the strongest influence on the main voice's or character's journey. You may also think of this as a persistent agent that shows up consistently through the main voice's or main character's journey. For now, place them in chronological order.

4. *Heightened dramatic tension scene(s).* In the journey to the want, there are surely some scenes where both are present: agent and obstacle, influencing the emotional/psychological want and motivation of the main voice or character, therefore increasing the emotional/psychological tension for the main voice or character. Select at least one scene that had the strongest influence over whether or not the main voice or character attained the overall want. This is what some authors call the climax, but I choose to call the heightened dramatic tension scene. This scene probably feels like a scene where the main voice or main character will either permanently get what they want, or not—or even more dramatically, where they will survive, or not.

5. *Revelation scene.* The main voice or character stands alone without obstacles and agents so that they can change on their own, make choices on their own, and have a revelation. In this one scene, the main voice or character interacts with something new or some new information that they didn't have before on their journey. In this moment, the voice or character chooses some old path or some new path that causes change— either as a person who now has new information and still chooses to get what they want in the old ways, or as someone who has new information

and chooses a new way of getting what they want. In your raw material, this scene is likely among the scenes from the Bringing Back the Chief's Stone Necklace Action and Write and the Releasing the Blame and Taking Responsibility Action and Write.

6. *Outcome scene.* One scene that shows the change that is a result of the revelation.

7. *Outcome action scene(s).* At least one scene that shows how the change will be sustained in outcome actions. This is where you show that the main voice or character has a new daily practice to sustain their new way of being. What does the voice or character now practice in order to sustain the change? Again, not all stories have this scene, but in Chapter 10 there is the opportunity to live outcome action scenes and then write those experiences.

EXAMPLE OF 7 PIVOTAL SCENES WITH NOTES FROM MY STORY "THE EMPTY NEST"

1. Initial wound. Hazel's mother dies when she is a young teen.

2. Increase of obstacle. Hazel's cancer diagnosis. Hazel's racket of seeing herself as more emotionally evolved than most people as an excuse to isolate herself.

3. Intro agent. Silas and her mother, Hazel in the woods.

4. Heightened dramatic tension. Silas and Corbin arrive at Hazel's door. Main character, agent, and obstacle are all present.

5. Revelation. Scene when Hazel visits her childhood home, which she has been afraid to do, and finds that her imagined consequences of revisiting her pain is much more damaging than the reality of what awaits her there. She releases her mother from abandonment blame. Agent and obstacle are removed so that the main character can change independently.

6. Outcome. After Hazel visits her childhood home, she decides to let someone into her secret protected reality and communicates with Silas so she won't be alone in her fear.

7. Outcome action. Hazel climbing the gorge with Silas and Corbin, the two people she now has in her life.

EXAMPLE OF 7 PIVOTAL SCENES WITH NOTES FROM FROZEN RIVER

1. Initial wound. Opening scene where the husband (Troy) has taken the money from the glove compartment, which leaves the main character (Ray) wanting the money back so she can get her double wide.

2. Intro obstacle. This is a very short moment embedded in the scene when Lila and Ray get to the river and Ray wants to turn back (the river as external obstacle). Ray's internal saboteur (internal obstacle) is her way of getting what she needs by going against the rules.

3. Intro agent. The scene when Ray goes to find her husband but meets Lila, who takes Ray to get what she wants by selling the car.

4. Heightened dramatic tension. The scene where it is Christmas Eve and Ray is desperate and the river is treacherous, and Ray and Lila traverse it anyway with some faulty outcomes. Main character, agent, and obstacle are all present.

5. Revelation. The scene where Ray and Lila get caught, but somebody has to be the scapegoat. Ray takes off, not across the river (obstacle is gone) but through the woods, leaving Lila to take the fall (agent is gone).

6. Outcome. The revelation and outcome scenes are combined. In the short moment of this scene, Ray has a revelation. We only see it in her stopping and in her puzzle-solving expression.

7. Outcome action. Ray uses her gift for scheming and hustling to come up with a plan where everybody wins, even Lila and the kids. Ray decides to take responsibility (a little time in jail) as a small sacrifice for everyone to get what they want. We know that everything is going to be all right when we see Ray's new family in place, living well and waiting for her to get out of jail. In the background, the single wide (a compromise to the double wide) is being hauled in. There is solace in the outcome action.

EXAMPLE OF 7 PIVOTAL POEMS WITH NOTES FROM WHAT IT TAKES:

1. Initial wound. I feel the poem "Fertility" is the initial wound, because it offers the moments of the father being absent from the voice, her mother and siblings, yet present for other loves. It is the wound that produces the "want to be wanted or loved."

2. Intro obstacle. "When They Tell Me." In this poem, the voice receives the diagnosis of her daughter's autism (in some ways she'd already known though it had not been proclaimed), and in "Sly Comfort," she feels her daughter pulling away from "two breasts, milk swelling in ducts" to self satisfy with her own thumb.

3. Intro of agent. Present in several poems is writing and literature and the ways they fulfill the want with connection with her daughter (in the poem "Angus Lost and Overdue"), the way they fulfill connection with herself (in the poem "Scripted"), and the ways in which journal writing holds the truth of her daughter's autism diagnosis (in "When They Tell Me") yet reading offers a way to have kinship with others over the diagnosis (in "The Challenge of Reciprocity: A Poem in Three Voices").

4. Heightened dramatic tension. The main character, agent, and obstacle are all present. I perceive the poem "Anteroom" as the poem of heightened tension, because it is when the "wanting to be wanted or loved" by the father ends, because of his passing, but "wanting to be wanted or loved" by the daughter begins, because of her birth. Though the father and the daughter trade off at times as being agent and obstacle, they are both present and causing the type of tension that we see, as Clarissa Pinkola Estés says within the "Life/Death/Life cycle" (127).

5. Revelation, outcome, and outcome action. The poems "Goodbye to Room 1116" and "Scripted" show the main voice self fulfilling her want for love, allowing herself the luxury of a hotel room, and allowing herself to lean on her inherited gift from her father—boldness, the "Just get the job done" attitude in order to return to her love of writing.

Now, copy from your original manuscript file the scenes that match the seven-scene/poem criteria and paste them after your 7 Pivotal Scenes/Poems list into your new document titled "Manuscript7Pivotal." Take the scene out if

1. It is repetitive (information we already have from another scene) and it doesn't advance the plot with new information about the character.

Sometimes, you can merge characters and situations. For instance, if the main voice or character had three partners in a short period of time that they had the same issue with, or if the main voice or character had ten cousins who held a similar significance in their life, these can be merged into one or a few characters. On the other hand, you can simply offer the most significant of these.

2. The scene branches off on a different personal plot and doesn't represent any aspect of this overall plot description.

Now, don't freak out if you find, for instance, that the initial wound scene was when the main voice or character was an adolescent, yet the increase obstacle was when the main voice was in their forties, as is the case with Hazel in "The Empty Nest."

The 7 Pivotal Scenes hold the structure for a longer work like a novel or memoir as well as for a shorter work like a short story or personal essay. With some personal plots, you will find that a lot of chronological space stands between the 7 Pivotal Scenes, but no worries; the point is to identify the story's plot structure, not to lay out the story—unless, as we'll discuss later, the 7 Pivotal Scenes are the short piece, with no extra scenes needed.

Also, remember we have several profound, life-changing ground zero initial wounds that send us off wanting something or desperately wanting to prevent something. For now, stick with writing about the events that are an outcropping of the initial wound from your stepping stones exercise. Don't discard the scenes you take out, but instead create an outtake file to keep them in as discussed in Chapter 5.

On the other hand, write-in if

1. You find that you don't have an example in your raw material of one or more of the 7 Pivotal Scenes.

2. You discover that a different event in your personal plot journey was much more significant, for instance, as your intro agent or intro obstacle scene.

Now that you have all of the pivotal scenes of your plot and then some, you'll find that you also have additional scenes in your raw material that work well to lead up to or away from some of the pivotal scenes.

In addition, let's take some time to talk about writing other scenes to continue advancing and also enhancing the plot.

Vocabulary: To **enhance the plot** is to take the base of the 7 Pivotal Scenes, which advance the plot, and to add scenes that offer additional insight into the main character's or voice's struggle toward their want, their agents and obstacles, and any other layers of their everyday life, including humor.

PROMPT 40: WRITE MORE SCENES TO ENHANCE THE PLOT

1. The nightmare. Many of us remember our nightmares, because they scare us witless. Utilize one of your nightmares that feels relevant to the plot (relevant to the want), and write it as a scene. Can you hear the scary music in the background?

2. The birth scene. Write the main character's or voice's birth, or perhaps the birth of a character who, by being born, became agent or obstacle in the main character's or voice's journey toward the want.

3. The death scene. Which death scene? The one that had some impact on the journey of the main voice or character as they reached for their want. Maybe it stopped them, added obstacles for them, or helped them to see clearly. Birth and death have the most catalytic effects on our lives, aside from acts of violence against us or profound acts of compassion toward us. The character is traveling along in a fairly predictable path, and like inertia, birth or death comes along and knocks them off onto a path that combines new wants, hopes, and fears with existing ones. One frequent use for the death scene is to show how one of your agents left the main voice's or character's life. For the main character or main voice to have full revelation, the main agent usually suffers some death, departure, movement, or removal. The same can be true for obstacles. In *Fifth Born II: The Hundredth Turtle*, the death of Lamont (agent) and the death of Loni (obstacle) both have profound effects on Odessa's journey, as does the birth of her son, Walton (new agent).

4. *The Funny Scene or Funny Write-In*: Some days, life is just difficult, but sometimes there are funny interjections. For instance, today, right in the middle of a very busy teaching day, a student e-mailed me, explaining that her "twitter thingy is damaged." I e-mailed her back and said she probably shouldn't tell people that. Humor gracefully interrupts the seriousness of real life. I used humor in "The Empty Nest," when Silas puts the flushing toilet ringtone on her mother's phone. This humorous write-in later pays off in the story. (We'll talk more about payoff in Chapter 18, The Craft of Scene Arranging.) In Chapter 5 of *Fifth Born*, "Gretal's Game" is comic relief that offers a humorous look at the interaction between the children. In the movie *Smoke Signals*, after Victor and Thomas decide not to respond to the racial comments that the men make on the bus, they talk about how the cowboys always win but then sing out on the bus about John Wayne's teeth. If you are writing a full-length novel, memoir, or collection of poems, it's a good idea to also have small scenes that are purely humorous or tongue-in-cheek, as well as the sprinkled-in humor.

Remember: These scenes can't be purely random. Any scene that you write should be instrumental in the main voice's or character's journey toward the want and therefore advance the overall plot, which is that paragraph at the top of your manuscript.

Even if you are writing a funny scene, it should offer us some understanding of the main character's or voice's wounds, wants, agents, or obstacles. For instance, though the chapter "Gretal's Game" is humorous, it offers the novel's largest plant of mother and home, which pays off in the last chapters of the novel.

These scenes can be strategically placed in your manuscript where they enhance the plot and offer cohesiveness to the scenes, transition, or comic relief.

Fetching Scenes that Enhance the Plot

Before the Stepping Stones Exercise, you had several writing prompts to help you produce raw material and to get you warmed up before the Stepping Stones Exercise. They were the Jump Starter Writings, Joys and Pains Exercise, Hope vs. Fear Exercise, Saboteur Writings, the Relationship Museum Exercise, and the Mirror Exercise.

From this raw material, you may find that there are scenes that are specific to some element of your overall plot. If so, pull them and place them where they enhance the plot. In other words, place scenes where they lead up to pivotal scenes and then progress toward the next pivotal scene.

HOW WILL YOU KNOW WHICH SCENES TO PUT WHERE?

The 7 Pivotal Scenes and their order should act as a guide with how to advance the plot. For instance, if an agent or obstacle shows up for the first time and will be a significant agent in whether the voice or character fulfills their want or a significant obstacle that prevents them from fulfilling their want, then you should introduce this agent or obstacle in one of the first scenes, not somewhere in the middle of the manuscript. And certainly don't introduce them for the first time during the heightened dramatic tension scene. Why not? It's not likely that a reader will feel tense about the potential positive or negative impact of an agent or obstacle if they are meeting this entity for the first time long after the journey of the voice or character is established. We don't hope for or have fear of things that we have no knowledge of.

Remember: You will rewrite many scenes, because with writing every day, your skill to wield beauty with your words will increase. Yes, you need to continue writing every single day in order to increase your capacity to shorten the direct line from the surface-level outer setting of your life to the deep internal setting of your life, and in order to increase your capacity to tell a story well with grace and eloquence. Writing every day helps you to climb to high heights while capturing the beauty of the climb, and to also tell of the time you fell down the mountain while capturing the beauty of the fall.

Remember: The 7 Pivotal Scenes anchor your overall plot. They act as guides as you begin messing around with lots of scenes and attempting to figure out what to keep and what to move. You at least know that there are seven scenes that are pivotal and will act as a point of reference for the plot.

Caution: In terms of scenes that advance the plot, please do not include a scene that offers us the setting. Some readers step away from the storytelling and offer pages and pages of setting. Readers have no tolerance for expository scenery writing without the internal significance of this scenery. In Chapter 14, I will offer you a much more effective way to allow the setting to exist simultaneous with the development of the main voice or character.

Where You Are in the Process

Before diving into the next chapter, I want you to congratulate yourself on what you have so far. Because you have 7 Pivotal Scenes that anchor your plot for a memoir or novel, or collection of poems, this alone can be (in draft format) a personal essay or short story, or chapbook, just by having the 7 Pivotal Scenes. You also have scenes that enhance the plot, and scenes inserted from your early prompt writing in this process. Though you will be adding more raw material to your manuscript in order to enhance setting and secondary characters, you already have the first skeletal draft of a full-length memoir or novel.

CHAPTER 12

The Macrocosmic Plot
and Its Planetary Scenes

Currently, in the file titled "Manuscript7Pivotal," you have your overall plot paragraph followed by bulleted descriptions of your 7 Pivotal Scenes, followed by the actual 7 Pivotal Scenes, arranged with other scenes that fall between, like your nightmare scene, funny scene, birth scene, death scene, or scenes from earlier writing prompts.

Your 7 Pivotal Scenes act as a point of reference while you take the journey to figure out which scenes to keep, which to move, and which haven't been written yet. There may be a few scenes that are flashbacks embedded into other scenes and some of these may be serving as pivotal scenes. If you have them listed and noted at the beginning of the manuscript, you are less likely to get confused. This is a little continuity lesson, which goes a long way after your manuscript grows beyond your own memory capacity.

Vocabulary: **Scene shaping** is the process of taking each of the scenes that you have written and examining them to see if they advance the plot (advance the main voice or character toward the self-fulfillment of their overall want) in the story.

In other words, since the story is about a personal want that was born from one of your initial wounds, you are examining each scene to see if it has anything to do with this particular journey the voice or character is on, from wound to revelation. If it doesn't, you are taking it out. If it does but it's missing some components, you're performing write-ins or rewrites.

Until you have shaped the raw material scenes into *microcosms of your overall plot*, you have little chance of merging the scenes with smooth transitions or juxtapositions that work well. In order to further understand which scenes advance the plot and which ones do not, you will need to examine each scene for the ways it mirrors the overall plot that you created in Chapter 11.

Yes, in answer to the question that you may be asking, sometimes you think you know the overall plot, then you arrange the scenes and—voilà!—a much deeper and emotionally true plot manifests and the true pivotal scenes emerge. Or, in most cases, revelations manifest that offer new writing for the newly realized plot; hence, the outtake file gets larger. The important thing is to make sure that you are deleting or adding scenes in an effort to tell a more authentic emotional and psychological truth but never deleting or adding in order to evade the emotional and psychological truth.

Scene Shaping:
Creating Microcosms of Your Overall Plot

Each of the scenes that you have written should possess these same elements from your overall plot.

EVENT

In each scene, something happens (an event). In the overall plot, this event is the initial wound, but in the scenes that you created from the stepping stones or in any additional scenes, this event (joyful or painful) is something that happened and triggered the same old want from the initial wound, or it might be a secondary wound that is incurred because of the peril the voice or character encounters in fulfilling the want.

A good example of an event within a scene is in Amy Tan's short story "Rules of the Game," when the event of Waverly winning her first chess game bolsters her confidence with the overall want of winning the life game against her mother. In each scene, whether it is a secondary wound or a joy that is the event, the event results in the resurgence of the want, and that want is linked to the overall want of the plot, which was caused by the initial wound of feeling dominated by the mother. After Waverly's joyful incident in "Rules of the Game," she wants to win against all of her opponents. That supports the overall want to win in the life game against her mother.

In my short story "The Empty Nest," the event of Hazel's cancer diagnosis triggers her want for family connection. Her initial wound of losing her mother and being abandoned by her father leaves her with an overall want for family, and the event of the diagnosis triggers those wants. It also brings to the forefront her internal saboteur, posed as an agent: the racket she runs where she convinces herself that other people are too emotionally and spiritually inept to be part of her life.

Mind you, all events inside scenes won't be as impactful as the initial wound event that drives the overall plot, or as impactful as a secondary wound which often shifts how the voice or character achieves the want. The most impactful events are likely the initial wound, followed by the heightened dramatic tension scene and any event that triggers revelation or outcome action. Within these impactful scenes, the event is often something life-changing, like birth, death, the threat of birth or death, or some violent or profoundly compassionate act that instigates loss or instigates healing.

Many of the scenes that fall between these scenes of impactful events are stepping stones where the event is a mild shift in the character's or voice's life, such as getting or losing a job or starting a new relationship. In *The Whale Rider*, Kahu's birth begins the novel and her presumed death ends the novel, with all other scenes sandwiched between the two impactful events.

As mentioned in the previous chapter, it's good to think of these most impactful events like the interrupting objects in the law of inertia. Things are in motion in life from some early wound and are going along on an even, monotonous plane, then some force (an event) impacts the character's or voice's movement and causes a slight shift in course on an otherwise monotonous journey.

Every scene should possess an event in order for the character to want and have a reason for their actions in the scene. You may find that you have scenes that don't possess an event per se, but do possess the reaction to the event. In these cases, you know that a write-in is necessary in order to place the event into the scene, or to merge the reaction with the event that the character is reacting to in order to render a full scene.

WANT

Within each scene, the main voice or character or a pivotal character wants something or wants to prevent something, just as in the overall plot. This want is tied in to the overall want that was born out of the initial wound. But in this one scene, the want has manifested differently according to the voice's or character's age or stage of development, or according to the event that has just impacted them.

For instance, in "The Empty Nest," the want for family manifests in Hazel's childhood prayer to go with her mother to the grave. In these scenes, the want is *not* fulfilled but annulled. Later, she fulfills her desire for physical closeness with one-night stands, but this doesn't fulfill the emotional want for closeness. As the story progresses, her daughter, who is a product of a one-night stand, becomes the family she needs, but then the child goes to college far away, and the starkness of the cancer diagnosis brings about the unfulfilled want again. So you see, each of your scenes must possess an event that causes the overall want to manifest again in a different manner as the voice or character grows, develops, or progresses toward self fulfilling the overall want.

In most poetry collections that follow the trajectory of a personal plot, the wound and want are from a personal plot in an era of the voice's life. Therefore, each scene or poem might manifest the want, but it might not harken back to a wounding event from childhood. For instance, in *The Father* by Sharon Olds and *What It Takes* by Grey Brown, the wounding events happen in the voices' adult lives, but the overall want is still thematically present as a foreboding, present or past want.

AGENTS AND OBSTACLES

In each scene, there should be something that helps (agent) or gets in the way (obstacle) of the voice or character fulfilling their want. For instance, in "The Empty Nest," Silas's desire to be away from her mother is an obstacle to the mother's ability to fulfill family through the daughter, but later, Silas's own search for family acts as agent and helps to fulfill the mother's want for family.

In other words, even the more subdued agents and obstacles affect the larger looming plot of the main character. In fact, if the plots of secondary characters have no bearing on the plot journey of the main character, take those characters and scenes out, because they do not advance the plot. We'll discuss more on secondary characters and their impact on character and plot development in the next chapter.

REVELATION AND OUTCOME

Most scenes won't hold a revelation, because the main voice or character usually experiences revelation only a few times throughout a novel, poetry collection, or memoir. These smaller revelations fully advance the plot toward the main revelation scene. With that said, there certainly should be an outcome for the main character or main voice in the scene where they either fulfill the want that they have within the scene or not, and the effort toward the want is then temporarily alleviated due to fulfillment or annulment. For instance, in one of the last scenes of *Cold Running Creek*, Lilly runs away assuming she has killed her husband. That event prompts her to want peace and the comforts of daily life on what she assumes is her last day of freedom. This self-fulfilled freedom prompts the revelation that she has in her power the option of not just running from her family but running from the oppressions of post–Civil War Mississippi. The scene and the novel end with the outcome action of this revelation, because the overall want of freedom is fulfilled as outcome.

So now, look for these plot elements in each of your scenes. Read each scene/event and see what the event is that caused a want that is a reflection of or exemplifies the overall want. Extend the writing of the scene to make sure that the want carries through from an event of something helping (agent) or something getting in the way (obstacle) straight through to their temporarily getting what they want or not (outcome). The only time that the outcome is not temporary is in the final outcome, where the overall want is fulfilled or annulled.

Remember that the want, just like all of the other elements of the scene, should be specific to the development of the main voice or character, and therefore specific to the overall want born of the initial wound in the overall plot. After all, each scene is a microcosm of the overall plot. Even if the scene is about a secondary character, that character's wants should be linked and have significance to the main character's or voice's wants. For instance in the novel *The Whale Rider*, the uncle, Rawiri, is the narrator but also a secondary character. He tells the story of his niece's journey from birth to being next in line as chief. There are scenes in the novel where we have his four years away in Australia and Papua New Guinea, but these years help us understand his new insights into the plight of his own people, his deep connection with Kahu, and the similar vision that the two characters hold.

Scene shaping is a great way to get you to enhance or eliminate scenes that you feel connected to because they simply tell us things about a character or a setting. When you go through your scenes, ask yourself these plot and character development questions regarding the main voice or main character:

1. What happened? (event)
2. What do they want in this very moment?
3. What gets in the way of the want in this very moment? (obstacles)
4. What helps them get what they want in this very moment? (agents)
5. Do they get what they want in this very moment? (outcome)
6. Are secondary characters developed in such a way that their relationship to the main character advances the plot? For instance, if we have the initial wound or profound joy scene or want scene of a secondary character, does this scene have an impact on the advancement of the main voice's or character's journey toward their want?
7. Is the want in the scene temporarily fulfilled or annulled? The scene is complete when there is a temporary advancement toward getting what is wanted, or when there is a temporary failure or regression from the want.

PROMPT 41: WRITE-IN THE MISSING PLOT ELEMENT AND MERGE RAW MATERIAL TO FORM COMPLETE SCENES

You will likely find yourself with pieces of raw material you thought were scenes but you realize have missing plot elements. You may have a scene that has an event, but you never show us the moment where the voice or character either got what they wanted or didn't. You may very well find that you wrote the rest of that scene as other raw material. Simply merge the two, unifying them with the same setting. If that makes a mess, rewrite the scene to contain the elements. If you find that your raw material is simply missing the elements of plot and that the missing material doesn't exist elsewhere, go back and write-in the missing plot elements for that event or rewrite the scene to include those elements.

Remember: Use an outtake file. This is a file (digital or hard copy) that contains scenes, or small parts of scenes that you don't need in your story because they don't advance this particular personal plot. You don't want to delete these scenes just yet, because as you know, they may round out or complete some other partial scene. But this writing simply doesn't seem to belong to this particular personal plot. An outtake file gives you a place to hold these scenes just in case you need them as reference or as raw material.

Don't keep these scenes in your manuscript, hoping that you will remember to go back and see if they advance the plot. This dilutes the plot that you are building with lots of unrelated information that comes between the events and the progression of the want.

You want to remove these mismatched writings from the manuscript so that the manuscript remains as clean and clear as possible. Don't try to be economical with thoughts like, "But that was two days' worth of writing; I have to make it fit in the manuscript." Take this writing out and put it in your outtake file.

Utilizing Theme or Motif to Assist with Scene Arranging

Once you identify that a theme or motif runs through the scenes (food, nature, love, freedom, travel, holidays) you can utilize that theme or motif to create cohesiveness. For instance, I realized that in *Fifth Born II: The Hundredth Turtle*, so much of the change in the character's life happens around Christmas and Thanksgiving because that's when she misses her siblings the most. This motif then helped me to shape some of the scenes and center the New York visits around Thanksgiving, which then helps the reader to follow the secondary character Lamont's changes from health to heartache to passing away.

Motif also helps you to focus the setting in a way that it carries the emotional refrain. For instance, it's Thanksgiving again, which means there are the smells and sights of fall again, but the emotional significance of this fall setting shifts as the characters arrive at this season with birth, breakup, or death.

Another wonderful example is in Alice Walker's essay "Beauty: When the Other Dancer Is the Self." She uses her age to offer the arrangement and progression of her life with the wound: "I was two," "I am eight," "I am fourteen," "I am twenty-seven." Similarly, in Sherman Alexie's essay "Indian Education," he uses the grade he is in school to advance the scenes: "First Grade," "Seventh Grade," "Twelfth Grade."

In Summary:

1. Don't forget the irony of saboteurs as agents and obstacles. As you work to shape your scenes, remember that what your main voice or character wants isn't necessarily what's good for them. Sometimes, their internal saboteurs are engaged in their attempts at fulfilling the overall want. For instance, in "Sonny's Blues," Sonny and his brother want out of Harlem but also want to be connected as brothers, but Sonny turns to drugs and his brother turns to a type of arrogance. Both the drugs and the arrogance cause the characters to go inside of themselves, and in doing so, they do not get what they want until they can engage more positive internal agents. Remember, back when you were creating your raw material, that in your stepping stones you sometimes took survival routes and turned an internal saboteur into an agent so that you could run your racket and get out of some mess or temporarily get what you wanted. That doesn't mean that what you got or how you got it was good for you, but it does make for complete emotional irony that you can lend to your voice or character.

2. With some of our stepping stones, we have gotten what we wanted in that moment, but perhaps we hurt someone else, even though hurting others isn't consistent with our personality (character development). In "Sonny's Blues," the main character feels that in his arrogance and his shutting emotions away, he hurt Sonny. Sonny as a secondary character feels that as he escaped into drugs he hurt many people, especially the main character. In the next chapter, we will explore the ways in which secondary characters and their wounds and wants impact the main voice or character.

3. Don't forget to think of the scenes and events that you put in chronological order as smaller microcosms of the plot that quite naturally advance the overall plot of the full-length work. The stepping stones advance the character to the moment at the horizon where they have the potential to do something new and change. In "Sonny's Blues," the club scene is the main character's horizon where he can do something different, support Sonny in his music and hear Sonny's pain, or he can turn this moment into yet another stepping stone where he is arrogant, critical, and emotionally shut down.

4. You may be tempted to abandon writing from your soul and to start writing a plot and trying to create some material to match it. In times like this, look to the first paragraph of your manuscript, the written statement of the overall plot from Chapter 11. The overall plot statement should help you keep the manuscript cohesive as you continue to write more scenes, and it will help you to stay emotionally true to yourself as you shape your personal plot into literary plot. If you need even more encouragement, seek out bios, documentaries, or interviews with the writers of our texts in common and see how James Baldwin, Amy Tan, Ta-Nehisi Coates, and others wrote from their emotional and psychological base.

What if the Scene Shaping Shifts Your Overall Plot Statement?

If you find that through scene shaping, you've discovered the deeper, more emotionally and psychologically authentic want that emerged from your writing, then that's when you shift the overall plot to reflect this discovery. But don't have that discovery and, rather than shifting, insist on just doing more of the same writing and fetching scenes that will fit the old plot.

For example, a student recently insisted that their want was "to be seen," but each of her scenes suggested that there was a more detailed want associated with a desire to ward off shame. She ended up uncovering a more detailed truth about a family secret that haunted her through her youth and launched her into a series of attempts to separate herself from her family and all who were privy to the secret. She had the courage to change her overall plot rather than insist on the safety of the original overall plot statement, which was fairly generic.

If you discover that there is a more significant initial wound, a more detailed want, and that you used the overall plot statement as a way to stay safe and to congratulate yourself for writing a full-length manuscript that isn't vulnerable, you are running a racket indeed.

Or perhaps you have written yourself to awareness and the old overall plot just doesn't match your new awareness of the true overall plot. Either way, it's not too late to do something about it. Simply know that the writing you did up to this point was to help you uncover the more authentic emotional and psychological truth.

Ignoring that you have discovered the more significant plot and insisting on economizing or staying safe will bring you to the same old dry writing that this book is designed to help you graduate from. Instead of relying on old saboteurish habits, create what will later become a classic because of its capacity to connect on the emotional and psychological level.

In short, don't misunderstand this chapter on scene shaping and scene arranging as the moment at which you abandon art. That opportunity will not arise in this book, not even when we get to the chapters on craft.

The Practice:
Increasing the Duration of Your Writing Time

At this point, you should be writing a minimum of four hours a day. When? I don't know your schedule, but make it happen. I'm holding myself to the same standard of daily practice.

Get up early, or turn off your favorite show and put the music in your ears and choose a line and get writing. Hide in the bathroom at work. Write on your lunch break. Talk it into your phone—whatever works, but integrate it and do it. Remember that the writing of this manuscript is a personal plot all on its own, and in order to get what you want (a full-length manuscript), you'll have to devise a daily practice that sustains your writing outcome.

Okay, as usual, shake off all of the ill messages of the saboteurs and get cracking with the writing.

CHAPTER 13

Secondary Characters

and Their Impact on Character and Plot

Characters

No need to create new characters. They are the people you've written about in the scenes of your raw material.

For Fiction Writers: With fiction, choosing a character or writing in third person is not the opportunity to abandon or distance yourself from the emotional and psychological truth. Nor is it an opportunity to use the character to philosophize about life to escape your own journey. You, you, you are everywhere. For now, you need only to change the names and look for photos of people who physically represent the real people (even if they don't have the same features, look for photos of people who have the same demeanor). If you have created a character that is based on an amalgam of two people, be sure to keep the emotional and psychological base of the character true. In the coming chapters, you will begin to lend your imagination and poetic license to the characterization of people, setting, and plot for the sake of crafting a story well told.

For Poets and Memoirists: You can opt to change the names and offer a disclaimer that you are doing so. Also disclaim that these events are as you remember them and not necessarily accurate from others' perspectives. Any one person's account of a relationship and its events is their perspective only, and therefore that memory is a form of fiction, yet also one's truth. Ironic, isn't it? But it does give you poetic license to offer your emotional and psychological journey for the sake of connecting with others.

Poetic license is one thing, but don't out and out lie. If you are going to make it up or claim that you did things that you didn't, then call it what it is—fiction—so that you don't end up with egg on your face. The only reasons that I can think of that someone would lie in the writing of memoir or even poetry are that they were creating fantasy or metaphor (in which case, these things should seem obvious), if they didn't take the time and do their research on the events of their own life, or if they were trying to inflate or deflate (saboteurishly) their own ego.

Caution: Be aware that your shame saboteur may show up and say you can't write about the real people until they are dead, because you are afraid of what will happen if people recognize themselves in your writing. Remind yourself that your writing is food, medicine, and kinship for someone who desperately awaits it, and the folks who don't want you to put it out there aren't the folks who are calling for it. Respond to the callers, not to the fears of your internal saboteurs or anyone else's. And always change the names to protect the guilty.

Secondary Characters

Remember we talked about how the internal obstacles and agents (saboteurs and gifts) and external obstacles and agents (physical obstacles and agents) can't be random? They have to be specific to what the main character or main voice wants or wants to prevent. Remember how in Chapter 8, we used the psychological research to discover and develop who serves best as main obstacles and agents in writing our personal plots?

So, if your main character or main voice is ever to discover the true meaning of their dilemma and have revelation and outcome, they are going to have to examine the joys and pains of their obstacles and agents. In other words, you will have to examine the psychological reasons why obstacle folks and agent folks in your life behave the way that they do and why they impress upon you or distress you the way they do. All roads lead back to you. It won't be enough to examine these people's psychologies; you'll have to examine their significance to you (the voice or character).

In "Sonny's Blues," we have the main character who better understands his own wounds and wants by looking at his brother's wounds and wants, and in the end sees how both are connected at the tragedies and joys (the blues) in their lives. In "The Moths," the main character is able to change and connect to her own nurturing side, when she sees the scars on her abuelita's body and knows that despite the pain of abuse, her abuelita was able to be nurturing, not hard and bitter.

Research the Wounds of Secondary Characters

In Chapter 8, you went to the library, bookstore, or online sources and looked for internal character development research (self-help research) for someone with an initial wound and a want like yours (main voice or main character). You sought self-help for the issue that you had as a result of the initial wound. In your research, you read personal accounts of what helped and hindered others with a similar wound and want, and you likely found information about the people in your life that helped (agents) and hindered (obstacle) with your issue.

Now that you are turning personal plot into literary plot, you will need to go back into that research and extend the research on the issues of these agent and obstacle people who are now secondary characters (if you are writing fiction) and secondary voices (if you are writing poetry or memoir).

You will be researching some of the wounding events that likely happened to a person who behaves like the obstacle person in your plot, and some of the wounding events that likely happened to a person who behaves like the agent person in your plot.

For example, in *The Whale Rider*, Koro Apirana (acting as Kahu's obstacle) is so hell-bent on finding the new leader because he has lived through the devastation of watching his people turn to commercialism and away from their spiritual roots. His wounds and wants are creating new wounds and wants for Kahu. The domino effect of emotional and psychological events is ultimately at the base of clearly drawn relationships in stories.

In order to scope a full universe of a story and in order to scope the full circle from wound to want to revelation and outcome in your personal plot, you'll have to develop empathy for the characters, even the obstacles, so that your readers can emotionally engage and have this same sort of empathy. You don't need to adore the perpetrator of your wounds, who is now the obstacle for the main voice or character in your manuscript, but you'll need to have enough compassion to know that all humans have an emotional and psychological past that informs their future, and in this case you intend to investigate for the sake of telling a story with depth, as opposed to just writing an exposé.

Toi Derricotte's poem "my dad and sardines" is a great example of revisiting the ways of secondary characters and voices in your life in order to understand yourself. She begins the poem by designing a small altar for her dad, then changing her mind about promises not to talk bad about him anymore. When the voice cannot find anything else in her house to eat but a can of sardines, the poem descends into a memory of her father and sardines and his self-indulgent ritual around eating them.

Your readers don't have to like all of the characters or voices anymore than you do; they just have to find them believable as humans. This means, for instance, that a voice or character can't just come off as an agent like Glenda the Good Witch—who appears out of nowhere for no apparent reason—or as an obstacle like the Wicked Witch of the West—who is bad to the bone for no apparent reason. Good for Gregory Maguire for picking up on the significance of an emotional and psychological base for secondary characters and writing *Wicked* and other novels as an extension of secondary characters connected to Dorothy's plot. Understanding the pains and joys of Dorothy's agents and obstacles helps us understand Dorothy's journey.

So, this exercise is more than mere research. By doing this research, you will likely have revelations about three things:

- Your own persistent wanting from people who don't have what you need.
- Your amazing ability to gravitate toward people who have exactly what you need.
- Your ability to have revelation and a redemptive journey when you find the humanity in an obstacle person.

Similar to our discussion in Chapter 8, where you researched the issues of the perpetrator of your wounds as a way of understanding your own, you will research the secondary characters, including obstacles and agents, in order to authentically build the emotional/psychological relationships that are connected to the main character's or voice's plot.

With my research in Chapter 8, my difficult discovery was that my father was well off, but his family wasn't. He wasn't gambling with the stability of *his* finances; he was gambling with the stability of his family's finances. He always ate well, dressed well, and drove a nice car. That breaks my heart in some ways, but it offers my heart a gift of awareness so that I can apply that heartbreak and revelation to my main character's understanding of herself.

Before we get started, let me caution you that this research isn't for you to expose the dirty reality of your obstacles and agents, nor is it for you to have some inside scoop that gives you a strange power over them. This exercise is for you to look at the wounds of the other players in your personal plot journey with the same compassion that you have looked at your own, so that as the writer of your story, you have the kind of omniscient emotional and psychological perspective of all of the characters, and you therefore have the empathy necessary to create with scope and depth that go far beyond exposé. This will help you write a story you and others find whole and can therefore grow from.

PROMPT 42: WRITE A LIST OF THE OBSTACLE'S BEHAVIORS

Write down the obstacle character's behavior. For instance, in my case, my father was the perpetrator of my financial initial wounds, and my mother was a secondary enabling perpetrator. For my father's behavior, I wrote down "inconsistent provider," "spends money on flashy things then is too broke to provide for children."

Research these behaviors as subject headings to read resources that will give you insight into the things that are likely to cause the behavior, help heal the behavior, and exacerbate the behavior. My research led me to resources about gamblers, including (ironically) the same book that I used for some of my internal research. *Mind over Money* by Brad Klontz and Ted Klontz states, "Betting on the horses or playing roulette is risk taking for entertainment, and within reason there's nothing wrong with that. But when risk taking becomes excessive, it can be very damaging . . . like taking your rent money or your child's college fund to the race track, or the broker's office." This was interesting, because I had completely forgotten about going to the racetrack with my father one time when I was young; Cahokia Downs was the name of the place. That memory led to many other memories of overheard conversations about the track and other things that, as a child, I didn't know were gambling.

PROMPT 43: WRITE THE SCENE OF THE OBSTACLE'S BEHAVIOR

Write a scene where you are in the midst of this obstacle character's or voice's behavior. Remember, first person, past tense. You can use minimal dialogue now, which we will discuss the proper use of soon in Chapter 15, Crafting Internal Character Development from External Stimuli.

Here is the raw, unedited version of what I wrote:

Cahokia Downs, the first time I went to the racetrack with Deddy, I felt special, his little girl. I was already eleven by then and as we rode across the Mississippi River to the Illinois side of the world. I just as soon could have been riding in a limo, like Annie after she found Daddy Warbucks, not like me riding in my father's Cadillac.

That morning after eating some sausage and cold grits, I held my belly still while we rode over the water, the car moving one way and the river under us moving another way.

Deddy said from the front seat one of his random sayings that was meant to teach me life lessons, "Don't never buy nothing on credit," and I said to the back of his Kangaroo hat, "Yes, sir," having only a vague idea what credit was.

The next morning when I stood at the back of the Kmart with my mother waiting for the layaway clerk, I told Mama, "Deddy said don't never buy nothing on credit." She giggled, a high-pitched sound escaping like air from a wild balloon, "That's a smart thing to say for somebody running from loan sharks and not wanting to leave any tracks."

So, that was some of his behavior scribed out in a scene where I was present. The event was going to the race track, what I wanted was to feel financially fabulous, and the scene ended with the annulment of that want and me standing in the layaway line hearing the truth of our circumstances from my mother.

I suppose he was gambling to appease some want, so I continued to research for the initial wound and to look for some of the childhood scenarios that led to gambling as a behavior. My father is twenty-four years deceased and I don't know anything about his childhood because he never talked about it, but my mother said that his mother left her kids alone a lot. I researched the 1920, '30, and '40 census and saw that my father's father was sixty-three when my father was born. His mother was a shocking twenty-nine years old at the time, some thirty-four years younger than her husband. She'd started having his children when she was around nineteen and he was around fifty-three.

I took that information and the idea of her not being home and speculated. It seemed likely to me that since he was a child in Mississippi in the 1920s and '30s, and the child of an elderly sharecropper whose young mother wasn't home a lot, he suffered from both parental abandonment and being deprived of fair wages for work. I simultaneously researched his childhood setting, a task we will explore in detail in Chapter 14, Setting and Its Impact on Character and Plot. As a Black male on southern sharecropped land, my father and his parents would have had no authority to seek help or justice. This important information led me to the next writing prompt.

PROMPT 44: WRITE THE INITIAL WOUND SCENE FOR OBSTACLES AS AN EXTENSION OF INTERNAL CHARACTER DEVELOPMENT RESEARCH

After you have identified the behavior of your initial obstacle person, and perhaps remembered and associated certain behaviors with things you remember about them, dig deep into the research for their initial wound. You might have to speculate based on the interviews and setting research, or you might already know the initial wound. If you are writing memoir, remember to add that this is speculation by saying something like, "Given the racist climate at the time, and the limited opportunities for his mother, I look at my father's picture and imagine the trials of his childhood."

This is a researched and more extensive version of the writing you did for Prompt 9 in the Mirror Exercise. This is an opportunity to link the wounds in the obstacle character's life as motive for their behavior in their relationship with you (as well as your story's main character or main voice). Based on what you perceive your obstacle character's issues to be, you will be writing an initial wound scene that can parallel that issue. There's no need to write an initial wound scene for every obstacle character, but certainly pick the ones who had the most impact on your personal plot.

Remember: You can use minimal dialogue now, which we will discuss the proper use of soon in Chapter 15. Place the writing in first person, past tense, with your writing from the perspective of the main obstacle character in your personal plot.

Yes, this likely will lead to feelings of compassion for yourself and at least a human empathy for your obstacle, since your issues and the issues of the people you seek out for relationships are inextricably linked. Sometimes, the inextricable link is through birth or parental relationships, adoption, or other relationships you didn't get to choose to be in, especially as a child dependent on adults. These relationships are part of your first family bonds, and you likely inherited your wounds through their reaction to their own wounds.

For instance, in "Rules of the Game," it is the wounds of war and being discriminated against by Americans that are elements of the rules of American life Waverly cannot seem to win, mostly because she has not yet understood her mother's wounds. In most of our relationship scenarios where we are wanting something and perceive an obstacle, someone's initial wound is causing negative behavior that causes your initial wound in turn, or causes your initial wound to be triggered.

PROMPT 45: WRITE THE INITIAL WOUND SCENE FOR AGENTS AS AN EXTENSION OF INTERNAL CHARACTER DEVELOPMENT RESEARCH

Based on what you perceive your agent character's issues to be, write an initial wound scene that would parallel that issue. No need to write an initial wound scene for every agent character, but certainly pick the ones who had the most impact on your personal plot.

You may find the agents' initial wounds became your initial joys because they were desperately seeking to prevent a similar wound from occurring for someone else, or you may find that these agents (much like yourself) found the gifts they possess as a result of their surviving the wound and have gifted those in turn to you.

PROMPT 46: WRITE-IN PARALLEL STEPPING STONES FOR OBSTACLES AND AGENTS

Go back and consider the scenes in your manuscript that were developed from your stepping stones. You will find that after your scene shaping, you wrote in or elevated the presence of obstacle characters or voices and agent characters or voices. Go back to those scenes and write-in or rewrite so that the want being sought by the obstacle or agent either clashes with your main character's or voice's want or advances their want accordingly.

Only write-in or rewrite scenes where you as the main character or voice are involved either through your future birth or actually being present, or the like. I say this because we are writing the wounds and wants of our secondary characters or voices only as they relate to the main character's or voice's wants. In my case, I want to be sure to write about my father's financial wounds and feelings of unpredictability from his parents, since these wounds caused him to behave a certain way and inflict similar wounds on me.

These character's or voice's movements in the story play a huge part in the journey of the main character or voice. One of the most powerful examples of parallel stepping stones that we have in our texts in common is in *The Whale Rider* and the parallel between Koro Apirana's fierce attempt to fulfill his want of finding a leader for the next generation and Kahu's fierce attempt to fulfill his want and to make him love her. Much of the dramatic tension of the story is caused by these parallel wants clashing, because he seeks a male leader and she is female. In Chapter 16, we'll talk more about the craft of dramatic tension and hope vs. fear.

PROMPT 47: WRITE-IN THE OBSTACLE'S GIFTS

Now, go back to these scenes of your parallel stepping stones with the obstacle person's stepping stones and write-in the obstacle person's gift of survival that is ironically linked to your gift of survival. You may find yourself going back to the raw material writing from Chapter 8 under the subheading The Ironic Origins of Some Internal Gifts. Here, you will find yourself sprinkling nuances into scenes to make the reader aware of the shared gifts that you possess as a result of the obstacle person's gifts. For instance, in *Rescuing Patty Hearst*, there are several scenes where Virginia's imagination, a gift inherited from the imaginative elements of her mother's schizophrenia, helps sustain her through emotional isolation, and we get the irony and tension that holds the story together where Virginia is afraid that this inherited gift of imagination is inherited mental illness.

If the obstacle person is one of the main voice's or character's first relationships, often the initial positive survival tools of the obstacle person are gifts inherited by the main voice or character. For instance, one of the great things that came out of my father's Depression-era living is his advice to never buy anything on credit. I have taken that with a grain of salt and purchased a house on credit, but when the financial crises of 2008 hit, I didn't owe any banks any money for car loans or credit cards, only my well-negotiated mortgage payment.

Because we are often linked with people either through our initial wounds or through our similar gifts, we can more fully understand our personal plots by understanding the personal plots of our obstacle characters and agent characters.

Again, keep all of these scenes, because even if you refer to them as internal memories or imaginings, writing the initial wounds and some stepping stones for secondary characters as they relate to the main voice or character offers the readers a feeling of authentic human struggle and triumph in all of its layered complexities, rather than a feeling of human exposé.

With our personal plots, some of you have the initial wound of a secondary voice or character being the impetus of the main voice's or character's initial wounds (for example, my father's pains led to his gambling habits, which became my initial wound of financial instability). It makes for great subplot for us to consistently see the personal journey of the obstacle person. Now, you don't want to offer the journey of secondary characters to the point of overshadowing the personal plot of the main voice or character, but offer them in such a way that the wants and fears of the main voice or character are pushed (shifted and redirected) by the growth, lack of growth, or any profound movements of the secondary character. For instance, my father's death shifted my personal plot and became a pivotal point at which getting what I wanted was waylaid and misdirected—thrown off track, so to speak.

In *Rescuing Patty Hearst*, around the middle of the book, Virginia has both parents living in the home again, and her mother is struggling to be normal and to forget about the secret war and about finding the war children. Even though Virginia has simply been humoring her mother all of this time, the loneliness of not connecting with her mother over the secret war, ironically, causes Virginia to become more devoted to finding the war children, even though she knows there are no children and even though she is going it alone. This becomes her best effort at staying connected to a mother who is struggling to resist the delusion of the secret war. When Virginia's mother shifts in behavior, this causes a shift in Virginia's way of dealing with her captivity.

PROMPT 48: WRITE SCENES OF SECONDARY CHARACTERS THAT ENHANCE THE PLOT

Write your secondary character's birth scene, death scene, funny scene, and any additional scenes where these events impacted the main voice's or character's journey toward the want. Make sure the main voice or character is present or eluded to within the scene. Remember, if the main voice or character is not present within these scenes, the scenes are likely to be a distraction from the plot rather than an advancement and enhancement of the plot. Therefore, it is best to embed scenes before the birth of the main voice or character within flashbacks or musings. This would be the case of writing about the secondary character's birth. We will work with how to do this in detail in Chapter 15, Crafting Internal Character Development from External Stimuli, which, among other craft elements, explores the proper use of flashback.

In Summary: This research and writing on secondary voices and characters is an extension of the research on your wounds and wants in Chapter 8. That research helped you to understand the full landscape of your wounds and therefore your wants. This extension of that research and writing will help you to see beyond the foreground of your landscape to the larger landscape where other people's root issues, and your main voice's or character's root issues, intertwine.

As the author of the work, you have to be capable of seeing the whole universe of the plot, including all of the many pivotal emotional and psychological players of relationship in each scene and their significance to the overall plot. In order to write in a way that offers you and the readers the potential to evolve, you must commit to the emotional and psychological research of your secondary characters in tandem with your own emotional and psychological research.

CHAPTER 14

Setting and Its Impact

on Character and Plot

The external setting isn't simply the place where the story unfolds. The setting is also instrumental to the character development and must be cohesive and relevant to the plot.

Researching your setting can provide the reader and you, the writer, with details that either you didn't remember or your circumstances prevented you from being aware of. It ensures not only that your setting is accurate with details that are of the time period of your story, but it ensures that your setting is relevant to the experiences of the main voice or character. You'll avoid losing readers who are distracted by the irrelevance of the setting, as opposed to being invested because of the relevance of the setting.

And setting research will also prevent the embarrassment of getting called on the carpet for not knowing what you are talking about.

Research the Setting for Sensory Details

What were the sights? The sounds (music and noise of the streets, fields)? Smells, textures, and tastes of the foods? Don't just rely on your memory. Researching sensory details of setting offers the reader a view of the main voice's or character's world as experienced through their emotional/psychological lens. You can use what is true of the setting to mirror the internal psyche of the voice or character. As you may have discovered in the self-help research, so much of how we perceive the exterior sensory details of our world is based on the state of our internal world.

For Example: In my short story "The Empty Nest," everything in Hazel's setting is bleak and colorless. It is winter during the scenes where she feels isolated and afraid for her physical health. I maintain these visual sensory details of her setting until the outcome action scene where the color green, which she has imagined as healthy, is all around her.

Research the Setting of the Events of Your Life

In researching the setting of the events of your life to understand the events of your main voice's or character's life, you are asking questions and digging for information to verify and clarify the events inside your relationships with the people in your scenes/events. This is an extension of the character research that you did in Chapters 8 and 13. Here, you are researching the setting of where these events took place. Similarly, you may discover details of events that you may not have been aware of. This may mean going to the hospital where you were born, or to the site of your elementary school and asking people questions about those settings.

PROMPT 49: WRITE BASED ON RESEARCH ON SETTINGS OF YOUR LIFE
Prompted by the research on the setting of the events of your life, write-in or rewrite scenes to include the setting. Always include sensory details

specific to the setting (sights, sounds, smells, tastes, textures). Although you have already done the writing of these events, don't just go in and add the details of the setting as write-ins. This will make for some disjointed writing, especially since it is the details of the setting that parallel the emotional and psychological details of the scene. For the sake of a well-written scene, jump-start and rewrite the scene with the significance of your setting research, being sure not to lose any of the other elements of your internal and external agents and obstacles.

The setting research is great inspiration. So, allow yourself to write not just for this one-time prompt, but save this as a prompt you come back to over and over.

For Example: In writing *Fifth Born II: The Hundredth Turtle*, I took a nostalgic and beautiful—yet painful—trip to Harlem, which is where my brother last lived before his death. There are nuances and details in the novel that are specific to the two characters' experiences where the external setting and internal emotions parallel in a way that I would not have been able to describe through the writing without making the drive to New York.

> After choir rehearsal, Lamont and I sat like pigeons on a wire soaking up the cold air of Harlem, the uneasy task of breathing first the stench of bus fumes, then the warmth of gingerbread cooking somewhere in the distance. Darkness fell and streetlights, fluorescent church signs, and liquor store signs illuminated like separate moons. The train was leaving Port Authority at 9 p.m., and like every year, we had our last moments on the stoop while I waited for Ella Mae to pack.

Research the History of Society-at-Large Events

This is different from researching the events of your more insular life. With researching the history of your setting, you want to know what was happening in greater society that may have paralleled or had some

impact on how you or other people were responding in relationship to
each other. This may mean looking through archived newspaper articles
—from the day you were born through to the days when you became
more aware of society-at-large—to see what has happening outside of
your insular life. It's surprising the impact this research can have on your
personal and literary plot, because it offers a larger context for the voice or
character than the insular context of their familiars. Most of all, it offers
social and historical contexts for our initial wounds, which are always
there motivating our wants, sometimes more than we acknowledge. Poet
Toi Derricotte believes "we carry the unfinished business of the past
forward. We are compelled to resolve, not only our personal wounds,
but the wounds of our ancestors. It's as if we have been sent on their
mission. We feel the painful wounds of history in our parents' bed" (21).

PROMPT 50: WRITE BASED ON RESEARCH ON SOCIETY-AT-LARGE
Prompted by the research on the history of society-at-large (the sociopo-
litical events, actions, and so on), do a minimum of six writing sessions.
Always include sensory details specific to the setting (sights, sounds, smells,
tastes, textures). These six writings should inspire the rewriting of some
scenes, or they may inspire the memory of certain important scenes that
you have not yet included. The history of society-at-large research is great
inspiration, so allow yourself to write not just for this one-time prompt,
but save this as a prompt you come back to over and over. Research can
enhance the story and help you understand sociological events that may
have been happening around you at a young age or that you may have
read about, but when looked at through the lens of your wants or your
character's wants, they can take on new significance and offer context.

For example, in Virginia Holman's *Rescuing Patty Hearst*, we experience
the kidnapping of young Virginia by her mother to participate in a secret
war (which is a product of her mother's schizophrenia). Later in the story,
the young Virginia takes pride in the secret war and embraces it as part
of her identity. These circumstances parallel the newsworthy event of
Patty Hearst being kidnapped and later embracing the war causes of her

kidnappers. The parallel to an occurrence in society-at-large enhances the story of the insular life of young Virginia by giving the private, insular events a societal context.

Also, in the writing of *Cold Running Creek*, I used the archives of the Work Progress Administration project and archives of slave documents at Duke University's Perkins Library to find out what would have been taking place in the lives of my characters in the 1800s. I found Choctaw slave codes. I didn't even know Native people participated in African slave labor. This became a major detail in the society-at-large that acted as agent to advance the main character's want at some points in the story, and acted as obstacle that marred the character's journey toward her wants in other points of the story. In other words, this information was very significant to the plot.

In Summary: In order to keep this research from adding tons of unnecessary details and text to your story, which can muck up and dilute the plot, ask yourself the following:

1. Are the events that occur in the main voice's or character's insular life, or in their society-at-large, consistent with the character's wants or with the character's mood or behavior? Do these events in any way parallel, reflect, or explain the events of the main voice's or character's insular life?

2. Is the additional societal information that I have included relevant to the plot? Does it take what I had with my story and elevate it with details that allow the reader to fully engage in the story?

If not, take out any setting details that don't enhance the reader's experience of the character's journey, and put them in your outtake file. This can be information that informs the author and makes it into the nuances of the story, but doesn't make it into the details of the story.

It's best if you can travel to these settings to do your research, but that isn't realistic in most of our lives. So, one of the things that I do is utilize photo archives of the people, places, foods, flora, and fauna of the area. I even look for well-rendered movies or documentaries of the place and time for my setting.

As you already learned through researching your initial wounds, research can be emotionally taxing, because you aren't just wondering what things looked like, you are wanting to capture the nuances of how the sensory details of place impacted the characters emotionally.

Allow yourself to take breaks.

PART FOUR

Craft Elements

to Bring about Literary Plot

In this book, craft is defined as elements added to manuscripts that enhance the reader's experience of an already whole raw work. Craft enhances and elevates that rawness to make it literary so that the manuscript is not just a story, but a story well told. These elements include but are not exclusive to the following:

- Internal character development motivated by external settings, which incorporates
  - › Dialogue
  - › Flashback
  - › Flash-forward
- Dramatic tension – hope vs. fear
- Poetics, which include

- › Metaphor
- › Simile
- Scene arranging for **arc**, which incorporates
  - › Theme
  - › Motif
  - › Plant and payoff (some refer to this as foreshadowing and payoff)
  - › Character tags

As I said in previous chapters, the overall want of the plot (the want born out of the initial wound) is the driving force of the plot. Like the elements of the plot, the elements of craft—sensory detail, dialogue, dramatic tension, metaphor and simile, theme and motif, plant and payoff, and even character tags—are all to be central to the overall want.

If you are a fiction writer, you will find that these chapters on craft are where your personal plot begins to morph into fiction, but it isn't random that this happens; it happens as a process of shaping the story so that it is told well, where each change or detour from the reality of things is done to enhance and advance the plot. This is also where it's good to let your imagination wander. Just make sure that the imaginative additions to the story don't simply become a last-minute way to steer away from the emotional and psychological truth.

If you are writing memoir, you will find that these chapters on craft are where your personal plot is elevated beyond a series of memories, and where the intent of craft helps you to enhance the reality without lying about the reality so that a story becomes a story well told. This is where your manuscript morphs into creative nonfiction.

CHAPTER 15

Crafting

Internal Character Development

Internal Character Development:
Building Parallel Internal Scenes from External Stimuli

In this excerpt from *Cold Running Creek*, Raven is having an external experience where her father is trying to communicate something about her survival. The external scene is filled with sensory details like sights, smells, touch, tastes, and **dialogue**. These external details, like the father's hair in the sunlight, the trees, and what the father says to her, are triggering her internal character response through an internal scene, which is also filled with sensory details. "Be brave," he says, and we then see what this omen means for her based on her past experiences.

> Late that afternoon he returned, slow in his stride, and when Raven went to collect the berries from the heavy thorned bushes, he came to her in the clearing of trees where the blackberry reached up and over to snag the ungraceful deer or small child.

"You are the oldest child." He held her face and looked deep into her eyes.

Raven saw a desperation and fear in his eyes that felt shameful to witness.

He whispered, "If we get separated in these days, know that I will wait for your spirit in the ancestral place."

Her mother's voice, "Mind your step," blending in harmony with his "I will wait for you." The sound of fear pounded in her chest.

"Be brave, child." He asked her to listen carefully and watch as he sketched in the dry earth. "Still water," he said, "where many things lay unsettled, tall trees with their roots above ground for fear of digesting the sins that lie beneath. This is the swamp. This is a safe place. You have never been there, but if we are separated, look for the flat green nuts of the water hickory and follow them to the swamp. Do you understand?"

Raven answered, "Yes," quickly, trying not to let her voice waver.

He went on, "In this place of exile, you will find safety. If there is trouble, you must take baby Dove and your brother, Golden, and run to this place. Are you listening?"

"Father, what about the other children?"

"They will be your uncles' charge. Listen to me, Raven," he scolded her, and the tears burned in her nose. She held her breath to keep the sorrow of her father's harsh tone from breaking her.

Change had been hard for her, never allowed to cry, the oldest child. "Be brave" he had said to her the day they escaped the relocation to the new Territory. Her clan eluded the army in a torrential rain that lowered like a veil. The army men called for a halt because the noon sky had turned evil, a rumble of thunder, an explosion like cannon fire, and the rain came down in gray sheets. It filled the dips and gullies with churned water that sunk the wagon wheels. Flashes of lightning spooked the horses.

Most of their clan was on foot behind the wagon. The army's men called for the assistance of every able-bodied man and woman to free the wagons from the deepening mud and to get the horses to safety. The rain hushed their commands and made the color of Choctaw skin and the color of white skin indistinguishable. Raven's inki knew that the confidence in the army men's voices was a mask over their anxiety, for they had not left territory familiar to Choctaw hunters. He did not need to say to Ishki what would come next. He and his wife unhitched two horses, one of them his own, and set them beneath the high pines near a deer path; the grandmother, two little cousins, Raven, with baby Dove on a crib board rode on one horse. The most recently walking child and Ishki on the other. "Be brave," he said before slapping the soaked hide; his wet hair and the horse's mane trailing in Raven's memory. The aunts and uncles ran with him, carrying the supplies they could gather quickly, and they were gone, shadows beneath the sheets of gray rain, between dark tree trunks, up a deer path, gone, to this place where Raven stood. Change threatened to stampede through the comforting rhythms of her new life again.

Raven's inki spoke solemnly now. "I am entrusting you with my plan for your survival. You must listen." But fear gripped in her chest, and her mind lingered on "survival," having seen that word wrapped like a blanket around death. (7–9)

This is an example of a flashback where an earlier wound is revealed in installments or as a full memory scene that is triggered each time particular things occur for the main voice or character. Another example is in the movie *Smoke Signals,* when Victor's initial wound of his father leaving is offered in installments. As the adult Victor hears Thomas's romanticized ideas about Victor's father, Victor flashes back to the scene of his father drinking with violent outbursts on the day his father left. This flashing back is also used to offer the wounds of other characters in the movie. For instance, the character Suzy hears Arnold Joseph's dog bark and flashes back to the scene of his dog barking on the day she found Arnold Joseph's body. External stimuli have stimulated internal scenes.

The external scene and its sensory details may also trigger an internal scene that is in the character's fantasy of the future. In this case, the internal scene is called a **flash-forward** because the voice or character fantasizes about something that has not yet happened and may or may not happen in the story. These flash-forwards sometimes foreshadow events that come to fruition in the story. Often, the potential outcome scene is foreshadowed through flash-forwards.

At the end of Part I in *Cold Running Creek*, Raven is an adult and is trying to impart this same information of running to escape pending danger to her daughter, Lilly. This time, Raven is flashing-forward:

"Mother." Raven was startled awake by Lilly's bright voice, the candle sleeping and the first hint of morning silver on Lilly's cheek, her voice playful and innocent. "Good morning, Mother. Did Father return last night? He and I must ride this morning. The air is good for flying." She laughed deviously, waiting for her mother to scold her for wanting to ride fast like a boy, but there was nothing, just the balmy, hesitant breeze of morning coming down from the North.

"Lilly, they are coming for you. I can see them, hooves making sparks on jagged rock." Raven hadn't planned to speak such words, but words and images merged and she could not distinguish between asleep, awake, and the space in between.

Lilly frowned. "They who, Mother?"

"You must listen to your mother, Lilly. Just listen this once, and don't ask questions."

Lilly's playfulness turned to the defiance that was new and solid in her. "I am to listen to my father as well, and he has told me to always wait, to be still. He talked to me before he left, you know? He said if you want to go on a trip, to stay, to wait for him. Even if you want to go to town, to wait. I want to stay and wait for him. I know they will come. I have seen it in my dreams too, Mother, but I will stand here and fight the Yankees with my father."

"Listen to me, Lilly." Only now did Raven feel the certainty, only now had she crossed the line of doubt, of knowing, of insanity, of clarity, knowing where time did not need the boundaries of the mind.

Raven listened and heard General Thorpe, Henry Trench, John

Bartlette's overseer, two young soldiers, exhausted, determined to finish what they had started.

"Lilly, the men who come for you are Confederate. I can smell the
sweat in their hair." Raven closed her eyes. "I can feel the grip on the
reins. They mean to take you." Raven's words slowed. "They mean to
take you."

Raven was sweating, her eyes pinched closed. Sweat soaked the under-
arms of the light blue cotton dress. She released the imprisoned breath,
grabbed the valise in one hand, Lilly by the arm in the other.

"Mother. Stop, please. Father said you are changing with age, Mother:
the forgetfulness, the speaking when no one is in the room." Raven had
not known her daughter's strength, ten years old now, growing strong
in her bone and muscle.

Raven heard a flood of noise, voices grunting. She saw in a flash of
sight; blood streaking down a saddle skirt.

"Stop it, Lilly. Come now, come." Raven hurried her grip, threat-
ening to pull the child's arm free from her body. (102–103)

The sensory details of the character's exterior world trigger the internal
past or future scenes that mirror the wound or the wants. In some cases,
the exterior sensory details illustrate the ways the voice or character is
choosing to survive the wound and progressing toward the want, or the
way the voice or character is giving in to the obstacles. In the example
above, the external sights and sounds trigger Raven's fear of moving
again and her horrible memories of the massacre, which foreshadow the
profound outcome at the end of the scene of not getting what she wants.

Keep in mind that this example is from the perspective of an omniscient
narrator. But you are writing in first person, past tense. Always use "I"
and always speak in your own voice as you work within this book. The
example is to show you external and internal scene. This combination
of external and internal scene is crucial in steering away from *telling* us
what the character is thinking, and instead letting us become part of the
internal landscape of the character's feelings.

CHAPTER 16

The Craft

of Dramatic Tension – Hope vs. Fear

Otherwise known as hope vs. fear, **dramatic tension** is typically stimulated in readers through one of three scenarios.

1. *Persistent obstacles of fear*. Dramatic tension (hope vs. fear) can exist when the reader is shown the life that the voice or character hopes for or wants but is then taken into the world of persistent obstacles of fear, where we fear the voice or character won't overcome their obstacles (because the obstacles are so rooted in the initial wound) but we hope that they will return to the good life that we have seen. *Bastard Out of Carolina* and *Fifth Born* hold this more persistent tension. The main characters, Bone and Odessa, live well in scenes when times are safe, because there are family members who love them and offer them that safety, but they more persistently live with daily fears that are born out of their initial wounds.

Bone and Odessa each hold on to the safety of their grandmothers, but both fear they will perish in their households because of the wounds inflicted by their dads. While the reader hopes for triumph over the fears and the obstacles representing them, the tension looms because the reader is as aware of the hope as they are of the persistent nature of the fear.

2. *Signposts.* These are warnings based on fears of other characters' experiences and are either heeded to fulfill our hopes or ignored to confirm our fears. In each scene, these signpost warnings are blatant or subliminal messages to steer the main voice or character away from obstacles and toward agents. The more the voice or character ignores or defies the warning, the greater the tension. It's the classic horror movie moment when the character runs from the monster to the kitchen where there's a knife on the counter (high tension), but then runs right past the knife (the signpost) and toward the stove where hot water is boiling (another signpost—high tension again). We hope for one outcome and fear another. This is a great way to display internal saboteurs you make the reader aware of but which the voice or character is not aware of. You can offer the warnings and signposts that agents in your life offered while you remained hell-bent on achieving the want through perilous means.

3. *Persistent agents for a persistent villain.* This is an ironic spin of the role of agents and obstacles. On rare occasions, there are few obstacles, yet there are persistent agents to aid a main voice or character to achieve horrible wants. We, as readers, end up hoping for obstacles to stop them but fear they will succeed toward an ill fate for themselves or others. This is typical of stories where the main character is a villain, like a serial killer or bank robber who has a long track record of successfully fulfilling their villainous want because they are aided by persistent agents.

One has to be careful with persistent obstacles and agents that they aren't so persistent the reader gives up hope. Always hold some bit of potential for positive change so that you hold on to the reader. There is tension, and there is tension that breaks and causes folks to lose hope or to feel such levels of frustration that they free themselves and close the book. You don't want that to happen, so you must play with dramatic tension (hope vs. fear) to achieve a balance that enhances the story as opposed to destroying it.

You may find yourself saying, "But, in my real life, I was hospitalized for seven hundred days, all of which I want to recount." That horrific situation may be true, but the reader won't be able to handle the seven hundred days with persistence toward hope. You'll have to cut their fears some slack and offer hope sooner.

When voices or characters in a manuscript hope for one thing and fear for another, so do the readers.

But how, as the writer, do you tailor these hopes and fears where necessary while staying authentic to the organic emotional and psychological journey of the main voice or character?

Organically Prompting for Dramatic Tension: Persistent Obstacles of Fear

To organically write-in this type of dramatic tension, you need only to recall Chapter 2, Warm-Up Prompts to Reveal the Irony and Tension of Your Dichotomies, and the Hope vs. Fear Exercise. Through that exercise, you considered ways that an obstacle is persistent because it is fear and therefore organically born of your wounds in life. You wrote at least one scene where you offered an event where what you hoped and feared was connected to your wounds. Because the wound is so indelible, and because the voice has yet to have revelations, the obstacle of fear also seems indelible and certainly persistent. An example of this indelible wound that causes the voice to desperately hope, is in the movie *The Pursuit of Happyness*, as Chris's initial wound is abandonment by his father, living in foster care while his mother was incarcerated, and abuse from his stepfather. This causes him to desperately hope to provide for his child and to desperately fear that his child will suffer a similar fate and end up in the foster care system.

PROMPT 51: WRITE-IN PERSISTENT OBSTACLES OF FEAR

To increase the dramatic tension of persistent obstacles in your manuscript, go back to your Hopes and Fears chart and look for these emotional and psychological hopes and fears that are organically persistent because the fear or obstacle is born of the initial wound. To increase the tension, increase the fear that the main character has, based on some fear that is persistent, indelible, and psychologically true as being born of the initial wound. As your scenes progress, increase the main character's efforts to traverse the obstacle. This will require either write-ins or, most likely, rewrites.

Signposts

We walk through our personal journeys looking for clues as to what we should be doing. An eagle in the sky, a snake at our doorstep. We wonder if it means we should date this person or that one, get a divorce, stop sleeping with a married person, have a baby, quit a job, write a novel, go back to school, and so on. We look for these signs to guide us away from obstacles and toward agents. All the while, we ignore the huge hints inside of our realities—the ones that aren't cloaked in metaphor and allegory.

For instance, a friend who is unhappy with his job had a mild heart attack clearly because of stress and the high-cholesterol foods he loved to indulge in (signposts pointing him toward a healthier work environment and healthier eating habits). But he chalked the heart attack up to genetics and went on eating barbecue every Friday, seeking signs from above on whether or not he should get a new job. In my short story "The Empty Nest," Hazel ignores the signs from her daughter that their lives are too isolated, ignores her own hand in her isolation, and cites others as being emotionally inept, all the while looking for signs of emotional connection.

Where there are ignored signposts, there are activities of denial where we get about the business of chasing our tails for what we want, rather than following the real signs and running in a straight line. That confusion makes for great dramatic tension.

PROMPT 52: WRITE-IN SIGNS AND SIGNPOSTS

To increase the dramatic tension in the scenes of your manuscript, examine your own life for times you have looked for signposts to direct you, yet all the while you ignored what was best for you. Write in or write new scenes associated with your overall want where you allow the reader to see the real sign that your voice or character should follow while they persistently follow their fabricated signposts of denial.

A very easy place to find fabricated signposts in your personal plot is in your big bag of internal saboteurs. One of my ways of ignoring that I need to make a change in relationship with a loved one is to look at all the ways that the loved one is inept, and I use that as a reason to stay away from them. All the while, I have a tendency to ignore how much I need the other person to fulfill my want for belonging. I used this of my particular internal saboteurs as another way to increase the dramatic tension in "The Empty Nest." The reader knows that Hazel needs to connect and to follow the signposts that point toward connection. Hazel knows that Hazel needs to connect, but she continuously follows the sign telling her that connecting with people isn't worth it. Play with writing and rewriting some of your scenes where these glaring yet denied signposts increase dramatic tension.

I suggest letting the dramatic tension of your story build on some combination of signs, signposts, and persistent obstacles of fear. For instance in *The Pursuit of Happyness*, Chris's persistent obstacle is a fear of losing his son, his hope is to get out of harm's way of poverty and become financially successful, and the signs and signposts that indicate that he is going in the right direction are offered by symbols of success like the red sports car and the happy exterior of people who have risen above his current circumstances.

I won't be giving you examples on how to prompt for persistent agents that aid the maladjusted wants of a persistent villain, because we have been on a writing journey to utilize personal plot to evolve toward a more whole, resolved self, not toward the devolution path of villains and rogues. Be satisfied that it's a type of dramatic tension that you may encounter as a consumer of art and that you may very well—outside of your work with this book—choose to craft.

This is another point at which your personal plot may take a shift. For the sake of literary plot and offering a story well told, you may choose to offer that you hoped your secondary character would follow the signposts. As we discussed before, it is understood that in memoir and poetry, we are talking about your perspective. Other real players in your personal plot may not have noted or noticed any signposts or warnings that were or were not being followed, and they may ask you to remove from your memoir or poetry that you were stressed over hoping that you or they would do different, do better. But it would be a mistake to let their fear of your perspective keep you from utilizing this organic tension to tell the story. Don't trade the dramatic tension that you felt in that moment for unanimous approval of reality. If you felt tension in your real life, you have an opportunity to organically convey that to the reader, which is much, much better than fabricating some dramatic tension just in order to utilize that craft element.

A wonderful example of dramatic tension is in Sharon Olds's poem "The Race" in her collection *The Father*. In this poem, she fears she will not make the cross-country flight in order to say goodbye to him before he passes away.

> goodbye to my body, goodbye to comfort,
> I used my legs and heart as if I would
> gladly use them up for this,
> to touch him again in this life.

For fiction writers, building the dramatic tension organically is your opportunity for what is called poetic license, where personal plot departs from biographical poetry and memoir and becomes fiction, because the way that you embellish your true hopes and fears is much more intriguing for the plot than what actually happened. For instance, in my first novel, *Fifth Born*, the older sister Tawanda *fears* for Odessa's daily survival and warns Odessa to find an extracurricular activity that the parents find legitimate so that she is able to be out of the abusive household. Odessa simply isn't capable of heeding that warning with all of the insanity that is happening around her, and though the readers *hope* she won't, Odessa falls prey to the father's abuse again.

In my real life, my sister didn't have enough insight to warn me, and I almost became victim to my father's abuse again but was saved by my ability to run faster than he could. But in the writing of the story, the plot advanced with much more of a dramatic arc as the character's escape came later in the story. Instead of building her escape in the place where one of my temporary escapes occurred, I built in that the sister warned Odessa (*fear*), and the scene ends when the father's abuse happens again, jeopardizing Odessa's *hope* for survival. The tension creates a pressure that must be released, but not too early, and then it becomes much more satisfying for the reader to see Odessa succeed at escaping the father's abuse later, because the reader has invested their *hopes* and *fears* in her journey. I haven't sacrificed the emotional and psychological authenticity of the dramatic tension and have kept the organic nature of it, but I have shifted and embellished for the sake of literary plot.

Sometimes, we as writers depart from the facts and say that it is in order to create compelling fiction, but it is really because we *fear* that people will think that what the main character chose to do is what we chose to do in real life, or we *hope* that we are more likely to get published if we leave out the most honest, yet embarrassing, part. Remember, even if you depart from the facts for literary reasons, maintain the emotional and psychological truth. Don't let your self-consciousness stand in the way of rendering a story well told.

Note: If you are having trouble finding places to increase the dramatic tension in your manuscript, look for these opportunities in places where you offered vague emotion for intense situations. Scout out phrases in your raw material like "I was afraid" and "there wasn't enough time."

CHAPTER 17

Poetic Language

and the Dual Purpose of Simile and Metaphor

Similes and **metaphors** are craft elements utilized to draw a comparison between two things and offer deeper or more universal understanding of a feeling, object, or concept. The only difference between the two is structural. Similes use the words "like" or "as" in making the comparison, while a metaphor says that one thing simply is the other, and the comparison is understood. For example, "We were vulnerable like birds in leafless trees" (simile) and "We were birds in leafless trees" (metaphor).

The purpose of simile and metaphor is to give the reader a deeper or more accessible understanding of the main voice's or character's environment, emotions, choices, and behaviors that are all based on their circumstances, and to offer information for what they *want* and what in their environment might be agent or obstacle to that want. For example, in "The Empty Nest," the metaphor that Hazel conjures for her uterus is from the photo in the exam room of a green forest of pine trees. She transfers this as a metaphor for her uterus, because she wants the doctor to find only healthy flora and fauna in there. This combines setting and metaphor toward a deeper, more poetic understanding of the character's want in this scene.

Simply put, if a simile or metaphor compares but isn't specific to the character's wants or wounds or their setting, take it out or rewrite it or don't use a metaphor or simile at all.

PROMPT 53 : WRITE-IN THE DUAL PURPOSE OF SIMILE AND METAPHOR

Do a search through your document for the words "like," "as," and "is" to find the similes and metaphors you used. Of course, some of the instances of these words won't reveal simile or metaphor, but this is a great way to seek them out in your manuscript. Do your similes and metaphors advance the plot and enhance character and setting development? If not, rewrite and replace them. For example, in "The Empty Nest," the following simile is used in one of Hazel's flashbacks about her nature adventures with Silas: "domed *like* a palm to hold the cave dwellers." This describes the cave they are in, but before and after the flashback, she is talking about her uterus and her womb, so the simile serves as internal character development to let the reader know that her uterus represents for her a place connected to all ancient things and the birth of her daughter—a space the two of them simultaneously inhabited for nine months.

If you search through your manuscript for metaphors and similes and find that, in fact, you didn't use any or you used very few, then this is a good time to look for those places where you struggled to convey something internal and intangible. Go back and write-in or rewrite these moments and compare that intangible emotion your voice or character experienced to something quite tangible that a reader can access and then connect to the emotion. When you read the above example of Hazel's intangible feelings about her uterus, note how these are described through a metaphor that equates her womb to the tangible ancient cave that she and Silas once visited.

CHAPTER 18

The Craft
of Scene Arranging

You have temporarily arranged your scenes chronologically, beginning with the initial wound scene, the oldest stepping stone scene of your past to the recent horizon issue scene, then the revelation scene, the outcome scene, and the outcome action scene, with other scenes sprinkled in where they best fit to enhance the story. You have also reviewed these scenes to make sure that among them, you have the 7 Pivotal Scenes that help anchor your plot.

All of the scenes of the overall plot—except the revelation, outcome, and outcome action—can be arranged any number of ways while keeping the overall plot description intact. But revelation, outcome, and outcome action have to remain as the last three scenes of a manuscript in order for the story to hold the reader's attention. Can you imagine if I'd started *Fifth Born II: The Hundredth Turtle* with offering you the scenes of how Odessa reconciled her heart around her brother's situation and her mother's life? What then would be the point of reading the story if the ending has been given away?

You may argue that in some books and movies, you begin at the end. In these cases, you are actually placed in the setting of the end, but have to journey through the entire story to have the revelation, outcome, and outcome actions that bring you back to that setting and the significance of that setting. It's okay to place the readers in the setting of the outcome at the beginning of a story, as long as the readers are not made aware of the revelation and outcome that led to that setting. The only reason that a writer should place a reader in the setting of the outcome at the beginning of the story is if this will cause the reader to engage in the story. For instance, if I began a story with the first setting being a Native American woman sitting in the Oval Office (in her rightful place) as commander in chief, this may be intriguing enough to make the readers want to go on the journey to find out what events, revelation, and outcome brought the setting of this outcome action.

I am going to offer you three craft devices that will inspire you to arrange your scenes in some manner other than straight chronology. Keep in mind that straight chronology is tried and true, but these three craft devices can be used in addition to or as an alternative to that method of arranging your scenes.

- Theme and motif
- Plant and payoff
- Character tags

Theme and Motif

As discussed in Chapter 12, theme and motif can be a way to arrange and order the events of your manuscript, but we didn't discuss the specifics of how this can be carried out.

THEME

Think of the theme as an intangible belief that helps you survive events like your initial wound and offers shape and philosophical containment for your story. What do I believe that helps me survive events like my initial wound? For instance, I believe that practicing the art of writing can help a person self define and therefore self propel their evolution. This can be distilled into a theme of "The Healing Power of Art." It is the theme of this book. A theme like "Freedom for All" is the distillation of my belief that we all seek freedom, no matter what social strata we stand on.

A theme can help you distinguish which scenes of raw material might best advance the plot. For instance in *Cold Running Creek*, all of the characters are seeking their freedom in some well-guided or misguided way. Keeping that theme of "Freedom for All" in mind helped me arrange scenes by focusing on the most significant scenes for my secondary characters. The scenes where General Thorp and Henry Trench are making power decisions based on maintaining the freedom they acquired were significant secondary-character scenes to keep, but scenes about General Thorp's childhood were put in an outtake file.

MOTIF

Think of a motif as the person, place, or thing that repeats and carries the intangible belief or philosophy of the theme while holding some psychological significance for the main character, like the chorus in a song or play. A motif then can help you express the theme through an established pattern in the story.

For instance, much of Part Two of *Cold Running Creek* is told through the motif (date pattern) of Lilly's birthdays. This repeated thing (her birthdays) holds psychological significance for her, but it is also a manifestation of the intangible theme—freedom. In the story, it is her birth that puts freedom into question for so many of the characters in the story. Born to a slave but the daughter of a wealthy landowner, is she free? Through this pattern of her birthdays, we are offered scenes that advance the main character and each character around the theme of freedom. The motif then offers the opportunity to arrange the scenes with the motif as the pattern for telling the story.

In the movie *Frozen River*, the theme is "Woman vs. Society," distilled from the belief that society is overwhelmingly treacherous for single mothers who often have to fend for themselves. The tangible object, the motif that carries this theme, is the frozen river. It is the obstacle that represents the treacherous nature of a single mother's survival, and it appears and marks each scene in the body of the movie. The stepping stones scenes of the movie are arranged around river crossings. Motifs can help to offer tangible patterns for the intangible themes of a story well told.

PROMPT 54: THEME AND MOTIF EXPERIMENT

Make a new file for your manuscript that you will use as a Theme and Motif Experiment. You may even want to title the file "ThemeMotifExperiment." Go to the descriptions above and consider the theme of your manuscript. In my case, practicing the art of writing can help a person self define and therefore self propel their evolution—"The Healing Power of Art." If you are having trouble identifying your theme, you may want to consider your beliefs. What beliefs help you to survive initial wounds?

Now, consider a motif (person, place, or thing) that may represent this theme. One place you can look for motifs is in your Relationship Museum from Chapter 4. Look in the column "My belief system" and see if there are objects (motifs) that are symbols of the theme of your manuscript. One of my objects is "My Writing Tools, Jump Starters, etc.," which is a manifestation of my theme "The Healing Power of Art." This helped me shape and arrange the chapters of this book along the pattern of my writing tools as exercises and writing prompts within those exercises. This pattern became the way I was able to arrange my chapters, which all hold the theme of "The Healing Power of Art." The motif gave me pattern and arrangement for my theme so that each chapter focuses on a set of writing exercises. It also helped me to take out exercises that were cute and fun but didn't have anything to do with the healing power of art.

So now, you may be wondering what to do with this information. Experiment with ordering your scenes and the arc of your plot utilizing theme and the repetition of motif as a container. For instance, in *Fifth Born II: The Hundredth Turtle*, scenes of negotiated and renegotiated family are organized around Christmas and Thanksgiving, because it is through this motif of the holidays that I am able to show the abstract theme that family is not made up solely of biological connection.

Identifying theme and motif at this stage in the crafting of the manuscript can help to order the scenes in a way that offers logical and accessible patterns (motif) for abstract, and sometimes lofty, philosophies (theme).

Caution: Remember to create a Theme and Motif Experiment file of your manuscript that is separate from your main manuscript file. After all, it's an experiment and some theme/motif arrangements don't work well for the telling of some stories.

Plant and Payoff

In Chapter 5 of my novel *Fifth Born*, "Gretal's Game," the Ella Mae game, appears to give comic relief and insight into the funny childhood dynamics that surround Odessa, even though when this scene occurs, she has already been molested once in the story. The Ella Mae game is a plant for what occurs in the last third of the novel, even though it appears as just a funny scene. This scene has to be planted in the story early enough in Odessa's life that we remember it when the name Ella Mae comes up again. If I had planted "Gretal's Game" before the first molestation, the reader would not likely remember the scene, because the tragedy of the molestation would nullify the name (Ella Mae) that comes up in "Gretal's Game." If I plant the game too late in Odessa's journey—for instance, after the uncle's murder when she is ten years old—that would be placing the plant right in the middle of the rising hope vs. fear, and the reader would sense that it is contrived as a plant thrown in carelessly to get them to remember something. Readers don't like to feel duped. They love to be surprised by something that they sensed was true. In the novel *Fifth Born*, the Ella Mae game is the plant, and Ella Mae the person is the payoff. This is part of scene arranging for story arc.

If you are at a loss for an object to plant that is authentic to the development of the characters and the plot, try going back to the Relationship Museum Exercise in Chapter 4. Whether you are writing poetry, fiction, or memoir, these objects already have a true emotional/psychological value for you and likely have been planted into your life in very organic ways. For instance, in my museum, there is the cell phone under my relationship with my daughter. Because it represents so much stress around power struggles over technology with her, I utilized it as a plant in "The Empty Nest." The cell phone and its ringtone were planted early in the story during the problem and struggle scenes, and they showed up at the end of the story as an object representing Silas (the daughter), who is part of the solution and outcome.

PROMPT 55: PLANT AND PAYOFF EXPERIMENT

Make a new file for your manuscript that you will use as a Plant and Payoff Experiment. You may even want to title the document "PlantPayoffExperiment." Go through your manuscript looking for a main object that represents the emotional relationship between the voice or character and their want, or an object that represents the voice's or character's relationship with a secondary character. Try your hand at planting the object and creating a payoff.

The best place to hide your plant is in plain sight. In the case of *Fifth Born*, I took the manifestation of the overall want (belonging, mothering) and hid it in plain sight within the story so that it could pay off as the fulfillment of the want later.

Caution: Remember to do this experiment with a copy of your manuscript. In the event that plant and payoff just doesn't work for you, you want to be able to go back to the original manuscript.

Character Tags

There are two sorts. **Shifting tags** are some of the most blatant yet famous character tags that signify a shift in the character or in the setting, like Harry Potter's scar, which aches when Voldemort is near. This character tag lets us know that something is about to happen. It's a way to give the reader some warning, control, or feeling of understanding of the main character's shifts in a story.

I am fonder of the second sort of character tag. **Habit tags** offer us physical manifestations of your character's internal character development. A great way to research some of your main voice's or character's habits is to go back to the internal character development research in Chapters 8 and 13. There, you may find physical habits that are specific to your main voice's or character's behaviors. These sorts of tags don't signify that something is about to happen, but they give us physical representation of shifts in a character's emotional state, like the ever-famous nail biting for a character who is nervous, self-conscious, insecure, and maybe even guilty of something, or the character with the habit of running their fingers through their hair because they are self-obsessed or hiding a crush.

A way to seek out character tags as objects that are authentic to your plot is to go back to the Relationship Museum Exercise in Chapter 4. If there is a relationship in the museum that is a voice in your memoir or representative of a relationship between two characters in your novel, you can pick out objects specific to that relationship as character tags. For instance in my museum, a black, waist-length leather jacket was under my relationship with my brother, and in the writing of *Fifth Born II: The Hundredth Turtle*, I used this object and other fashion choices that the brother makes as a character tag for the many shifts and dimensions his identity experiences as he progresses toward death.

Character tags are simply physical behaviors or physical traits or choices that are specific to a character's wounds and wants. These characteristics repeat because they are part of a behavior profile, and they signify a shift in the character or in some aspect of the setting that triggers their behavior.

PROMPT 56: CHARACTER TAG EXPERIMENT

Make a new file for your manuscript that you will use as a Character Tag experiment. You may even want to title the copy "CharacterTagExperiment." Go through your manuscript looking for habits or physical traits or choices that can be embellished to prompt shifts in the character, or to illustrate the voice's or character's internal behavior. It may be helpful to go back to the internal character development research in Chapters 8 and 13 to see if there are objects or behaviors that are specific to someone with wounds and wants like your characters'.

In Summary of Scene Arranging for Story Arc: It's best to do these prompts of arranging your manuscript as experiment files, so that in the event one of the experiments works: fabulous. But in the event that they all fail, you can go back to your chronologically organized original.

In Summary of Craft: All craft devices are to bolster and enhance the plot; they assist in driving the wants in the overall plot. If there is a craft device that is in play but isn't specific to the plot by driving the overall want, take it out.

Caution: If you have skipped ahead and read any of these craft techniques, do not attempt to begin writing your manuscript here based only on craft suggestions. That will likely create some very contrived, non-organic, non-authentic writing and will go against the themes of this book. Instead, find as *plants* the ideas and exercises early on in the book that *pay off* in these last chapters. Go back and do the cumulative work and enjoy the discoveries.

CHAPTER 19

The Self-Edit

and the Peer Edit

Let's work first with some more Zelda-ized definitions.

Content Edit: The content edit is concerned with the *craft* of telling a story well and is a major part of the writing. This edit entails working with all of the craft elements discussed in Chapters 15, 16, and 17 to ensure that the story is well told and that the plot is cohesive and compelling from beginning to end. With a good content edit, you will ensure the following:

1. *Parallel internal and external settings*. Both settings work in parallel to advance the plot through the personal plot journey of the main voice or character and include the proper use of dialogue, flashback, and flash-forward.

2. *Dramatic tension*. The journey's hope vs. fear offers the reader the

rise and fall of emotional tension similar to the ebb and flow of human growth in a true-to-life personal plot.

3. *Compelling language and poetics.* These are a sensual and pleasant medium for carrying the sometimes difficult-to-witness writhing of a human journey. These spoonfuls of sugar help the reader walk through a course of want-driven actions, and include the proper use of simile and metaphor and the proper and effective use of dialogue.

Copy Edit: The copy edit is concerned with the *believability* and *continuity* elements of telling a story well, and it entails checking the effectiveness of the craft elements discussed in Chapter 18—theme and motif, plant and payoff, and character tags—all toward enhancing the readability of your story. This is also where fact-checking and researching *now* spares you massive embarrassment *later*. Here's what a good copy edit should establish:

1. *Believability of setting.* For instance, in the writing of my novel *Fifth Born II: The Hundredth Turtle*, I had to find out what the hospital that is referenced in the story was called in the early 1980s, because the name of that hospital in Harlem changed several times over the years.

2. *Continuity of setting.* For example, if you call wool "linsey wool" in Chapter 3, then you better call it that in Chapter 4 as well.

3. *Continuity of time.* For instance, if a character is twelve years old in 1970 and is twenty years old in 1980, this is an error that can be caught with the fine-tooth continuity checking of the copy editor.

4. *Readability and flow.* Lastly, this phase of a copy edit is concerned with the flow, readability, and ability for the reader to draw the intended meaning from the story. For example, with this edit, you may find yourself having to experiment with toning down the use of dialect and colloquialisms, or perhaps inserting more dialect and colloquialisms, all for the readability of the manuscript. This is also the place to ask if the themes and motifs, plants and payoffs, and character tags (if you used them) feel authentic or contrived.

Line Edit: The line edit is concerned with the *mechanics* of telling a story well:

- Spelling, grammar, and punctuation
- Word usage
- Tense
- Perspective
- Consistent spelling of proper nouns that are exclusive to the story.

For example, *Fifth Born* had to be vetted for the spelling of "Deddy," which was the proper noun used for the father. In *Cold Running Creek*, multiple checks had to occur to assure the "I" in Ishki and Inki were capitalized when referring specifically to *the* mother and father and low-ercased when referring to mothers and fathers in general.

The line edit is always the last edit that I do as the author, because I don't want to be distracted from the flow of the art by the mechanics of it all, and it also offers me the opportunity to clean it up before giving it to those who will read for content editing and copy editing, who may get distracted by errors in the mechanics. Yet, after I have made corrections, I call for another line edit to clean up any mistakes I made during my corrections. The point of any edit is to hone the manuscript so that the reader's attention is kept locked in to the story, as opposed to the reader being conscious of the writer and their missteps and their interesting craft choices that bring attention to themselves.

Vocabulary: A **read-through** is a thorough read of the entire manuscript in order to familiarize yourself with the story you are telling or to edit for particular elements of the story. In order to do a thorough **self-edit** (content, copy, and line edit), you will do ten read-throughs of your manuscript.

You might be thinking, "I don't want to do ten read-throughs!" But remember, in order to end up with full command over this manuscript and to know it as well as you know your own home (be able to walk around inside with or without sight or hearing and know where everything is), you will need to be able to navigate through your manuscript in this same way—with complete familiarity.

I. READ-THROUGH TO REACQUAINT

The first is a full read-through of your manuscript in order to get reacquainted with the overall plot of the story you are telling and to highlight the places in the manuscript that feel like they need work because they do not advance the plot. You don't want to start editing the manuscript yet; just read through and perhaps highlight in order to have a feel for the whole piece, and to know and understand what scenes were included and the order that you settled on.

2. READ-THROUGH TO CONTENT EDIT AND ASSESS 7 PIVOTAL SCENES

Label the 7 Pivotal Scenes in your manuscript. (See Chapter 11 for further guidance on 7 Pivotal Scenes.) Of course, you will want to remove these labels before giving the manuscript to a reader; this is to assess if they actually still exist in the manuscript. You have done plenty of fiddling around with your manuscript since Chapter 11 and there may be missing pivotal scenes. If there are missing scenes, you know you have writing to do, or you have outtakes that need to be fetched and tailored with transitions and continuity to fit where they belong. Of course, there will be many scenes that fall between these 7 Pivotal Scenes, but they all should advance the plot by moving the story forward in the development of the voice's or character's wants that progress toward revelation and outcome.

If there are scenes that don't advance the plot, put them in your outtake file. Keep in mind that you have done several write-ins to enhance each of these scenes. They have progressed in their depth and scope since Chapter 11. At minimum, you want to make sure that you have the following:

1. *Initial wound scene(s)*. One or a series of initial wound scenes that caused a loss and therefore a want or need.

2. *Increase of obstacle scene(s)*. In the series of events that are the journey to obtain the want or need, some external things or beings got in the

way (obstacles), and some internal beliefs and behaviors got in the way (internal saboteurs). Choose the obstacle scene(s) from your raw material that had the strongest influence on the main voice's or character's journey. For now, place them in chronological order.

3. *Intro agent scene(s).* In the journey to obtain the want or need, some external things or beings helped (agents), and some internal beliefs and behaviors helped (gifts). Choose the agent scene(s) from your raw material that had the strongest influence on the main voice's or character's journey. For now, place them in chronological order.

4. *Heightened dramatic tension scene(s).* In the journey to the want, there are surely some scenes where both are present: agent and obstacle, influencing the emotional/psychological want and motivation of the main voice or character, therefore increasing the emotional/psychological tension for the main voice or character. Select at least one scene that had the strongest influence over whether or not the main voice or character attained the overall want. This is what some authors call the climax, but I choose to call the heightened dramatic tension scene.

5. *Revelation scene.* The main voice or character stands alone without obstacles and agents so that they can change on their own, make choices on their own, and have a revelation. In this one scene, the main voice or character interacts with something new or some new information that they didn't have before on their journey. In this moment, the voice or character chooses some old path or some new path that causes change— either as a person who now has new information and still chooses to get what they want in the old ways, or as someone who has new information and chooses a new way of getting what they want. In your raw material, this scene is likely among the scenes from the Bringing Back the Chief's Stone Necklace Action and Write and the Releasing the Blame and Taking Responsibility Action and Write.

6. *Outcome scene.* One scene that shows the change that is a result of the revelation.

7. *Outcome action scene(s).* At least one scene that shows how the change will be sustained in outcome actions. This is where you show that the

main voice or character has a new daily practice to sustain their new way of being. What does the voice or character now practice in order to sustain the change? Again, not all stories have this scene, but in Chapter 10 there is the opportunity to live outcome action scenes and then write those experiences.

3. READ-THROUGH TO CONTENT EDIT AND ASSESS FOR MISSING SCENES IN THE PLOT

So, there are the 7 Pivotal Scenes, but there are many other scenes that also progress the plot, tell the story, and take us from one era of a main voice's or character's life to the next era; all are scenes that advance the plot and progress and evolve the want toward revelation. Remember the 7 Pivotal Scenes work as an anchor for all scenes that advance the plot, but all scenes must advance the plot.

In my years of teaching and reading participants' manuscripts, one of the consistent issues I notice is that the early edits of their work are missing the emotional undergirding of the most significant scenes. By this, I mean in writing the manuscript, the author has managed to leave out the most significant years in the main voice's or character's journey, because these scenes are the most difficult ones in the personal plot of the author. The plot caves in like a rotten floor if there are missing undergirding scenes.

For Example: When I was writing *Fifth Born II: The Hundredth Turtle*, I went through several drafts of the book, creating ways in which the character Lamont died without the main character, Odessa, witnessing it. These characters were based on my brother and myself, but they weren't us, so my logic was that it would be fine to write Lamont dying in New York while Odessa was in Mississippi. My colleagues who read and gave notes on the novel consistently said that Odessa's character felt less substantial after the brother's death, or that she lacked authenticity in her grief. I tried and tried to write around the issue without having to overhaul the plot, but I was wasting time and energy. When I finally got out the Kleenex and wrote the death scene that was closest to my own emotional truth, the authenticity shined light on the inauthentic state of half the manuscript. Finally, I also rewrote several scenes that came before and after Lamont's death so that I could fix the systemic problem of the novel, which was my emotional distance.

So, the task then is to read through your manuscript and ask yourself if you have left out the part that is difficult to tell. You can usually find that difficult-to-tell part hiding behind your sense of *shame* saboteur or your feelings of *grief*. The second task is not to waste time moaning and groaning about what you'll have to tear out in order to write in the missing truth. The manuscript isn't its strongest self until it sits on the foundation of solid emotional truths. Go back to Chapter 3 and read about your shame saboteur and all of the other saboteurs, and ask yourself if your saboteur is covering up some of the truth that you need as your best scenes.

4. READ-THROUGH TO COPY EDIT FOR BELIEVABILITY OF CHARACTER DEVELOPMENT

This will send you back to your internal character development research in Chapters 8 and 13 as you answer one question for yourself: would someone with my main voice's or character's issues behave this way?

5. READ-THROUGH TO CONTENT EDIT FOR SETTING

See Chapter 14, Setting and Its Impact on Character and Plot, and leave yourself notes. Search for words like "house," "sky," "car," "room," actual places or settings. When you examine the settings of the manuscript, enhance them for internal character development. In other words, be sure that the things the voice or character notices, including the character's surroundings, are consistent with the character's wants or with the character's mood or behavior. If your settings feel more arbitrary, rework them to make them consistent and significant to your voice's or character's journey. Ask yourself, "For each external thing that the character or voice notices, do they have an internal reason for noticing this thing connected to their wounds, wants, obstacles, or agents (connected to the plot)?"

For Example: Everything in Hazel's first-person accounts of her setting is bleak and colorless until the action outcome scene (the inside of the cabin, the woods, and so on). The settings are a manifestation of her mood.

6. READ–THROUGH TO COPY EDIT FOR BELIEVABILITY OF SETTING

This will send you back to Chapter 14 and your setting research as you commit to answering for yourself, Does the setting interact with and enhance the voice's or character's wants? Does the setting in any way reflect and put into historical or social context what is driving the voice's or character's wants?

7. READ–THROUGH TO CONTENT EDIT FOR DRAMATIC TENSION

Each scene is a microcosm of the overall plot where the overall want is manifested in some way. That want becomes clearer in each scene when we delete moments that aren't specific to the tension between the main voice's or character's want and the things that help or hinder. Go through each scene and increase the obstacle, or increase the agent and the main character's resistance to the obstacle or adherence to the agent. As mentioned in Chapter 13, you may also want to explore parallel yet divergent wants of two characters as a way to enhance the dramatic tension in all of the scenes of the story. The best example of this from our texts in common is the parallel in Kahu's wants and Koro Apirana's wants in *The Whale Rider*.

After you have edited for this, strip away all extraneous characters other than the obstacle, agent, and characters that increase their tension in the scene. This will increase the dramatic tension in the scene and make the want more sharp. Dramatic tension builds when secondary characters and the settings shift (both are part of the main character's exterior setting). And when these things shift, the main character's wants shift—hence the tension. See Chapter 16, The Craft of Dramatic Tension – Hope vs. Fear.

Note: The content edit for secondary character development, for setting, and for dramatic tension go hand in hand. They can be handled together in one edit, because the main voice's or character's want is temporarily fulfilled or not fulfilled in each scene because of shifts in the setting or in the secondary characters.

Note: It is in the revelation scene though that the main voice or character permanently shifts with their want, and the dramatic tension is then felt by the secondary characters, whose beliefs may topple under the weight of the main character's revelation. For instance, in *The Whale Rider*, when Kahu has the revelation that she must ride the whale back out to sea, Koro Apirana's belief that a boy-child will lead them crumbles.

8. READ-THROUGH TO CONTENT EDIT SIMILES AND METAPHORS

See Chapter 17, Poetic Language and the Dual Purpose of Simile and Metaphor, and leave yourself notes. Search for the words "like," "as," and "is" in search of the similes and metaphors you used. Of course, some of the instances of these words won't reveal simile or metaphor, but this is a great way to seek them out in your manuscript.

Ask yourself upon each encounter: Does this simile or metaphor advance the plot or enhance character and plot development? Are the comparisons specific to the setting, to the character's behavior as they journey to fulfill their want?

The comparisons should not be for comparison's sake but should be dual purpose: they should help the reader understand an emotion, object, or situation better, but they should also give us information about the character or setting. For instance, it would be silly to say, "I was calm, like a snowy day in December," if the story is set in Phoenix, Arizona.

For Example: In "The Empty Nest," the following simile is used in one of Hazel's flashbacks about her nature adventures with Silas: "domed like a palm to hold the cave dwellers." This describes the cave they are in, but before and after the flashback, Hazel is talking about her uterus and her womb, so the simile serves as internal character development for the literal place inside the character that is threatened with disease.

9. READ-THROUGH TO CONTENT EDIT FOR PROPER USE OF DIALOGUE

There is nothing worse than dialogue where we read one person say something, then read, "said Herman." And then the other person says something, and we read, "he said." You are the writer with a full emotional, psychological, and spiritual scope of the characters and their full history of experiences, including the wounds and wants that drew them to each other. You have the power to give us much more than what they said.

The proper use of dialogue in literature is the same as true-to-life dialogue. We say things to each other because we are motivated by what we want the other person to feel or think. As the writer, please offer this information to the reader before or after the person opens their mouth. Give us the psychological and emotional context of their words by showing us the memory, fantasy, or thoughts inside of their head before they speak.

Another option is to show us the character's response through their body language. Similarly, when someone says something to us, we hear it through the filter of our wants and wounds, our joys and pains. So, when someone is spoken to, give us the internal reaction of memories, fantasies, or thoughts that are stimulated by the words spoken to them. Think of dialogue the way you think of setting. The external setting stimulates internal scenes, but in this case the characters that are speaking to each other are external setting for each other and therefore stimulating internal responses for each other. Chapter 15, Crafting Internal Character Development from External Stimuli, explores the proper use of dialogue with details that will help you accomplish this read-through.

It's funny that after thinking about dialogue as stimuli for internal setting, it seems like common sense that this is true, but we were all taught some dry old, boring, unrealistic way to offer dialogue. Go ahead and edit for this and make a commitment to offer dialogue from now on in the proper way—the way that humans really relate to each other.

10. READ-THROUGH AND CORRECT FOR LINE EDITS OF MECHANICS

Read through your manuscript for errors with grammar, punctuation, spelling, and word usage so somone else may read without the constant distraction of errors. You will want to complete a line edit by yourself before giving the manuscript on to readers. Most of what you'll ask of them is a good copy edit. Because you are so close to your manuscript and have done so many read-throughs, you won't catch all of these issues, but you should be able to catch enough so that the manuscript is readable, and your readers and editors will likely catch the rest.

Improving upon these areas of your manuscript through a self-edit will take days, maybe even weeks or months, because you will be led to rewrite scenes or passages for better storytelling. So, I want to express the importance of conducting your own very thorough content, copy, and line edits before giving the manuscript to your incredibly important peer readers, who will be instrumental in catching issues of believability and continuity with your manuscript you are too close to see, and in preventing the manuscript from being an embarrassment when you are seeking publication. It goes without saying then, that you don't want to hand your readers a manuscript that is such a disheveled mess that they lose faith in your ability to tell a story well. They will be expecting a manuscript—yes, one that needs work, but one that they can still enjoy while they read and offer notes.

Remember how we talked about how your manuscript is food, medicine, and kinship for some anonymous audience? Your peer readers are the first of that audience; they are helping shape and clarify the manuscript for you, but they will also be the first people who have the opportunity to experience your art.

Once you learn how to do your own content, copy, and line edits, you can push past first draft to second draft, and you will learn how to recognize what's missing in your manuscript.

Peer Readers

I refer to a **peer reader** as a friend or colleague (not someone who you have deep, long-term emotional ties to) who is professional in their specific field of expertise, can read your manuscript, and give you detailed feed-back that will help you improve upon, clarify, and tighten your story.

Earlier in this book, we discussed the ways in which your writing is food, medicine, and kinship for some often-anonymous reader. Those people have called for your work and you have answered the call with an emotionally, psychologically, and spiritually authentic story of your human experience. To get the story fully told—and told well—there are some puzzling jobs involved that you are likely too close to the manuscript to resolve through the self-edit.

Yes, again, you get to practice your vulnerability. One of the stages of completing the full-length manuscript is to involve peer readers in the process. It's like being called on to bake the one and only cake for your sister's wedding and having good enough sense to offer some sample cakes and get feedback before the main event.

I use four peer readers. First, I give the manuscript to someone who can line edit and correct the manuscript for grammar and spelling so that the other readers don't end up so distracted by the errors that they can't engage. Then, I simultaneously give the manuscript for copyediting to three friends or colleagues:

1. One who is brilliant at catching continuity issues in a manuscript associated with moving parts, like age, dates, and so on. This person is the one who, at your book club, noticed that the character was thirteen years old in 1861 and twelve years old in 1862.

2. One who has similar emotional, physical challenges as the main voice or character. Yes, even if these are your emotional, physical challenges, you want someone with the same challenges to read for believability and to see if you have conveyed the feelings and issues fully. You are so close to the story that you may think you have shared your joys and pains with your issue when you have not.

3. One who lived or lives in the setting(s) of the manuscript during the time it is set. This doesn't mean giving the manuscript to someone from California if your manuscript is set in South Central Los Angeles.

It means giving the manuscript to someone from South LA who lived under the same socioeconomic constraints as your character during the same time period. As we know, regions change over a period of time. Yes, even if you grew up in South LA, you only had one perspective of that time and place. You want to be sure to offer the truest experience so others from that time and place don't point out the shortcomings of the manuscript's setting but instead feel connected to the manuscript's setting.

Now sit back and relax for a few weeks. Let your peer readers give you guidance for your next full edits on the manuscript.

What to Do When Peer Readers Return Your Manuscript

Make corrections based on those you feel are truly helpful to the plot, but don't make any corrections that you instinctually feel should remain. Instead, get a second or third opinion. Sometimes, I override my instincts and take the advice of others if I believe one thing is truly helpful to the plot but three readers have suggested an opposing thing. This is when it's important to put our intent aside and allow for what our first readers have discovered to be the truth. In other words, don't be hard headed.

What to Do with the Manuscript You Outgrew

What do you do if the peer edit or some other form of the edit reveals that what you have is not the art of it but instead an exercise in getting at the art of it? In other words, what do you do if you have an almost-finished manuscript that doesn't fit what you now understand about how to make good art?

Put it in a file cabinet to keep it as a memento of how you have grown as an artist, but for goodness' sake, don't try to salvage the work of your learning moment by trying to turn it into the masterpiece itself.

Sometimes, we are learning so fast that the old manuscript has lost its relevance, except as a learning tool, before we can even finish it. Often, we don't realize this until peer readers get ahold of it and do what we have asked by giving their honest opinions.

You don't have to finish that old thing just because you started it. It served its purpose, and now you are on to write the real art. If you have done all of the exercises of this book and find that this scenario is true for you, go ahead and use what you now know and take nine months or so and write the whole manuscript from this vantage point of having done this book and having all of the guidance from your peer readers.

Here are some things I have said, and others in my tutelage have said, in response to those peer readers who suggest we start over and write the true art:

- I have to keep working on this version of the story, because I'm committed to the character.
- I have to see this through so I know how the story turns out.
- The character has a life of their own; I'm just following.
- This is a good story; people just aren't ready for it.
- My reading group (of people who are afraid of their own emotional shadows) love the book.
- My reading group (of people who are always self examining and adjusting accordingly so that they live emotionally aware lives) are overcritical and pompous and that's why they don't get the artistic significance of this story.
- They're all jealous (those who think you should ditch the manuscript and start over).
- My agent is addicted to unrelentingly grim stories.
- My agent is addicted to fairy tales.

It's also okay to say that you wrote what you wrote on your way to some artistic truths but discovered on the way that what you were writing wasn't the manuscript itself but practice for the manuscript—or perhaps it was a lesson in how to let yourself write from the authentic base of your emotions, psyche, and intellect combined.

When we grow, it's hard to stop the old behaviors that belong to our previous way of being. You are walking around now, fully aware of at least one of your personal plots, its wounds and gifts, but it might be hard to stop speaking the language of the version of yourself who wasn't aware. Don't reflect upon your manuscript in the old ways, in the language of denial and blame. Let your manuscript stand in the light all pretty and ugly, and have the courage to work on it until it is honestly a story well told. If your peer readers say the manuscript isn't what you believe it to be, it's time to bravely work on it until it becomes the art that's being called for.

CONCLUSION

Spinning
Straw into Wool

Many edits will follow—second, third, twentieth drafts. Don't pretend that the story is ready if it isn't; that's like trying to serve a cake that is raw in the middle. Conversely, don't pretend that the manuscript isn't ready when it is; that's just allowing your fear saboteur to take over the end of the writing process, which is publishing.

Remember, don't let the defenses that have stayed too long and become saboteurs keep you from showing up in your creative life in the same state that you arrived in this embodied life, naked. In this state, you are most vulnerable and most capable of offering your brilliance.

There are going to be times when you feel spun around and won't remember why you're doing these new self-fulfilling behaviors. Your saboteurs will pop up and you'll be listening to those voices of your old way of being at the same time that you're listening to the new voices of your greatest gifts, and you'll feel completely confused. In those times of being spun around, remember the goal—your outcome action—in the way that a good dancer focuses on a steady point, a spot on the wall so that they don't get dizzy in the spinning. The other thing to do is to remember that anything that doesn't advance your personal plot of self fulfilling the want with your gifts is likely the old saboteurish voices talking.

Last but not least, know that the journey you have taken, allowing yourself to feel and remember and have divergent emotions of joy and pain, and hope and fear, is an affirmation of your humanity, and the expression that you make from that journey is art.

By taking the journey of *The Soul of the Full-Length Manuscript,* you have turned into a different kind of writer, aware of not just the outer world, earthly details of your personal plot but also the inner-world, psychological, and spiritual details of your personal plot, each informing the other into a whole artistic awareness.

You can now use your personal plot to spin straw into wool for blankets to keep yourself and others warm. It can be ground into flour for baking the bread from which you and others feed. Or dried in the sun, like may-apple root, and crushed into powder to purge the ailments from bellies.

I've enjoyed our journey. May the instinct to want for what you already have, guide you in your positive evolution.

GLOSSARY OF SHARED VOCABULARY

7 Pivotal Scenes: Scenes that anchor your overall plot and act as guides as you begin manipulating your raw material to figure out what to keep and what to take out. These seven scenes will act as a point of reference for the plot.

1. *Initial wound scene(s).* One or a series of initial wound scenes that caused a loss and therefore a want or need.

2. *Increase of obstacle scene(s).* In the series of events that are the journey to obtain the want or need, some external things or beings got in the way (obstacles), and some internal beliefs and behaviors got in the way (internal saboteurs). Choose the obstacle scene(s) from your raw material that had the strongest influence on the main voice's or character's journey.

3. *Intro agent scene(s).* In the series of events that are the journey to obtain the want or need, some external things or beings helped (agents), and some internal beliefs and behaviors helped (gifts). Choose the agent scene(s) from your raw material that had the strongest influence on the main voice's or character's journey.

4. *Heightened dramatic tension scene(s).* In the journey to the want, there are surely some scenes where both are present: agent and obstacle, influencing the emotional/psychological want and motivation of the main voice or character, therefore increasing the emotional/psychological tension for the main voice or character. Select at least one scene that had the strongest influence over whether or not the main voice or character attained the overall want. This is what some authors call the climax, but I choose to call the heightened dramatic tension scene.

5. *Revelation scene*. The main voice or character stands alone without obstacles and agents so that they can change on their own, make choices on their own, and have a revelation. In this one scene, the main voice or character interacts with something new or some new information that they didn't have before on their journey. In this moment, the voice or character chooses some old path or some new path that causes change—either as a person who now has new information and still chooses to get what they want in the old ways or as someone who has new information and chooses a new way of getting what they want. In your raw material, this scene is likely among the scenes from the Bringing Back the Chief's Stone Necklace Action and Write and the Releasing the Blame and Taking Responsibility Action and Write.

6. *Outcome scene*. One scene that shows the change that is a result of the revelation.

7. *Outcome action scene(s)*. At least one scene that shows how the change will be sustained in outcome actions. This is where you show that the main voice or character has a new daily practice to sustain their new way of being. What does the voice or character now practice in order to sustain the change? Again, not all stories have this scene.

Action and Write: Can be flipped as Write and Action. These are writing prompts where you must first do the action, then write about the emotional journey of doing the action as the first step toward writing outcome. In other cases, you must first imagine and write the next step, then take action and live it as the first step toward writing outcome.

Agent: A person, place, or thing that helps you out in this world, particularly in your healing from an initial wound.

Arc: The arrangement of a story using elements such as chronology, theme or motif to enhance story meaning for the reader.

Art: The offering of your experiences through a medium like writing, dancing, teaching, carpentry, and so on. The purpose of art is to make yourself vulnerable about your experiences here in life, to have the *courage to be vulnerable* about those experiences so that you can connect with others who came here solo like you and will leave solo just like you.

Bibliofusion: Consuming literature written with personal plot as inspiration for creating literature with personal plot.

Character Tag: A craft element that utilizes reappearing physical traits of a character that, when they appear, signify a shift in the character's internal or external setting (shifting tags) or represent habitual, physical representation of a character's emotional state (habit tags). Examples include Harry Potter's scar, which aches when Voldemort is near, or the ever-famous nail biting for a character who is nervous, self-conscious, and maybe even insecure.

Content Edit: The edit concerned with the *craft* of telling a story well. This edit entails working with all of the craft elements discussed in Chapters 15, 16, and 17 to ensure the story is well told and the plot is cohesive and compelling. A good content edit will ensure the following:

1. *Parallel internal and external settings.* Both settings work in parallel to advance the plot through the personal plot journey of the main voice or character and include the proper use of dialogue, flashback, and flash-forward.

2. *Dramatic tension.* The journey's hope vs. fear offers the reader the rise and fall of emotional tension similar to the ebb and flow of human growth in a true-to-life personal plot.

3. *Compelling language and poetics.* These are a sensual and pleasant medium for carrying the sometimes difficult-to-witness writhing of a human journey. These spoonfuls of sugar help the reader walk through a course of want-driven actions, and include the proper use of simile and metaphor and the proper and effective use of dialogue.

Copy Edit: The edit concerned with the *believability* and *continuity* elements of telling a story well, all toward enhancing the readability of your story. This is where fact-checking and researching *now* spares you massive embarrassment *later*:

1. *Believability of setting*. For instance, in the writing of my novel *Fifth Born II: The Hundredth Turtle*, I had to find out what the hospital that is referenced in the story was called in the early 1980s, because the name of that hospital in Harlem changed several times over the years.

2. *Continuity of setting*. For example, if you call wool "linsey wool" in Chapter 3, then you better call it that in Chapter 4 as well.

3. *Continuity of time*. For instance, if a character is twelve years old in 1970 and is twenty years old in 1980, this is an error that can be caught with the fine-tooth continuity checking of the copy editor.

4. *Readability and flow*. Lastly, this phase of a copy edit is concerned with the flow, readability, and ability for the reader to draw the intended meaning from the story. For example, with this edit, you may find yourself having to experiment with toning down the use of dialect and colloquialisms, or perhaps inserting more dialect and colloquialisms, all for the readability of the manuscript. This is also the place to ask if the motifs, themes, plants and payoffs, and character tags (if you used them) feel authentic or contrived.

Craft: Elements added to manuscripts that enhance the reader's experience of an already whole raw work. Craft enhances and elevates that rawness to make it literary so that the manuscript is not just a story but a story well told. These elements include but are not exclusive to the following:

- Internal character development motivated by external settings, which incorporates
  › Dialogue
  › Flashback
  › Flash-forward

- Dramatic tension – hope vs. fear
- Poetics, which includes
  › Metaphor
  › Simile
- Scene arranging for arc, which incorporates
  › Theme
  › Motif
  › Plant and payoff (some refer to this as foreshadowing and payoff)
  › Character tags

Dialogue (proper use of): A craft element that allows the reader to hear the voices of the characters and understand their emotional and psychological responses to each other. The proper use of dialogue is the same as true-to-life dialogue. We say things to each other because we are motivated by what we want the other person to feel or think. As the writer, you have the opportunity to offer the psychological and emotional context of the speaker's words by showing us the memory, fantasy, or thoughts inside of their head before they speak. Similarly, when someone is spoken to, give us the internal reaction of memories, fantasies, or thoughts that are internally stimulated by the words. Think of dialogue the way you think of setting. The external setting stimulates internal scenes, but in this case, the characters speaking to each other are external setting for each other and therefore stimulating internal responses for each other.

Dramatic Tension: Otherwise known as hope vs. fear. Dramatic tension is typically stimulated in readers through one of three scenarios:

1. *Persistent obstacles of fear.* Dramatic tension (hope vs. fear) can exist when there are persistent obstacles, and we fear the main voice or character won't overcome them but hope they will. Both *Bastard Out of Carolina* and *Fifth Born* hold this more persistent tension as Bone and Odessa live with daily obstacles, while the reader's hope for triumph and fear of doom grows.

2. *Signposts.* These are warnings based on fears of other characters'

experiences, and they are either heeded to fulfill our hopes or ignored to confirm our fears. In each scene, these signpost warnings are blatant or subliminal messages to steer the main voice or character away from obstacles and toward agents. The more the voice or character ignores or defies the warning, the greater the tension. It's the classic horror movie moment when the character runs from the monster to the kitchen where there is a knife on the counter (high tension) but then runs right past the knife (the signpost) and toward the stove where hot water is boiling (another signpost—high tension again). We hope for one outcome and fear another.

3. *Persistent agents for a persistent villain.* On rare occasions, there are few obstacles, yet there are persistent agents for a main voice or character who has horrible wants. We, as readers, end up hoping for obstacles to stop them but fear they will succeed toward an ill fate for themselves or others. This is typical of horror stories where the main character is a villain who has a long track record of successfully fulfilling their villainous want because they are aided by persistent agents.

Enhance the Plot Scenes: Taking the base of the 7 Pivotal Scenes and adding scenes that offer additional insight into the main voice's or character's struggle toward their want, their agents and obstacles, and additional insights into any other layers of everyday life, including humor. This may include, for instance, a nightmare scene, birth scene, death scene, or a funny scene.

Event: A fully rendered internal and external moment where this moment and its temporary outcome mirror the overall plot.

Flashback: A craft element that utilizes a memory, fantasy, or musing from a character's past that is triggered from things in the character's present external environment. These memories, fantasies, or musings are embedded as short scenes directly into the outer scene where the memory is triggered. Often, the initial wound scene is best told in installments or as a full memory scene that is triggered each time particular things occur for the main voice or character.

Flash-Forward: A craft element that utilizes a fantasy of future events that is triggered from things in the main voice's or character's present external environment. These fantasies are embedded as short scenes directly into the outer scene where the fantasy is triggered. Often, the potential outcome scene is foreshadowed through flash-forwards.

Gift(s): Also internal agents. Think of gifts as survival tools you embody that are of some long-term good for you and perhaps others. Your artistic ability is a gift that helps you express and therefore survive life experiences, but it also helps others survive once they have consumed your art.

Heightened Dramatic Tension Scene(s): Scenes where both are present: agent and obstacle, influencing the emotional/psychological want and motivation of the main voice or character, therefore increasing the emotional/psychological tension for the main voice or character. Select at least one scene that has the strongest influence over whether or not the main voice or character attains the overall want. This is what some authors call the climax, but I choose to call the heightened dramatic tension scene.

Initial Wound: An event that has a long-term, significant impact on your emotional, psychological, and spiritual development. The initial wound results in a significant loss and that loss causes a want, and that want drives and motivates you on a journey to fulfill the want. The initial wound is the primary event of any of our personal plots.

Internal Agent(s): Also gifts. Think of internal agents as the survival tools you embody that are of some long-term good for you and perhaps to others. Your artistic ability is one of your gifts or internal agents that helps you express and therefore survive life experiences, but it also helps others to survive once they have consumed your art.

Internal Character Development: Internal scenes that are happening inside of the main character's mind that parallel and are a response to the external stimuli. Developing the character internally means researching their emotions and psychology, and adding to your writing their thoughts, memories, or fantasies. In short, as writers we forget to write the feelings of our characters in some way other than creating an internal monologue that we put in italics. Instead, it is important to show what someone is feeling by showing us the scene that is happening in their heads, which is their psychological and emotional response to what is happening around them. This requires that we delve into self-help books for a more in-depth understanding of what helps and hinders someone with their issues.

Internal Saboteur: The voice that tells you that you can't have kids and write, work a job and write, take care of your elderly parent and write, or write at all. Keep in mind that the voice is just a henchman for the ill messages of the past. As a result of having people who exacerbate our wounds—be they our intimate nuclear society of family or the society-at-large—we may become convinced that despite our obvious power to multitask, endure profound trauma, and survive while showing ultimate mental and psychological strength, we are weak. Over time and as we grow from children into adults, most of us have a tendency to maintain these saboteurish myths regardless of whether the people who instilled the original ill messages are alive or dead. In their absence, we perpetuate the negative messages ourselves.

Jump-Start: Utilizing a Jump Starter in order to stimulate and motivate your artistic writing.

Jump Starter: Artistic inspirations to get you into the writing of your prompt. You might prompt yourself to write your birth story, and you just sit there thinking about the fact that you don't remember being born, or thinking about the story that you've been told over and over. All that pondering, but your little car is sitting on the track and you haven't gone anywhere yet. Jump Starters are bits of artistic inspiration from other sources like photos, music, and lines of poetry that are already published or presented as being in the creative zone. You use these if the prompt doesn't immediately spark the desire to zoom off down the track and write. Jump Starters, just like jump-starting a car, can take you from a mundane brain into the artistic zone in seconds and can prevent you from fiddling around, wondering how to start or what to say about an event.

Line Edit: The edit concerned with the *mechanics* of telling a story well:

- Spelling, grammar, and punctuation
- Word usage
- Tense
- Perspective
- Consistent spelling of proper nouns that are exclusive to the story.

Loss: Emotional, psychological, or spiritual depletion as a result of an initial wound.

Main Voice or Main Character: Terms I use to distinguish between the "I" in poetry and memoir (main voice) and the "I" in fiction (main character).

Metaphor (proper use of): A craft element that draws a comparison between two things and offers deeper or more universal understanding of a feeling, object, or concept. The only difference between metaphor and simile is structural. Similes use the word "like" or "as" in making the comparison, while a metaphor says that one thing simply is the other and the comparison is understood. For example, "We were vulnerable like birds in leafless trees" (simile) and "We were birds in leafless trees" (metaphor). The comparisons should not be for comparison's sake, but should be dual purpose: they should help the reader understand an emotion, object, or situation better but should also give us information about the character or setting. For instance, it would be silly to say, "I was calm, like a snowy day in December," if the story is set in Phoenix, Arizona.

Motif: People, places, or things that hold repetitive representation of the theme while holding some psychological significance for the main character. A motif then can help you express the theme through an established pattern for telling the story. For instance, much of Part Two of *Cold Running Creek* is told through the motif (date pattern) of Lilly's birthdays. This repeated thing (her birthdays) holds psychological significance for her, but it is also a manifestation of the intangible theme—freedom. In the story, it is her birth that puts freedom into question for so many of the characters in the story. Born to a slave, but the daughter of a wealthy landowner—is she free? Through this pattern of her birthdays, we are offered scenes that advance the main character and each character around the theme of freedom.

Obstacle: A person, place, or thing that gets in the main voice's or character's way, particularly obstructing their path to healing from an initial wound. This may also be a person, place, or thing that exacerbates an initial wound.

Outcome: The moment when the main voice or character turns the awareness of revelation into action for change and evolution.

Outcome Action: Comes after the revelation. The outcome action is the part where readers are left satisfied that things will be okay because the main voice or character's change is sustained through their new plan or new way of being. Some stories won't have an outcome action scene and may end in a cliff-hanger, which leads you to believe that perhaps the main voice or character will revert back to the stepping stones of their plot and that their outcome will not be sustained. Others may end offering that the main voice or character had a negative reaction to the revelation and outcome.

Outtake File: A file that contains writing that you don't currently need but you don't want to delete just in case the writing is valuable later. If you create an outtake file, title and date it, for example, "Outtakes 12-10-16." This will alleviate any panic you have about tossing writing.

Overall Plot: Fundamentals of a story. In this book, overall plot refers to

- Who is the story is about? (main voice or character)
- What pivotal, difficult, life-changing event happened? (initial wound)
- What was lost and what did the loss leave the voice wanting? (motivation)
- What helped fulfill the want? (agents and gifts)
- What got in the way of fulfilling the want? (obstacles and internal saboteurs)
- What revelation changed the course of the voice and their wants?
- What was the outcome to this journey?
- What was the outcome action that shows the outcome will be sustained?

Peer Reader: A friend or colleague (not someone who you have deep emotional ties to) who is professional in their specific field of expertise, can read your manuscript, and give you detailed feedback that will help you improve upon, clarify, and tighten your story.

Personal Plot: The process of creating literature by writing an impactful event, writing the journey of wanting what was lost in that event, and then living and writing a revelation and outcome where there is a shift in understanding about the wound and the want, as well as a new way of being.

Plant and Payoff: A craft element that utilizes a scene or object planted (or placed) early in a story, which reappears later in the story where the full emotional significance of the object or scene is revealed. This causes the reader to experience, along with the characters, time-released revelations about the true meanings of things in the story.

Practice: A consistent, repeated action that helps you sustain the change that you've had through your outcome. For instance, you may begin jogging every day as a practice to sustain your outcome of weight loss.

Prompts: Equivalent to the tiny bits of intent for your writing, a direction to go in. For instance, a prompt may be "Write your birth story."

Racket: Your attempt to turn some self-defeating behavior, which may have benefitted you in the short term and infrequently, into a long-term, stable solution for getting what you want. The difference between internal saboteurs and rackets is duration. A racket then is when you sign up your internal saboteurs (which are usually short-term survival methods) to do the work of agents (which are long-term fixes).

Read-Through: A thorough read of the entire manuscript in order to familiarize yourself with the story you are telling or to edit for particular elements of the story. In order to do a thorough self-edit (content, copy, and line edit), you will do ten read-throughs of your manuscript. See Chapter 19 for details on the ten read-throughs of a thorough self-edit.

Revelation: A moment in your life when you come to understand an initial wound, what helps with the healing, what gets in the way, or how to fulfill the want caused by the initial wound.

Scene: A fully rendered internal and external moment in fiction or memoir where this moment and its temporary outcome mirror the overall plot. In poetry, scene often translates into a whole poem where there is temporary outcome. For instance, in Sharon Olds's poem "The Race," there is the outcome of her making the flight and seeing her father again before he passes away.

Scene Shaping: The process of taking each written scenes and examining them to see if they advance the plot (advance the main voice or character toward the self-fulfillment of their overall want). In other words, since the story is about a personal want that was born from one of your initial wounds, you are examining each scene to see if it has anything to do with this particular journey the voice or character is on from wound to revelation. If it doesn't, you are taking it out. If it does but it's missing some components, you're performing write-ins or rewrites.

Shape-Shifters: Internal saboteurs that shift when the characters or voices shift. They elude your intelligence and good instincts, and like the bamboo chopped from the garden, they pop up again, having run underground undetected by your common sense. You recognize a behavior that doesn't serve you well, so you stop only to find that you are practicing that same behavior under an even more agent-like cloak.

Simile (proper use of): A craft element that draws a comparison between two things and offers deeper or more universal understanding of a feeling, object, or concept. The only difference between simile and metaphor is structural. Similes use the word "like" or "as" in making the comparison, while a metaphor says that one thing simply is the other and the comparison is understood. For example, "We were vulnerable like birds in leafless trees" (simile) and "We were birds in leafless trees" (metaphor). The comparisons should not be for comparison's sake but should be dual purpose: they should help the reader understand an emotion, object, or situation better but should also give us information about the character or setting. For instance, it would be silly to say, "I was calm, like a snowy day in December," if the story is set in Phoenix, Arizona.

Spelunking: A metaphorical way to help you deal with your fear that you will go crazy or be stuck in some perpetual state by spending time deep in your memories. If you are going into deep caves, you should wear a headlamp and a utility belt. You should bring matches, a torch, a raincoat, and food pellets that can sustain you for days and days if necessary—you get the picture. You get equipped for the mission at hand.

Theme: A craft element that utilizes one of the intangible beliefs that helped you survive events like your initial wound and offer shape and philosophical containment for your story. What do I believe that helps me survive events like my initial wound? For instance, I believe that practicing the art of writing can help a person self define and therefore self propel their evolution. This can be distilled into a theme of "The Healing Power of Art." It is the theme of this book. A theme like "Freedom for All" can help you to know which scenes of raw material might best advance the plot. For instance, in *Cold Running Creek*, all of the characters are seeking their freedom in some well-guided or misguided way.

Threshold of Learning: A metaphorical way to describe the fear blockage between where you are and what you want. Think of the threshold of learning as a door with all of the scary faces and memories moving around on it. Whenever we're about to learn, we encounter our worst fears and stand at this door just shivering, but we aren't learning unless we are challenged. Once we open that door, we are on the other side of a new piece of our evolution. The point at which we have the potential to learn in all relationships is this same threshold. Only discernment through self-exploration can help you open that door by revealing the difference between real scary faces on that door and the scary faces of memories and experiences long since passed.

Want: The motivating force for a main voice or character, who desperately wants to gain something lost in an initial wound event or desperately prevent some similar event or similar initial wound feelings from occurring.

Write-In: What I call producing events or scenes with some intentional prompting that I think may advance my plot and get at more of the want for my character or voice. Sometimes, these are also writing moments where I write what I believe to be the missing scenes or the missing element of the scene. I also call it "write-ins" when folks meet up at my studio, a coffee shop, a library, or somebody else's living room alone, with a friend-writer, or a group of other writers, and park themselves there for four hours straight without anything else that they can do except drink tea or coffee and go to the bathroom. No talking, just writing.

The Zone: That place where you have let go of all self-consciousness and you are just creating from your depths without editing, thinking, or being on the surface of the moment. When you use the Jump Starters in Chapter 1, you are essentially grabbing a zip line. You are standing on one ridge, not in the zone, and the poet, photographer, or musician who created the inspiring art is in the zone on the other side. You choose a line, look at a photo, or turn on the music, and instantly you are in the zone too, and can write.

BIBLIOGRAPHY

Alexie, Sherman. "Indian Education." In *The Lone Ranger and Tonto Fistfight in Heaven*. New York: Atlantic Monthly Press, 1993.

Allison, Dorothy. *Bastard Out of Carolina*. New York: Dutton, 1992.

Baldwin, James. "Sonny's Blues." In *Going to Meet the Man*. New York: Vintage Books, 1995.

Brown, Grey. *What It Takes*. Cincinnati, OH: Turning Point Books, 2010.

Coates, Ta-Nehisi. *Between the World and Me*. New York: Spiegel & Grau, 2015.

Derricotte, Toi. "my dad & sardines." *American Poetry Review* 33, no. 1 (2004): 35.

Estés, Clarissa Pinkola. *Women Who Run with Wolves*. New York: Ballantine Books, 1992.

Farrokhzad, Forough. *Sin*. Translated by Sholeh Wolpé. Fayetteville: University of Arkansas Press, 2007.

Frozen River. Written and directed by Courtney Hunt. 2008. Culver City, CA: Sony Pictures Home Entertainment, 2009. DVD.

Gardner, Chris, Quincy Troupe, and Mim Eichler Rivas. *The Pursuit of Happyness*. New York: Amistad, 2006.

Holman, Virginia. *Rescuing Patty Hearst*. New York: Simon & Schuster, 2003.

Ihimaera, Witi. *The Whale Rider*. Orlando, FL: Harcourt, 2003.

Lockhart, Zelda. *Cold Running Creek*. Hillsborough, NC: LaVenson Press, 2007.

———. "The Empty Nest." *Referential Magazine*, March 21, 2014. http://referentialmagazine.org/zelda-lockhart/

———. *Fifth Born*. New York: Atria Books, 2002.

———. *Fifth Born II: The Hundredth Turtle*. Hillsborough, NC: LaVenson Press, 2010.

———. "Untitled." In *259 West Bute*, edited by Arnoux, G. C., N. Girault, J. Green, K. Hagerman, and H. Jacobs, et al, 25–27. Norfolk, VA: Old Dominion University, 1990.

Olds, Sharon. *The Father*. New York: Knopf, 1992.

The Pursuit of Happyness. Directed by Gabriele Muccino and written by Steven Conrad. 2006. Culver City, CA: Sony Pictures Home Entertainment, 2007. DVD.

Sendak, Maurice. "The Shape of Music." In *Creators on Creating 1997*, edited by Frank Barron, Alfonso Montuori, and Anthea Barron, 127–28. New York: G. P. Putnam's Sons, 1997.

Shakur, Tupac. *The Rose That Grew from Concrete*. New York: Pocket Books, 1999.

Smoke Signals. Directed by Chris Eyre and written by Sherman Alexie. 1998. Burbank, CA: Miramax Home Entertainment, 2000. DVD.

Tan, Amy. "Rules of the Game." In *The Joy Luck Club*, 89–101. New York: Putnam's, 1989.

Viramontes, Helena María. "The Moths." In *The Moths and Other Stories*, 27–34. Houston: Arte Publico Press, 1995.

Walker, Alice. "Beauty: When the Other Dancer Is the Self." In *In Search of Our Mothers' Gardens*. San Diego: Harcourt Brace Jovanovich, 1983.

ABOUT THE AUTHOR

ZELDA LOCKHART holds a PhD in expressive art therapies; an MA in literature; and a certificate in writing, directing, and editing film from the NY Film Academy.

She is author of *Fifth Born*, a Barnes & Noble Discovery selection and finalist for debut fiction from the Zora Neale Hurston/Richard Wright Foundation. Her novel *Cold Running Creek* won an Honor Fiction Award from the Black Caucus of the American Library Association. Her third novel, *Fifth Born II: The Hundredth Turtle* won a finalist award from the Lambda Literary Foundation and secured her position as Piedmont Laureate in North Carolina. Her fiction, poetry, and essays appear in several anthologies as well as in periodicals like *Chautauqua*, *Obsidian II*, and USAToday.com.

Lockhart is director at Her Story Garden Studios: Inspiring Black Women to Self-Define, Heal, and Liberate Through the Literary Arts. She continues to lecture and facilitate writing workshops across the US on issues specific to the human struggle and on ways that consuming and creating literature are good for what ails us. She welcomes visits to her websites:

www.ZeldaLockhart.com
www.HerStoryGardenStudios.com
www.LaVensonPress.com

CPSIA information can be obtained
at www.ICGtesting.com
Printed in the USA
LVHW031919070922
727805LV00003B/276

9 780978 910266